understanding human behavior

An Illustrated Guide to Successful Human Relationships

COLUMBIA HOUSE / New York

Editor	Nicolas Wright
Deputy Editor	Susan Joiner
Senior Designer	Stewart Cowley
Art Editor	Mary Cooper
Art Assistant	Jeff Gurney
Editorial Assistants	Mundy Ellis
	Sarie Forster
	John Moore
	Michael McIntyre
Picture Research	Diane Rich
	Hazel Robinson
	Paul Snelgrove
Editorial Director	Graham Donaldson

Production Manager: Warren E. Bright
Cover Design: Harry W. Fass
Cover Photo: Harry W. Fass

contents

introduction

The man and woman who achieve complete sexual harmony have the basis of a firm and lasting marriage. There may be other difficulties but they are unlikely to undermine the relationship in the way an unhappy sex life does. For once sex goes wrong the marriage itself is threatened.

And one of the greatest threats is posed by the frigid wife. The reasons for her frigidity are usually complex but with help and understanding she can overcome them. In the third volume of *Understanding Human Behavior* we discuss the problems faced by such a woman, explain what causes them and suggest how to deal with them.

We also show what happens to a marriage when a couple become bored with each other. This is nothing unusual. It happens to everybody at some time or another. But not everybody tries to alleviate their boredom by rushing into an illicit affair. If they do then their troubles are just beginning!

Do you like hurting people? Or perhaps you enjoy being hurt yourself? Inflicting and receiving pain has long been accepted as a normal aspect of sexual relations — but within certain limitations. The difficulty is in deciding when those limits have been reached. *Understanding Human Behavior* explains where normal standards end and deviance begins.

Most people have heard of Pavlov's dogs. But how many know who Pavlov was and why his experiments with dogs became so famous? Volume Three discusses the significance of his findings and the way in which they affect us all.

(continued)

There is hardly any more superstitious group than actors and actresses. To them green is an unlucky color, real jewelry should never be worn on stage and any production of Shakespeare's *Macbeth* is always fraught with disaster. Read *Understanding Human Behavior* and find out why.

Our highly informative and fascinating series in the Question and Answer section continues with ESP — extrasensory perception: what it is, when the research began and how it is regarded by serious scientists.

Other articles in Volume Three include: memory — and how it works; impotence; nymphomania; Freud's Oedipus complex and Havelock Ellis — described as the greatest sex reformer of his time.

— The Editor

Robin Clifford

The Secretary...

We all know the "perfect secretary." She is, after all, easily recognized—a pleasant, efficient and attractive woman. But do we know what makes her what she is? Why, for instance, is she almost invariably single? Why is she content to remain in the background? And why does she find it impossible to establish a meaningful sexual relationship?

Tell the average boss that the "perfect secretary" is a professional virgin and he will vigorously protest—at least until his mind comes back down to mundane things like work. Then even he would admit that, fantasies aside, it might not be a bad idea.

But where does such a woman come from? Some would say she is born and not made—that her childhood prepares her for the role of the ideal secretary. The only skills she needs when embarking on her career are shorthand and typing. She already has the temperament and instinct to do the job well.

The classic perfect secretary is relatively easy to recognize. She is invariably pleasant and is often extremely attractive as well as being neat and efficient. Rarely is she a married woman.

Take Miss Parsons. She is both a servant and a mother to her boss, Mr. Anderson, and he feels that he could not do without her. She has created a world in which he is happy and effective at his job.

Type Cast

Miss Parsons shields Mr. Anderson from unwelcome callers and unnecessary intrusions on his time. And she is always courteous and discreet. She uses the same tactics to gently correct his frequent mistakes. But she never allows him to get the impression that she considers him anything but superior to her in every way.

Content to go on working quietly in the background, she would never dream of trying to get the upper hand with Mr. Anderson. Miss Parsons is, in fact, like the perfect nineteenth cen-

tury servant—reliable and content with her station in life.

Miss Parsons is ideal for Mr. Anderson because, no matter how efficient *she* is, he will never feel that she constitutes a threat, but will know that, with her protection, his inefficiency will be hidden or kept in check. She is a force to be reckoned with if she feels that her boss is threatened in any way.

And Mrs. Anderson is happy too for Miss Parsons certainly has no sexual interest in her husband and never will have any.

Miss Parsons is typical of the sort of woman who makes the perfect secretary. No wife would have to worry if she went off on a business trip with her boss. Not even soft lights and sandy beaches would change her attitude to her boss.

Being a mother to Mr. Anderson satisfies Miss Parsons the most. But this is not because she is compensating for a desire to have children—it is a lack of desire for children of her own that makes her the person she is. According to some psychological theories, women who are perfect secretaries will sometimes speak wistfully of marriage and children, but they are not being sincere, although they might think so at the time. They gain immense fulfillment from their jobs and are usually extremely happy.

Bluestocking

They are never neurotic, as they would be if they were trying to sublimate or deny subconscious desires. Many people never come to terms with their mental or emotional needs, nor manage to find the ideal fulfillment of them, but these women often do.

A woman such as this does not always turn to secretarial work—she could also become an extremely efficient hospital matron or a faultless children's nanny. But in today's commercialized society, there are more such women in offices than in any other professional sphere.

Before World War I, this type of woman would have become a nanny

Florence Nightingale was so dedicated to her life's work that she willingly gave up marriage and a family—or probably, like the perfect secretary, she never even considered the idea.

John Freeman

or a governess. Florence Nightingale, a woman of outstanding organizational ability, turned down many offers of marriage and put her career as a nurse first. Other women would choose to mix marriage and a career because giving up marriage would be a sacrifice.

How does a woman who is a perfect secretary achieve fulfillment and satisfaction without sex? The theory is that the sexual side of her being is not properly developed. The explanation as to *why* it is not properly developed is not so simple, nor is it totally understood, but it is almost certain to have occurred in infancy.

Sometimes a female baby, at the breast stage, develops a slightly distorted image of its mother. This image is created by a mixture of prebirth mental programing and the baby's early, unfocused sight of its mother. No child is born with a totally blank mind; it has a certain amount of what could be termed "race memory"—just as a baby bird is born with an instinct to migrate and an ability to sense direction. If this prebirth mental programing is a bit off key, the image of the mother can be far different for one baby than for another. The mother of the ideal secretary appears as a "phallic image" to her child.

Also, the mother's own personality will affect most of the subsequent early conditioning. An earthy, very "motherly" parent will cancel out this situation without ever knowing the slightest thing about it. But a more socially sophisticated woman—who might not be such a good mother—may not be able to manage it.

The woman who is a perfect secretary almost always has a mother who could be described as a bluestocking—an intelligent, cultured woman, well-read and interesting in conversation. She is more of a wife than a mother to the child. The child has a love for her mother different from the usual dependence. It is thought that she subconsciously sees her mother as possessing a phallus, a kind of infant sexual development and identification that usually exists between a baby and its father.

Phallic Mother

The theory of the "phallic mother" was first developed by the female students of Freud. As a concept, the idea of the female phallus has run through traditions, fairy stories, superstitions and art for many centuries. The broomsticks of witches were carved to represent the head of a penis. In ancient pictures of goddesses, the serpent,

symbol of phallic power, is usually present.

This lack of normal sexuality is not sexual repression—that would cause great problems and lead to a need for treatment—it is simply arrested development due to the very early confusion. And it leaves the child, when adult, without the sexual facet which is such an important part of most people's make-up.

This asexual type of personality can be male or female. They are often among the happiest members of society, gaining their pleasures and fulfillment from work rather than from sexual relationships. In this way they are free from the physical, mental and social problems which invariably surround sexuality.

The psychologist Carl Gustav Jung had a theory that children often live out some aspect of their parents' personalities which has been repressed or which circumstances have prevented from developing. The psychology of a child is closely linked to that of its parents. Any problems, either personal or existing between the mother and the father, are often transmitted, subconsciously, to the young child. The child then either suffers from the effects or allows the problem to become part of its own personality.

Nurse Mother

In one of his papers, Jung cites the case of a nine-year-old girl who ran a low temperature and was not fit to attend school for several months. No apparent cause could be found. But the parents, convinced their child knew nothing of their problems, were unhappy together and wished to divorce. They had been postponing a decision because they did not want to hurt the child. Then they finally made a firm decision to separate and told the child that she would have two homes and two separate parents. Her health improved, and the physical symptoms of the vague illness disappeared.

A baby that has gone through early sexual confusion will be a child who is subconsciously affected not only by what its mother says, but even more so by what its mother *is*. The girl destined to become a perfect secretary finds her mother interesting and intelligent (almost as she would normally find these qualities in a mate) and never quite throws off the phallic image she has of her.

The boss, then, becomes part of a reversible mother-child relationship. The perfect secretary gives to her boss *not* what she would like to give to her *own* child, but what she wanted to get from her mother—constant protection and support. Because of the primitive level of the condition, the relationship takes on the reversible element so that, as well as being cast in the role of child, the boss is also the symbol of the phallic mother.

He is the child in need of help and assistance *and* the mother figure, complete with phallus, who gives both guidance and protection. The secretary is creating, within the office environment, the nursery situation from which she never really progressed and within which she and her boss play their equivocal roles.

Virgin Territory

Outside the office, the perfect secretary is also excellent at organizing her life—and everyone else's. She is ideal material for helping on committees or in any sphere of social life. Her relationships with men must, necessarily, be rather empty because of her inability to take them to their deepest meaning through sexual fulfillment. But that does not mean that she is not an interesting and amusing companion, only that she will be more stimulated by going out to dinner with an intelligent and entertaining man than forming a sexual relationship with him.

For her, caresses are acceptable but any attempt at intimacy beyond that is out of the question. While the man will probably look on a pleasant evening together as the preliminary to sexual enjoyment and fulfillment, for her the evening out is fulfillment in itself.

She will almost always remain a virgin and, if she wishes to be happy, she ought to make sure that she organizes her life so that this is possible. These women do, occasionally, marry and are often lured into marriage by the thought of other people's children. They do not want to have

The desk will give her away. If spotless, the chances are you have struck gold. She is superefficient and unobtrusive with it; she is the office almanac with the answer to every problem; she is the boss's confidant and adviser, undercover agent and bodyguard, ego booster and scapegoat, first aid post and ultimate weapon. She is a mother rather than a vamp, she is every boss's dream, she is . . . the perfect secretary. An untidy desk? She will be nowhere near as efficient but is probably ten times more interesting!

children of their own any more than they want sexual intercourse with a man. But, if they meet a widower or a divorcé with a young family, they are very likely to fall in love with him. It is not a pure and simple love of the man, it is a reflected love directed mainly at his children.

Such a woman is capable of mental love in all its forms but physical love can never be a happy thing for her, no matter how kind, gentle and patient her husband or would-be lover is.

Love without Fire

If she does venture into marriage, problems can arise which would make psychiatric treatment necessary. Take for example the case of a very attractive woman in her forties who had backed out of one marriage as a young girl and then became accustomed to the life style of a single woman. She was courted by a widower but could not make up her mind about marriage. He was a wealthy man with a good social position and her relatives and friends (well-meaning but lacking wisdom) urged her to marry him.

Still unsure and fearful, she visited a fortune teller who told her that the man would shortly die. She married him but her unwillingness to participate in the sexual side of marriage came as rather a shock to him. A few months after their marriage the husband, in a high state of unrelieved sexual excitement, had a coronary thrombosis and died. The woman was a relatively wealthy widow but the guilt feelings which the whole series

Many girls take up secretarial work but few give their lives to it. Only in her attitude can you distinguish the perfect secretary from the others. The normal girl (this page) tends to put her life interests above her job and appears at work dressed to attract men, whereas the perfect secretary (opposite page) will usually seem more severe. At parties she will talk to members of her own sex, while the less-dedicated girl will prefer to chat to men. If the perfect secretary suffers from anything it is the strain of being too perfect, for while the normal secretary relaxes waiting for her boss, the perfectionist worries if he is late. When the boss is out, the average secretary is likely to make private phone calls, but not the perfect secretary. She will use the extra time to catch up on her backlog of work.

of events had thrown up inside her resulted in her seeking psychiatric help.

One of the most famous heroines in English literature is a classic example of this kind of personality, and it is significant that her creator never took her beyond the vows of marriage and into the nuptial bed. The character, of course, is Jane Eyre. She falls in love with Rochester as part of her relationship with the child she is teaching and then eventually marries him when he is the blinded, helpless creature she can devote her life to looking after.

There is no sexuality in the character of Jane Eyre at all. She never has even the slightest desire to take Rochester as her lover—her feelings for him are not in the slightest carnal. The ordinary sexually motivated reader is left to believe that the story ends happily. But, considering Jane Eyre's personality, the marriage could not have had a fulfilling sexual side.

Satisfied Secretary

Today there are many jobs and careers open to women and those who do not wish to marry can be perfectly happy in their work. Before the emancipation of modern woman, marriage was an experience to be endured and many women were unhappy all their lives. The Victorian idea that women ought not to find sex enjoyable, in fact, stemmed from this type of woman. They are always, if married, adept at concocting excuses for avoiding sex. They will have countless sick headaches or the symptoms of endless illnesses.

Happiness is very simply a matter of understanding yourself and adapting your life in the light of that understanding. This is simple to say but the most difficult thing in the world to achieve. The perfect secretary usually manages to understand her needs and desires in a superficial way at least. If she has a satisfying job, a good boss, a decent income and some interesting friends then she is indeed lucky—because she will have met all her mental and emotional needs. But if she tries to do something which is alien to her make-up, like accepting marriage, she will build up problems for herself.

A boss ought to be very grateful to have her around and his wife can be thankful that she does not have to worry. Friends and relatives of this sort of woman ought to encourage her to enjoy a wide social life but should discourage her from getting into a situation in which sex must play even the smallest part.

Robin Clifford

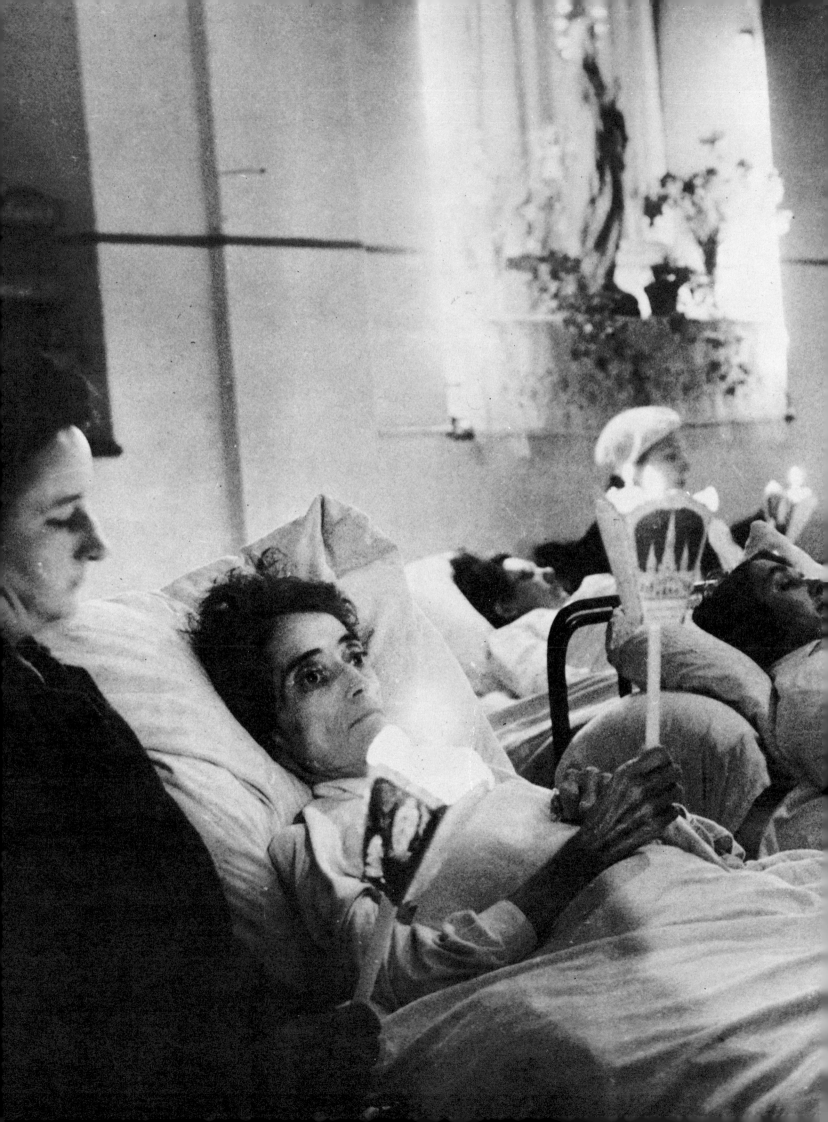

Mind over matter?

Man does not live by science alone and many of his ailments are treated by unorthodox methods. Even in our so-called civilized Western society there are men and women who refuse to visit a doctor. Instead they place their trust in "folk medicine" and attention from unconventional healers. In this they are no different from uneducated, primitive tribal peoples.

This morning countless people in many parts of the world woke up feeling unwell. They suffered from a variety of ills which ranged from serious ailments to less serious complaints. What is interesting is how they dealt with their illness and the steps they took to regain their health.

In a village on the African continent one of the leaders of the community woke up with intense pain in his right side. As his forefathers had done, he went to the witch doctor although there was a modern hospital within a few miles of the village. He knew that the doctors could deal with his body's complaints but the witch doctor could rid him of the evil spirit causing him pain.

In a small town in upstate New York a man woke his wife to complain of severe pain in his right side, the same condition suffered by the village leader. She called the doctor and later in the day he went to hospital with appendicitis. The African saw the man he had been taught to seek for help and so did the American. Both had one thing in common—a belief or faith that a particular person could cure them with skills that they alone possessed.

Most people living in industrialized societies have a certain degree of faith in their doctors, but others rely on folk remedies or other systems of medicine to put things right. Some people refuse to see a doctor, preferring to treat themselves or to see the practitioner of a healing art not recognized by the medical profession.

The man or woman who is consulted by a sick person will approach the illness in one of a variety of ways. If he or she is a registered practitioner, the patient may be prescribed drugs or sent along to a specialist for detailed investigation. A nondoctor, that is one who does not have a medical degree, might focus treatment on a single—perhaps nonmedical—aspect of the patient's problem.

Witch Doctor

A witch doctor might try to influence the spirits or gods who were affecting the sick person. A faith healer would treat the spirit of the person itself. The number of ways in which a sick human being can be treated illustrates how much superstition influences us during illness.

To most Africans, God, in one of his many manifestations or called by one of many names, is an ever-present

E. E. Evans-Pritchard

being. His priests (medicine men and witch doctors) are recognized leaders of the tribal community.

The African pagan (like the pagan everywhere for that matter) believes in a polytheistic system in which a chief god presides over lesser deities, rather as a king ruled over his domain in ancient times. The lesser gods—the spirits of the earth and the ghosts of departed heroes—are thought to be much more sympathetic than the supreme being. They can be flattered, wheedled and even threatened.

Estimates give the number of non-Christians and non-Moslems in Africa as 157,031,000 or over half of the total population. These pagans feel they can only stay healthy by keeping in touch with the gods through the medium of the medicine man or witch doctor.

These religious officials, who are found throughout pagan Africa, have always been popularly presented in the West as bogymen dressed up in absurd masks, feathers and animal skins, who leap about to the accompaniment of drums. They are alleged to deal in pure mumbo-jumbo in order to hoodwink the superstitious savages who are under their spell.

Preventive Medicine

The fact is that these priests fulfill a useful function in all primitive communities. It is true that their skills, methods, medicines and cures do not conform with modern science. But this is not the fault of the medicine men. Until European doctors arrived on the scene, the Africans had no alternative but to put their trust in those members of their tribe who had some understanding and some control of the physical and mental ills that afflicted the community.

In other words, where malign spirits seemed to play so great a part in men's lives, specialists were needed to study cause and effect; and over the centuries there emerged a class of men who appeared to have some skill and some success in the prevention and cure of sickness. This was the origin and role of the medicine man.

Left: In 1858 St. Bernadette saw visions of the Virgin Mary at Lourdes in southern France. Now millions of sick people like these invalids make the pilgrimage in hope of a miracle cure.
Right: African witch doctors possess powers of healing and are believed to gain knowledge from the spirits. A witch doctor will dance himself into a trance during which he will visit the spirit world.

In some cases, the medicine man has developed effective cures based on his knowledge of drugs derived from plants. From centuries of experiment and observation, he has developed a stock of drugs for such day-to-day needs as inducing vomiting in the case of poison; purgatives for ridding children of worms; sedatives for quietening hysterics; and potions for chest colds, headaches, whooping-cough, dysentery, snake bite, swellings and stings.

Plant Potions

If his remedies were all totally ineffective, the medicine man would quickly lose his standing in the community, as a doctor would in ours.

It must be admitted, however, that the medicine man also relies for his cures on his special brand of hocus-pocus, as an examination of his "little black bag" would reveal. It contains a fantastic collection of trivia—bits of bone, wooden figures, lumps of old iron, shells, beads, feathers. A great deal of the medicine man's treatment is psychological and belongs to the sphere of faith healing.

Some Western observers of his methods, particularly in the case of neurotics, go so far as to say that he has as much success as our psychiatrists, if not more.

All European observers agree that the African's obsession with witches is the most evil aspect of paganism. Yet the witch doctor, like the medicine man, is not at all the ogre of popular imagination. He flourishes in primitive societies because of the belief that both the spirit and the human world are peopled by two opposing forces—the good and the evil. The witch doctor is on the side of the good, and his chief job is to protect the community from evil spirits and wicked men.

He must always be ready to cope with mysterious events and diseases, like the death of a chieftain, sudden fevers, barrenness in women, sterility in men, mental disturbances and all other calamities believed to be caused by witches.

In such cases his standard practice is to "smell out" the evil-doer by the ancient and barbarous method of "trial by ordeal." This usually consists of administering poison either to the suspects or to their animals, and the degree of the sickness resulting is considered infallible evidence of guilt. Just to make sure there is no mistake, a confession is extorted from the accused by torture. The punishment for witches is death.

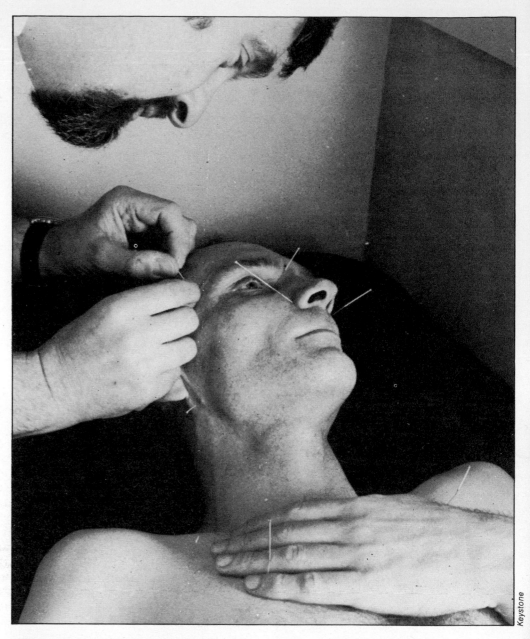

Keystone

A decade ago, acupuncture (the ancient Chinese practice of regulating the body by probing its energy channels with needles) was regarded by Western doctors as so much mumbo-jumbo. Today they are not so sure. There is some evidence that acupuncture can be successfully used in anesthesia, and it may even cure certain minor ailments.

African medicines are of two kinds. Straightforward potions and drugs distilled from plants and roots, prescribed in much the same spirit as Western medicines, are given for simple ailments; and magical potions or powders concocted from strange ingredients are prescribed for more difficult cases.

Examples of the latter potions are the various concoctions used for warding off evil spirits or giving a man protection from his enemies.

From northern Nigeria comes this secret formula:

Cut off the head of a snake and in it plant the seed of the swamp dock. Bury the head in a grave which must be seven days old. Pour water on it for three consecutive nights. When the plant has grown to a height of three or four feet, go again to the graveyard and strip naked. Pull up the swamp dock and use it as a girdle. If anyone attempts to attack you, the girdle will become a snake that will bite your enemy.

We can see from this formula that medicine in Africa is more magic than science. Knowing nothing of bacteriology, the medicine man relies to a great extent on psychology and faith, hence the hundreds of spells and

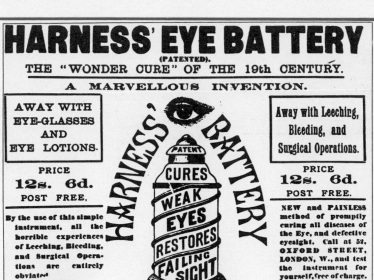

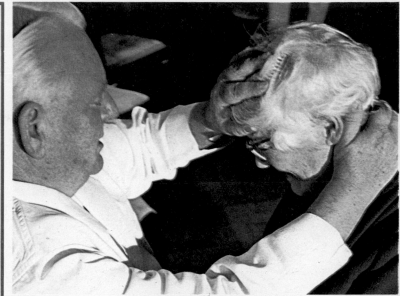

HARNESS' EYE BATTERY
(PATENTED).
THE "WONDER CURE" OF THE 19th CENTURY.
A MARVELLOUS INVENTION.

AWAY WITH EYE-GLASSES AND EYE LOTIONS.

Away with Leeching, Bleeding, and Surgical Operations.

HARNESS' BATTERY

PATENT

CURES WEAK EYES RESTORES FAILING SIGHT

52, OXFORD St. LONDON. W.

PRICE 12s. 6d. POST FREE.

By the use of this simple instrument, all the horrible experiences of Leeching, Bleeding, and Surgical Operations are entirely obviated.

PRICE 12s. 6d. POST FREE.

NEW and PAINLESS method of promptly curing all diseases of the Eye, and defective eyesight. Call at 52, OXFORD STREET, LONDON, W., and test the instrument for yourself, free of charge.

REDUCED FAC-SIMILE OF HARNESS' EYE BATTERY. WILL LAST FOR EVER

PAMPHLET POST-FREE.

EYES
SUCCESSFULLY TREATED.

HARNESS' EYE BATTERY is perfectly safe to use, even by children of tender years, the application being entirely under the patient's control.

HARNESS' EYE BATTERY, in addition to PREVENTING and CURING DISEASES OF THE EYE, will cure asthenopia, and POSITIVELY RESTORES WEAKNESS OF VISION, whether resulting from advancing age, or from that general nervous prostration which prejudicially affects the optic nerve. It also speedily CURES SPECKS BEFORE THE EYES (Musca Volitantes), so generally complained of by those suffering from early excesses and in a low and nervous state. Such patients will find in HARNESS' EYE BATTERY an absolute remedy for the malady, which is a real and not, as supposed, an imaginary one, and shows undoubted local manifestation of a debilitated state.

HARNESS' EYE BATTERY is sent, carefully packed, with directions for using it, post-free, on receipt of 12s. 6d.

HARNESS' EYE BATTERY is admitted to exercise a rapid influence upon the complex system of nerves, blood-vessels, fluids, and membranes constituting the most wonderful of Nature's mysterious mechanisms. Almost every disease of the eye can now be successfully treated by the systematic use (according to directions) of HARNESS' EYE BATTERY, which can be applied at any time, as is sufficiently portable to be conveniently carried in the pocket, and may be used by any person from infancy to old age, with perfect safety.

Stated simply, this is a system of curing diseases and weakness of the eye, and restoring normal acuteness of vision by assisting Nature, through influencing the circulatory functions to convey to the affected region a sufficient supply of healthy blood, and thus to annihilate the morbid and stagnant conditions which foster and maintain disease.

The Medical Battery Co., Ld., 52, OXFORD St., LONDON, W.

charms, one for almost every event.

According to Margaret Mead, in *Coming Of Age In Samoa*, the secrets of healing in Samoan society are passed down the generations by the older women of the community. Now, gradually, Samoan nurses have been trained and the people are learning to bring their sick to government dispensaries for treatment rather than trying to bring about cures through native remedies, mostly of a herbal nature. The nurses also go out to the villages to see the sick. But, despite the increase in the number of nurses practicing modern medicine, older Samoan women still carry on the art of healing through herbal remedies which have been proven by constant use down the years.

Of interest is a woman's power during times of illness and death. The sister of a man who becomes sick must formally swear that she holds no anger towards him as that emotion is considered a powerful force in Samoan society. In fact, the whole family is brought together in a ritual in which each member is asked to deny or admit that he or she holds anger against the ill individual. The idea is that a confession of anger on the part of any member of the family

Many old-fashioned remedies can be dismissed as quackery but to ignore all unorthodox cures like faith healing (right) may be a mistake. Today, even if the whys and wherefores are not understood, there is growing recognition that healing techniques not found in medical textbooks seem to have some beneficial effects.

constitutes an explanation of the malady. Anger, in this case, is the source of infection.

The field of fringe medicine includes a wide variety of theories of healing outside the orthodox Western sphere. The theories range from the medically sound to others which might at best be described as whimsically strange if not instances of outright quackery.

Faith Healing

Meanwhile, other systems of medicine, like acupuncture, are slowly becoming acceptable as modern medical techniques. To countless others naturopathy (that is, the treatment of ailments through proper foods, massage or exercise to aid natural healing) has proved effective. Herbal medicine is sworn to by innumerable people in

many parts of the world. The herbalist claims that his skill, which is largely inherited, can be used to concoct recipes which will assuage or cure a large number of ills.

Thousands of people have testified that faith healing works for them—yet its effectiveness, by its very nature, is incapable of scientific proof. What cannot be disputed, however, is that faith healing is a great source of hope to the otherwise hopeless.

Despite the fact that modern orthodox medicine is coming up with an increasing number of successes in its battle against disease, fringe medicine is enjoying a universal growth in acceptance. Belief is a key factor in the effectiveness of many of the methods often frowned on by the medical profession. Those who practice these methods usually have unshakable confidence in their techniques. Their patients, especially if they experienced cure, tend to become passionate advocates of the methods. But modern medical men, trained to check and check again, are sometimes extremely skeptical of many aspects of fringe medicine.

Even so, it is now accepted that psychological causes play an important part in the development of a disease, and that faith in a way of treatment can be instrumental in bringing recovery. Indeed the modern doctor has long used placebos, or preparations of little or no therapeutic value, to treat patients who believe they are receiving medicine which will help them. The patient often recovers spontaneously in this way.

Faith healers claim to have, usually in the absence of medical knowledge or skills, the gift of healing; methods of treatment vary with the individual healer but in general they are not appropriate to orthodox medical practice.

Convincing Cures

Attitudes about the faith involved in healing (that is, belief held in the absence of, or in spite of, logical argument based on available facts) vary so widely that it is not even possible to establish that such belief is an essential element in the process, either for the healer or for the patient. Neil Bayon and Maurice Colinon worked experimentally as healers during recent years, without the slightest faith in their powers, but both achieved considerable reputations.

One authority suggests that the study of healing and the study of cures is by no means the same thing, and that spontaneous recovery may be one of the reasons why no rational theory of healing exists. It is difficult to define a boundary between paranormal healing and orthodox medical practice.

An orthodox doctor giving a patient a placebo in the hope and expectation that the sufferer will benefit by being humored in this way is a good physician. Similarly the faith healer may believe that he is doing something positive and his actions and his belief may also serve as a placebo, with the result that the patient feels better.

Theories are continually being presented. Sigmund Freud began writing about conversion hysteria (a loss of physical function resulting from an emotional disturbance in the absence of disease) as early as 1886, reviving modern interest in ancient rites.

Within recent years a vast amount of work has been done in the field of psychosomatic medicine. Briefly, psychosomatic diseases are those in which harmful local changes occur in an organ, usually as a result of psychic stress. Both hysterical and psychosomatic disorders are, at least in their early stages, reversible and it is very likely that some of these illnesses

Uprooting a mandrake was, according to popular belief, a dangerous business since the plant gave a shriek which could kill a man. On the other hand, the roots of the plant had a curative value.

lend themselves more readily to the unspecific methods of the faith healer.

George Groddeck has been called the father of psychosomatic medicine. This assessment is largely based on his paper *The Psychic Origin and Psychoanalytical Treatment of Organic Disease*, written in 1917, in which he says, "I consider it a basic and dangerous misconception to suppose that only the hysteric has the gift of making himself ill for whatever purpose.

"Every man has this ability and each uses it in an extension beyond comprehension. In being ill a distinct purpose is served." He goes on to say, "A great many miraculously easy cures which we credit to suggestion or to the personal influence of the doctor are basically to be led back to the sudden realization . . . that man will no longer need this or that protection."

In *The Unknown Self*, a selection of his writings, Groddeck added that a patient "may reject the methods approved by scientific and ordinary

experience and choose to be cured by other—in some cases quite ridiculous —means, or without any assistance from other people . . . may work out his own salvation by using the conditions of his own environment."

The theory does not explain why the will to health may be aroused by unorthodox approaches after conventional methods have failed, but it does illustrate the possible complexity behind the simplest symptom.

The will to health may finally express itself in the patient who has failed to gain relief of illness in the usual medical environment; and even though such a patient may say that he does not believe in faith healing, he has, usually unconsciously, reached the point at which he *must* become well. And this is the time when the healer may contribute to the reversal of a psychologically based illness or to the mental well-being of a patient suffering from organic disease.

Auto-Suggestion

It should be remembered that there is a common prejudice against neurosis and neurotic symptoms, implying that they are in some way less respectable than organic disease. Whatever the cause, the symptoms are just as real for the patient. Pain hurts.

Suggestion is, of course, relevant to both orthodox and unorthodox healing. Argument still continues about the basic mechanism of hypnotism, which can certainly be used for the removal of symptoms, sometimes dramatically. The removal of symptoms, which is of the greatest importance to the patient, rather than the removal by psychological methods of the cause of symptoms, has become academically respectable over recent years. This replaces the earlier assumptions that the relief of symptoms without insight into the nature of their origin would result in relapse or in a group of new symptoms.

It has not so far been possible either to prove or to disprove that faith healing cures organic disease, and further investigation is needed, particularly in the rigorous following-up of claims of reputed unorthodox cures. But man does not live by science alone, and so long as the obvious safeguard of medical supervision is respected it is unlikely that faith healing can do any harm.

Indeed it can lead to an improvement in the emotional state which is in itself a good thing in that it makes life easier for the sufferer even though it may not basically affect his physical condition.

Steve Bicknell

Affairs & why

Are you bored with marriage? Do you long for the excitement of an illicit affair? If you do, don't worry—it's not at all unusual. But if you give in to your impulses after a few flirtatious lunches it could mean the end of your marriage. Do you really want that?

Certainly marriage is not what it used to be. A look at the divorce statistics proves that. In 1948, when Kinsey published his report, one out of every nine marriages ended in the divorce courts. By 1972 the ratio was one in four.

To many it is fashionable to divorce. And to many others it is just as fashionable to have affairs. Or rather to have them in a noisy way. Men or women who do not hop into bed with someone else, and stoutly say so, tend to be regarded with a certain pitying dismay.

No doubt about it then—having affairs is popular. And those who would not have dreamed of straying from the straight and narrow a generation ago are clearly going to think about it now. But they will probably only think about it.

This is because the factors that lead to unfaithfulness are many and complex, very compelling and deep-rooted, and infinitely more significant than a change in fashion. However, given the other factors, the more permissive social climate of today is probably one of the reasons for the popularity of affairs.

From Pill to Pillow?

But freedom to talk about someone else's affair of the heart at dinner parties is not reason enough to cause an otherwise constant person to betray all that seems most dear and sacred.

The Pill has had the blame for an increase in promiscuity and marital infidelity laid at its rather battered door, probably with little genuine cause. No one is going to leap into bed with someone other than their husband or wife simply because they can be sure of no nasty consequences nine months later.

Before discussing why there is an increase in extramarital sex, if indeed there is, it is useful to try to discover why there is any at all. Ask the pundits and they will provide many and varied theories. But ask the people who actually do have affairs with other people's husbands and wives and you will get a rather narrower line of reasoning. They were, they will tell you, bored—bored with their mate, and with the sexual relationship they had with their mate—bored with the humdrum routine of married life, be it ever so happy—and bored with the rather limited social horizons of that life as well. They longed for some excitement, both emotional and sexual, and some reassurance that they still possessed the ability to inspire that excitement.

But, then, we all get bored. We would all like the excitement and the reassurance of a little sexual adventure now and again. So why do we all not turn into sexual adventurers?

Well, many of us do, of course, but many of us do not, and in examining the reasons why not, we begin to see the reasons why more clearly too. Fear is the greatest deterrent, probably—fear of getting caught, of throwing away everything, of hurting innocent wives, husbands and children. There is also the fear of getting hurt yourself, although that is usually more remote.

Wishful Women

Nevertheless, if it is fear that is stopping you, the urge to stray cannot be particularly strong. The conviction that it is only other people who get caught is a fairly deep one; it always seems terribly easy at first to be discreet and tactful, and there is beginner's luck to spur you on as well.

And, in any case, many people start a relationship without ever intending it actually to be an affair. A few flirtatious lunches seem totally in order—and it is only when they start to get boring too that bed seems the only place to be.

Then again, if you start an affair because you have fallen deeply in love (less likely, but still fairly possible) fear will not be a deciding factor. All is fair in love and war and this is both. And if it is unfair to your spouse, the cause is so noble it is worth it. Love makes us appallingly selfish.

Women are more likely to be afraid of starting an affair than men, and with good reason. They are more

The eternal triangle has provided the theme for many a good plot but in practice seldom provides happy endings for those involved.

likely to be caught. It is easy for a married man to have an extramarital love life during office hours, pleading long business lunches. But this is difficult for a woman, for who will hold the fort and the baby for her as the passionate hours roll away? She has no secretary to placate her husband with bland lies, nor any nonexistent meetings to attend—unless, of course, she is a business person herself. The married woman with a career is in the same advantageous position as a man. This may be one of the social reasons for the increase in extramarital sex.

Now that women are people in their own right, and not simply either wives or waiting to become wives, they can conduct their own lives and careers more or less as they wish. They are free to enjoy their own money, their own time and, if they wish it, the comparative freedom to conduct an affair of the heart.

What is more, with this new freedom to act, they have found freedom to think. And they are thinking of things that were fairly unthinkable before—like themselves, their own desires, and their own boredom with a too-familiar though well-loved spouse. Instead of remaining resentful and jealous over the kitchen sink, they can go out and be unresentfully carnal over the lunch table. An oversimplification, of course, but the fact remains that the physical ability (in the sense of being, quite literally, physically available) to have an affair is for most women a phenomenon of the last couple of generations.

Loyal is Royal

If fear does not deter you, what will? Perhaps a nobler emotion altogether, a funny, old-fashioned sentiment called loyalty. To the loyal, the crime is not getting caught, it is doing something to be caught at. You do not commit the crime because that in itself would damage the relationship. You would not be the same singlemindedly loving person if you loved someone else—you would have sold out, betrayed the ideal, and never mind if anyone found out or not. Things would never be quite the same again. Such idealism is rare, precious and hard to find; to live up to it requires great maturity and tenacity of purpose. And it is considered less and less important, such faithfulness and loyalty. So long as you do not hurt anybody else, goes the argument, what harm is done?

Yet another deterrent is the dread of the complications, the intrigue, the

network of lies that will inevitably accompany any extramarital relationship. Most people's lives, particularly if they have children, are involved enough without the added demands of a clandestine relationship. But for many, a double life has its charms. Booking tables at hitherto unknown restaurants, earmarking a rendezvous, driving off for half an hour's secret bliss, all this has a remarkably uplifting effect on a jaded spirit.

Wife Swapping

Possibly the main reason a man opts for extramarital sex is to prove himself—again. He has the sense that his life is slipping away, particularly if he is middle-aged. He panics and wonders what he has been missing. A wife, however loving and loyal, will ultimately and inevitably fail to thrill totally to her husband's advances; and he will need to be sure that he still has the ability to evoke that excitement.

Women feel this need, too, although men can never quite believe it; but the need can be more simply satisfied. Words of love and admiration coming from a new man in her life will reassure a woman.

Undoubtedly, the less happy a marriage, the more likelihood is there of sex taking place outside it; and yet you will find many people, who enjoy an otherwise apparently good marriage, claiming that an extramarital relationship has recharged their sexual batteries and enriched their marriage. Those who participate in wife-swapping claim that it provides all that is best in extramarital sex without endangering a marriage—because it is all completely open and above board.

Granted it allows sex to take place between a man and a woman without deception or complicated arrangements. But it provides none of the other enticements—romance, intrigue, the excitement of a new relationship, or love. So it really cannot offer very much to the bored, the disgruntled, the unappreciated, the depressed, the panic-stricken, or the insecure. If your husband or your wife does not wish to sleep with you often enough for your liking and in every other way you are happy, then perhaps wife-swapping parties are for you. Otherwise, perhaps not.

Yet another factor in the sex-outside-marriage syndrome is the current obsession that people have these days with themselves. Never before have men and women been more aware of their complexities, their needs, their subconscious—and indeed conscious—desires. Our attitude to ourselves is a bit indulgent: we should not, we feel, be deprived of too much, for fear of what it might do to our development as personalities. We need reassurance, satisfaction, sexual fulfillment, lest we become withered and wretched. So who are we to deprive ourselves? And so we lurch forward into all kinds of self-indulgent forays, for the good of our psyches—and very nice it can be, too, to have such a sop for the conscience, when, like old-fashioned loyalty, it rears its cumbersome head.

And what of the deeper reasons, the ones we are scarcely aware of? There is a kind of person, according to the psychiatrists, who can only love some sort of forbidden object—somebody with a "don't touch" label. It is a kind of unresolved Oedipus complex. These people have never really recovered from being in love with their mother or their father; they are constantly searching for someone who is also taboo. These are the people who have multiple extramarital affairs, and clearly it is a much more serious condition than simply being bored.

And at the end of your affair, then what? Three things might happen: your marriage might break up, you might confess and hopefully receive forgiveness, or you might keep silent. Silence is undoubtedly the best thing all round—if you can do it. Not many can though. Most people, again according to the psychiatrists, have a terrible desire to confess and be punished and to atone for their sins.

One of the most startling aspects of the Kinsey Report was its revelations about extramarital intercourse. Top: The graph shows how experience in extramarital intercourse among women increases from the age of 16 to 30—though in the days of tighter social convention, the total amount of extramarital intercourse remained less than in freer times. Figures for ages 26 to 30 in the youngest group are not shown as at survey time the marriages were of too short duration for data to be collected. Below: The graph compares extramarital relationships among men and women showing that while extramarital activity increases among women as they get older, the reverse is true of men. The statistics showed that by the age of 45 more women than men are involved in sex outside their marriage.

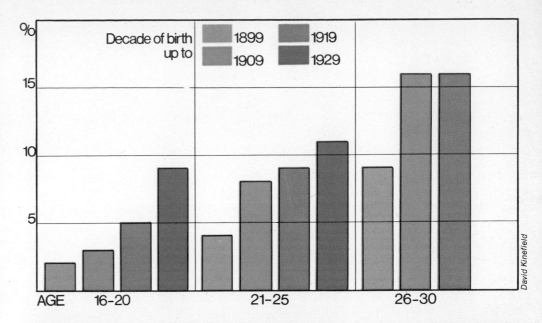

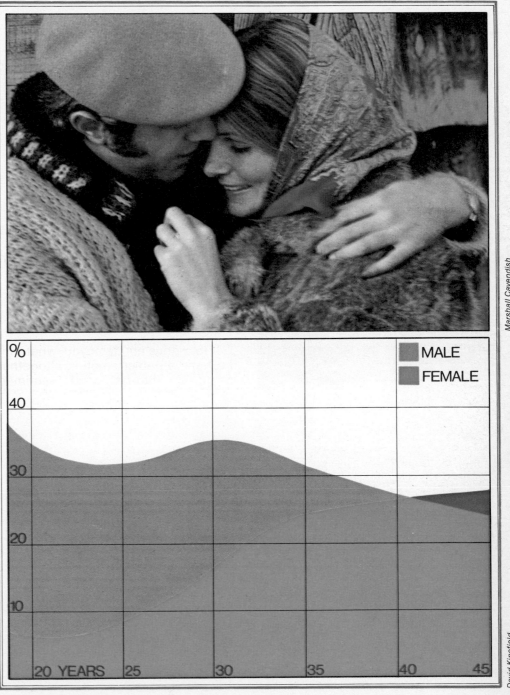

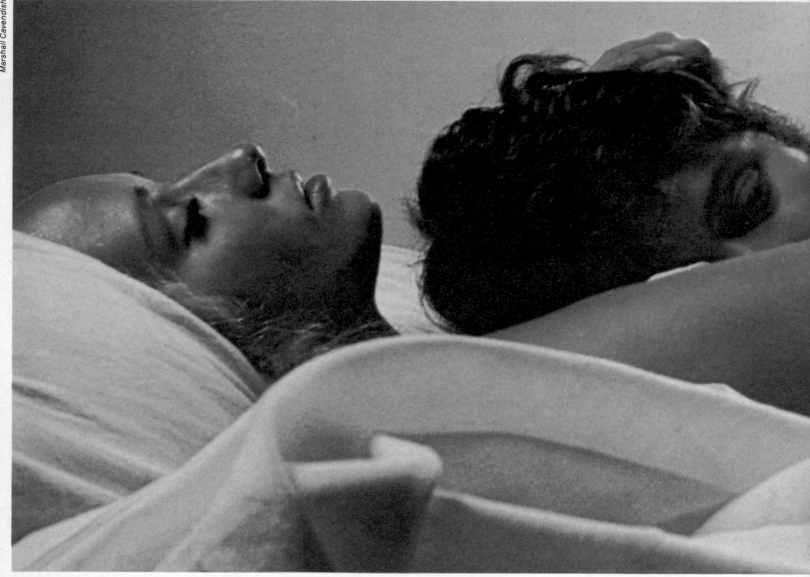

This is not helpful and not kind—and the wronged and innocent party in the affair deserves better than that.

Remaining silent is not easy—but neither is it cowardly. You may avoid some rows and recriminations, but so do you avoid the satisfaction of saying, even as you apologize and prostrate yourself, "Well, somebody else did want me." The advantage of keeping silent is that you retain your options, you can change your mind, decide perhaps one day to tell, although you would probably be ill-advised to do so. But once you have spoken you cannot change your mind; you cannot say no, you did not really do it, or really mean it. It is done, and that is it, and the damage is finally wrought. No amount of apologizing or justifying will make the other person feel any better—or you for that matter.

The $64,000 question, perhaps, is whether men are more likely to stray than women, and wouldn't we all like to know? Kinsey's figures say that they are, that they do, and by precisely twice as much; but if the suppositions here are correct—and they probably are—the gap has narrowed somewhat. Still there are more erring men between the sheets than erring women.

Revenge: Sweet and Sour

Despite all that Germaine Greer, the Women's Liberationist, would have us believe, it is probably quite true to say that women are more satisfied in their lives by the home and the family than are their husbands. And this has nothing at all to do with the fact that they are bored beyond endurance by that home and family a great deal of the time. A woman who has given birth to and reared a child or two, who has successfully conducted a happy family life for a decade or three, and who loves and is loved by her husband, will consider herself fulfilled in the long run. For that accomplishment is still what she is basically about. Men have no such totally reassuring tasks to perform and their role in the family as provider is less fundamental. So, for men, the roots of contentment in marriage are not quite so deep—and the plant is a little more easily uprooted.

Also, women are undoubtedly more emotional about sexual relationships than men. They need to feel, if not in love, at least romantically aroused, before they will consider going to bed with somebody other than their husband. Men need only feel sexually aroused. Of the two kinds of arousal, sexual excitation is a lot more easy to come by.

Apart from falling, or feeling she is falling, deeply in love, a woman will rush into an extramarital bed at high speed for another reason: revenge. Hurt and betrayed wives are easy prey for seducers. They seek reassurance that they are still desirable, and also want to pass on if necessary some of the pain they feel. It is an act that says "See if I care" and "Anything you can do I can do better," and the more people that can see her doing it the better, the more she likes it. But often revenge is sour, and the bitter taste remains in everybody's mouth.

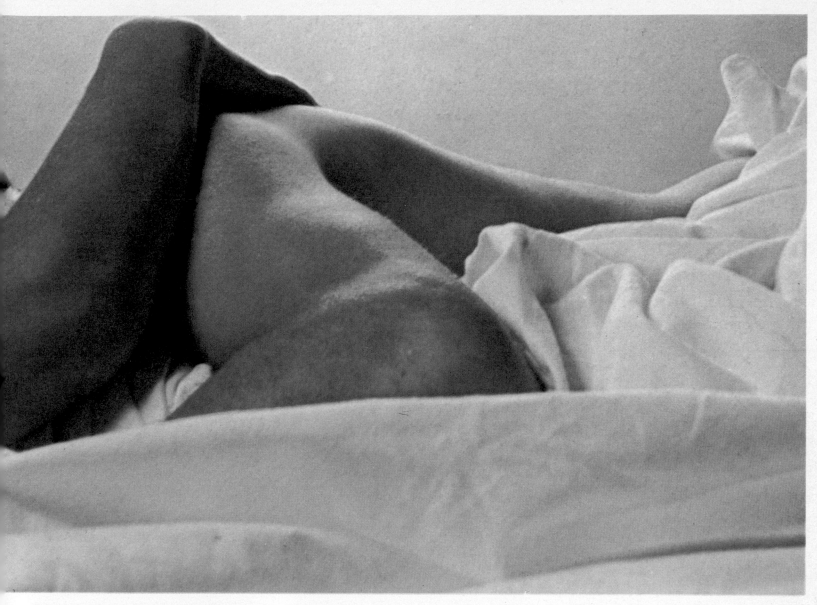

Does sex outside marriage free the horse from its carriage? Studies show that extramarital affairs can occasionally revive an ailing marriage but usually too much is at stake to justify the experiment.

Adultery is often a symptom that something is wrong rather than the sole cause of marital breakdown. The healthy marriage will survive the isolated affair, but not a series of clandestine relationships. If one or both of the marriage partners are leading a complicated love life, then perhaps they should never have married and it would be best to split up. Frequently there are complex psychological reasons for such sexual promiscuity and these can mar a marriage beyond hope.

Of course an affair can lead insidiously from flirtation to a much more disastrously deep involvement, and from there to the divorce courts. But even then it is hard to imagine that the original marriage was particularly good. For it is only in women's magazines that people fall passionately in love overnight. As far as most of us are concerned such a relationship grows a little more slowly, however powerful the sexual attraction may be, and there is time to draw back, to evaluate, and, hopefully, to decide that what we already have is worth settling for. If it is not, then that is another story, in another women's magazine, and we are back with the original and rather shaky marriage.

And where, you might wonder, does all this rapture begin? In the office? At a party? Across a crowded holiday beach? The answer is all three, and more besides. People meet their lovers where they meet their husbands and wives, which is anywhere and everywhere they happen to be. There is undoubtedly a high likelihood of people becoming involved with their fellow workers, because there is so much common ground, and a high exposure rate to one another day by day. Wives with husbands in high-powered or high-pressure jobs are inevitably at risk here, because it is so hard for them to share or even to appreciate the problems and the stresses that are ever-present—while Miss Smith, the secretary, finds it extremely easy. But the secretary is an overrated danger. The fellow executive with whom there is so much common ground and common purpose is a far greater threat.

Seven Year Itch
And, then again, does the itch really become unbearable after the proverbial seven years, or is it sooner—or even later—than that? Certainly where the cause is boredom, weariness or staleness, the period towards the end of the first decade of marriage is a particularly "accident prone" time. The first tender and careless rapture is over, and *ever* after seems a long time to live with just one person, however happily. Women are particularly restless at this time, with their children growing out of dependence and babyhood and departing to school. Variety brings spice to life —spice often hot to handle!

Kobal

Sex & Bargains

Marriage is often described as "licensed prostitution." And although most women would recoil from the implication, there are still those who regard sex as a highly negotiable asset. The husband who has been cajoled into painting the bathroom ceiling might well find his reward in bed even though sexual bargaining like this could end in a devalued relationship.

Successful hustlers have learned one basic principle—offer a person what he or she wants and the money will flow to pay for it. The stronger the desire, the easier it is to tap the reservoirs of cash—and if the desire is for sex the possibilities for extortion are virtually limitless. The call girl in a mink coat knows it and so does the gigolo dangling chunky gold bracelets. More surprisingly, in marriage, too, sex may be used as a bargaining counter.

To some extent every marriage is a sexual bargain in which husband and wife agree to look for economic and emotional security together. But despite the traditional jibe that marriage is licensed prostitution, the husband does not "buy" his wife's sexual favors, nor does she pay for a roof over her head by activities in the marital bed.

Male and female roles in modern Western society may imply that the husband pays the bills while the wife looks after the home and the children, but their sexual enjoyment of each other is shared and not linked to material contributions.

Some people, however, take a narrower view of the marital contract and for them sex is an asset that has a definite value and an exchange rate calculated in goods and services. Harold had become used to his wife Diana pulling on a long nightgown before coming to bed—and more often than not muttering that she was too tired to make love. He had also become used to her complaints that he never gave her expensive jewelry, although she knew as well as he did that they could not afford it.

Then one day Harold won a casual

sweepstake at his office and found he could buy the necklace that Diana had pointed out in the local jewelry store. That night Diana got into bed wearing nothing but the necklace and whispered that he still looked as handsome as he had on their honeymoon. To Diana, one necklace equaled one night of love-making.

This attitude can reveal itself even before marriage. A young woman, for example, may insist on a proper number of visits to the cinema, expensive candlelit dinners and bouquets of flowers before agreeing to make love.

Although less open about the connection between sex and money, she is not many steps from Mae West's Diamond Lil. To the comment "My goodness, those diamonds are lovely" she happily replied, "Goodness had nothing to do with it." Carried to the extreme, these demands may include a marriage proposal, with its guarantee of lifelong security, to trade against sexual capitulations.

The Price of Love

Sexual bargaining can spread into all areas of a relationship, and spending money on entertainments or gifts is only one form of payment. Jane had very high standards of housekeeping, her curtains and carpets were always spotless and everything had its place. Jeffrey was happy to talk about new furniture and decorations, but tended to sit around and rest after coming home from work rather than starting on Jane's schemes.

One evening, Jane announced: "We must paint the bathroom ceiling." Jeffrey had his reply ready: "I'll get around to it soon." That night Jane turned over and rolled away from him as he tried to embrace her in bed. "You're always ready for that, aren't you?" she said. "Why can't you put some of that energy into keeping the house nice?" The next evening Jeffrey painted the ceiling, and Jane was there when he finished to lead him to the bedroom.

The way the bargain is struck, or the pressure applied, may be a long way from the finger in the mail order catalogue and the insincere "I'm sure you'll find it worth your while" of the real gold digger. But to the partners the implications, although not spelled out, can be quite clear. A woman's tight smile when her husband begins a story at her expense warns him against finishing it if he hopes to make love to her that night. A man's refusal to kiss his wife when he leaves the house in the morning aims to get her to change the weekend arrange-

ments she has been planning on.

The sexual bargain may even be about sex itself. "David's always been a bit shy and straightforward," said Sheila. "We're really quite well suited to each other. But then he began talking about how our love-making might be more exciting and made hints about some underwear he'd seen. It seemed silly to me—our love-making had always seemed to satisfy both of us—but he virtually refused to make love to me for a while. Eventually I bought a black lacy bra and pants and let David know I was wearing them. He almost drove me into the bedroom."

In light-hearted ways using the wiles of sex in other areas can be fun. Cajoling, hinting and promising are close to flirting and if both partners are aware of what they are doing—one influencing, the other being influenced—it is an enjoyable game. Choosing where to spend a holiday, or when to visit each other's parents, becomes a shared decision linked to the couple's sexual awareness. The one seducing has his or her attractiveness confirmed, the one seduced has the pleasure of granting a wish.

Many everyday situations contain some element of sexual bribery and few people mind the hint of untold pleasures in a pair of fluttered eyelashes or a deliberately husky voice as the request for a special favor or privilege slides in.

The Language of Love

Some married couples actually prefer exchanging tokens of love to trying to talk directly about complex emotions. Such couples may develop a language of their own involving presents and tasks carried out, sex given and withheld, in which they communicate without embarrassment. Each knows what the other means.

Preparing a favorite meal or arranging a visit to the theater becomes a pleasant bribe which says: "I've done this because I want to make love. Will you?"

Exploiting a partner's sexual desires, however, rather than just acknowledging their strength, is likely to cause serious difficulties. Then husband and wife no longer share their decisions and enjoyment of sex. They are continually in conflict and cannot see how they might compromise. Coercion as a way of life, one partner forcing the other to make every adjustment, is not a recipe for a happy marriage.

Immaturity is the thread that runs through most of these forms of bargaining with sex. "How can I get the

most out of marriage?" asks the childish mind, and replies, "By holding my partner to ransom." The man who believes that paying for his wife's new dress automatically entitles him to sexual intercourse as and when he wishes, and the woman who seduces her husband as a way of persuading him to buy a new washing machine, miss the possibilities of cooperation.

The Threats of Sex

The bargain may even be a way of avoiding adult responsibilities and returning to a less-demanding childlike state. Eric Berne in *Sex in Human Loving* suggests we all have elements of child, adult and parent in our psychological make-up. The childlike person forces the partner into the parental role and then tries to manipulate the "parent" through the emotional blackmail of withholding sex. Unconsciously he or she argues, "Parents give their children what they want and I want . . ." Sex is a more powerful weapon, however, than any infant's tantrums.

After Charles and Mary had seen their son off to college, Charles decided to turn the empty bedroom into a workroom. It was something he had always wanted and he enthusiastically threw himself into buying tools and ordering a work bench. Then Mary's mother began talking about how lonely she was now that her husband had died and Mary suggested she might come to live with them—in the spare room.

"Charles agreed at once," said Mary. "I suppose he felt he had to. But then he began to sulk. He'd be quiet all evening—except to say perhaps he'd have been making something if there'd been a room he could work in—and then he'd get into bed and just go to sleep. He wouldn't even kiss me goodnight.

"In the end I arranged for Mother to go into a home—she's very happy there and we can afford it—but I wish we'd talked about it properly instead of Charles having to have his way to bring our relationship back to normal."

One way that sex can become a form of payment is through a misguided and oversimplified view of male and female roles. A man may believe he has continually to demonstrate his ability to support his wife. He decks her with jewels, provides a new fur coat at Christmas, the latest models of kitchen equipment and so on. His wife's natural pleasure leads to lovemaking and gradually the couple come to link his expenditure with her compliance. They may even boast

Kobal

Men are conditioned to believe that strong, silent types get the girls and may think they can trade one act of courage for an adoring embrace. This form of sexual bargaining means that a man might find himself playing a part for which he is by nature unsuited.

about his conspicuous expenditure.

A woman who imagines the husband's contribution to marriage is the money he earns, and the wife's her physical charms, may demand a series of gifts almost to show that he is keeping to the bargain—if the flow of gifts stops, so does the love-making. In this situation, if the man or woman is also driven to "keep up with the Joneses," the couple are sitting on a sexual time bomb. The payment for sex will eventually become too great.

For some people this may actually be the aim. They use sexual bargaining as a way of avoiding love-making. For whatever reason they turn against sex—distaste, boredom, an affair outside marriage—they suggest an impossible bargain to camouflage the withdrawal. "I will make love if you will do this, or this or this."

In other cases, the sexual bargain, although still linked to immaturity, may have a positive value by helping one or both partners overcome reservations about sex. The ideal is an acceptance of sex as a central and enjoyable part of marriage, but some people fear the strength of their own emotions and find difficulty in expressing sexual feeling.

Business Partnership

For them, exchanging sex for rewards paradoxically loosens the chains of sexual inhibition. Love-making that was difficult to enjoy for itself alone, because it involves an unacceptable loss of control, becomes legitimate when it has a double purpose. The thought of gaining a television or a piece of costume jewelry allows release to otherwise inadmis-

sible sexual desires. Sex, somehow, is not so sinful when it is for business purposes.

Some insecure couples may actually build a stable marriage in this way although otherwise unable to sustain an intimate relationship. Emotional blackmail of any kind—and sexual bargaining relies on blackmail—requires that the victim accepts the situation. He or she must think that any alternative would be worse. The blackmailer demands and the victim gives because any resistance might destroy the marriage. The two collaborate in a game that neither can win in order to avoid the responsibilities involved in a mature relationship.

People like this may be frightened to engage in open conflict because they think marriage should be continual bliss. Any dissension, they believe, conjures up the specter of divorce. They may never realize the potential rewards of cooperation just because they are too frightened to disagree.

Deirdre's father had been a hard-driving businessman. When she married John, a teacher at the local school, she realized that he was a much gentler man but assumed that the responsibilities of a house and a growing family would give him ambition. John, however, seemed quite content to continue working at the school—he enjoyed being a teacher despite the low salary.

Then Deirdre turned on the pressure. First it was remarks about how nice her best friend's house looked, then it was complaints about making do on a teacher's earnings. "I didn't marry you to live in poverty," she said. "You can't expect me to enjoy making love in a secondhand bed."

John began tutorial work in the evening, and when this, too, seemed not enough took on a job as barman at the weekend. Soon he had the money for a bedroom suite, but he was exhausted every night and his teaching had begun to suffer. John felt he could not complain that Deirdre wanted the living standards she had been used to. His acceptance of Deirdre's insistent demands prevented them from seeing that they might be happier if they postponed the chase

Sexual politics make strange bedfellows! To strike a bargain outside the bedroom a woman may gear herself to her husband's particular sexual tastes. This often gives pleasure to both of them but can mean trouble when black lace equals blackmail.

after money while John worked for qualifications that would gain him promotion.

Both men and women may attempt the emotional blackmail of sexual bargaining. An insecure man, for example, may resort to sexual bargaining in marriage just as he is tempted to make unfair emotional demands of friends and colleagues at work. But the impetus comes from the feeling that there is no other source of power and this more often applies to women than to men. John Scanzoni, associate professor of sociology at Indiana University, points out, in a book subtitled *Power Politics in the American Marriage*, that, in overall terms, women in Western society earn less than their husbands and have less access to resources outside the marriage. Social conventions almost *expect* them to seek influence through the wiles of sex.

Power Behind the Throne

In the past, a woman's political power has been linked to the bedroom rather than the hustings. Lysistrata called upon the women of Greece to withhold sex from their menfolk until they refrained from war. The struggle for influence at the court of Louis XIV was between his mistresses, not his ministers. And behind every great man, according to the cynics, was a woman who had traded her virginity for a share of greatness.

It is hardly surprising that a housewife today might feel that only by rationing sex can she affect her husband's decisions and stop him from taking their sexual relationship for granted.

Jacqueline and Tom had been married ten years and Tom had gradually slipped into staying late at the office, eating a quick meal when he got home and slumping into bed. At the weekend he would take Jacqueline out for a meal and then routinely make love to her.

Jacqueline's resentment built up until one Saturday she pushed him away as he tried to cuddle her in bed. "Why don't you ever ask what I want?" she said. "We make love when you say, we go to the places you like. Don't think you can go on like that!"

An emotionally mature couple will "make a bargain" with time and plan a happy future together (below), instead of trying to manipulate each other. A poor young man (right) may burn himself out working late hours to buy the expensive gifts his wife demands. But this bargain will cost him too much. His income rises but he will not have leisure to enjoy it (see chart). An understanding wife will realize that though income may decrease initially, a period of education or poorly paid experience is an investment for the future and will mean more money and leisure later. Yet, if she were understanding, she would not have demanded gifts at all.

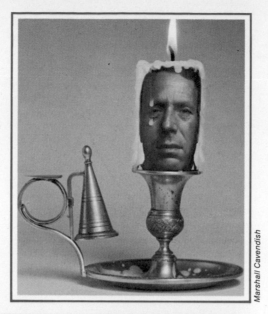

Marshall Cavendish

Marshall Cavendish

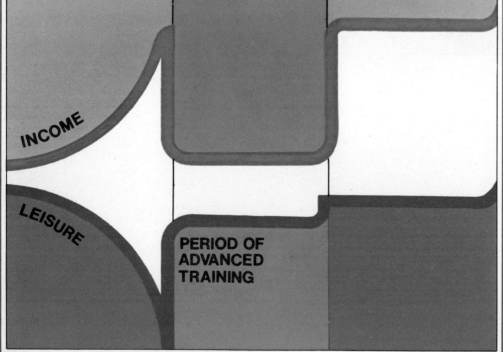

INCOME

LEISURE

PERIOD OF ADVANCED TRAINING

David Kinefield

Over the next few weeks Tom began to ask her opinion more—and seemed to take more interest in satisfying her during their love-making. Jacqueline might have altered Tom's selfish behavior earlier if she had felt able to criticize him openly. She had not believed he would listen unless she applied some kind of pressure.

The need to bargain with sex reflects immaturity and an underassessment of personal worth that can stem from an unbalanced upbringing. A child raised in an insecure home, perhaps one where the parents often quarrel and give little time to playing with the child or where a divorced father or mother appears only occasionally, may come to associate love with gifts: the very presence of the parents is a precious gift.

In such situations, a child who learns that demanding "rewards" is the one sure way of getting attention may learn techniques of emotional blackmail at an early age. "If you love me you will give me a tricycle, a doll, a candy" is the forerunner of the adult's demands for material proof of love. In another case a child bribed to achieve a parent's high expectations may continue "achieving" and seeking rewards in adult life.

At a later stage, an insecure adolescent may discover the power of sex. To a young person who has never before felt able to control any part of his or her environment the results can be intoxicating—gifts are proffered, requests complied with, insults meekly swallowed.

Suddenly sex appeal becomes an antidote for personality deficiencies and the worlds of the cinema, of advertising and so on apparently confirm that sex is the currency for every payment. Some people remain at this stage of semimaturity and will continue to exploit sexual relationships in adult life—the power is there and they cannot resist using it.

Once a couple recognize in their own relationship the destructive spiral of demand backed up by sexual threat, followed by surrender and then yet greater demands, what can they do? Perhaps the first step is to make sure that *both* actually know what is happening.

The man or woman who is held to ransom and does nothing to avoid it chooses to devalue the relationship and takes some of the responsibility for later problems. Discussion may be painful but carries the assumption that both partners want a deeper emotional involvement that will give their relationship a secure base.

Oedipus explained

According to Freud we are all obsessed with our parents in early life. Little boys become sexually interested in their mothers and jealous of their fathers. In girls the reverse is the case. The way we learn to cope with these emotions affects us for the rest of our lives.

Ask a little girl whom she would like to marry when she grows up and the answer may well be "Daddy." Equally, small boys may have the same feelings towards their mothers.

Parental reaction, naturally enough, is to pass off such statements as a joke and no adult would be inclined to take them seriously. If one *did* take these desires seriously the implications would be startling. It might, for example, be concluded that small boys regard their fathers as sexual rivals, and that in the same way girls are jealous of their mothers. Freud, who took everything seriously—even jokes, developed the theory that every child does indeed harbor very strong feelings for the parent of the opposite sex.

He suggested that if growing up proceeds naturally, these feelings are resolved by the child learning to identify with the parent of the same sex. However, in some cases, said Freud, these desires persist—albeit at an unconscious level—and result in excessive love of the mother and pathological hatred and envy for the father in the case of boys. This he termed the "Oedipus complex" after the ancient Greek legend of Oedipus, who killed his father and married his mother.

In girls, who may be excessively jealous of their mothers, it is called the "Electra complex."

Freud maintained—much to the horror of his contemporary world—that all of us are subject to these complexes in early life, and that our subsequent psychological development depends a great deal on how we come to terms with these powerful emotions, of which we may not ever be consciously aware. It is just these kinds of "unacceptable" feelings which we repress.

Some say he has an Oedipus complex and has never outgrown his need for a mother figure. Others claim that such a relationship can be as fulfilling as one between two people nearer the same age. Is this match by conscious choice or due to some early maladjustment?

There is no way of confirming Freud's theory in the way that a theory in physics can be confirmed. If we cannot recognize it in ourselves, we certainly will not see it in others. But there is another kind of test. Does the theory help to explain some aspects of everyday behavior?

Oedipus Complex

A simple observation provides a clue. Quite early in his career, Freud noticed that nearly all his neurotic women patients said that they had been seduced by their fathers. Obviously this was not really true, and Freud pointed out that the "memory" must represent a wish, concealed even from the patient. These memories were part of the evidence for the existence of the Oedipus complex. The other evidence was somewhat piecemeal.

It is generally agreed that male

Marshall Cavendish

homosexuals are usually devoted to their mothers. The reason given is that they have been unable to find a woman who could match their mother's standards. This, however, is absurd. Mature people do not fall in love and marry as a result of listing the qualities of the partner. What we are really saying is that the adult has never outgrown his sexual attachment to his mother.

Meaningful Dreams

The Oedipus wish turns up, of course, in dreams, and Freud quoted a good example. One of his patients dreamed that he was having an affair with a woman whom someone else wanted to marry. He was worried that the other man might find out and cancel the proposed wedding. So, in his dream, he behaved extremely affectionately to the other man. He even kissed him.

Like most dreams, this one was based on fact. The man *was* having an affair. But from this point on, the dream broke away. He was having an affair with a married woman, whose husband, a friend, seemed to suspect him. And, the crucial difference, the husband was ill and expected to die soon. The man certainly hoped to marry the woman when she became a widow.

His situation was normal and at least partly honorable, and there is no obvious reason why it should have been disguised in the dream. But, as Freud points out, the man unconsciously "wished" to kill the husband to have his wife, or at least he wanted him dead. This is exactly the situation of the boy in a family, and the man reacted as he had in childhood. He was extremely fond of his father.

Some of Freud's best examples come from his own memories. He quotes what he calls an anxiety dream: He saw his mother, with a peaceful, sleeping expression on her face, being carried into the room by two strange, tall people with birds' beaks. They laid her on the bed. She appeared to be dead. Freud, who was seven or eight at the time, woke screaming.

We all know what Freud means by an anxiety dream—it is a dream that is peculiarly disturbing and leaves a feeling of dread behind. Years later, Freud worked out what his dream represented. Parts of it he recognized easily. The strange people came from Bible illustrations, and his mother's expression reproduced a glimpse Freud had had of his grandfather, in a coma, a few days before his death.

An artist's conception of the development of the Oedipus complex in a male child in relation to his parents. The reverse is the same for a girl. From the changing position of the lines, it can be seen that a boy is furthest from his father as a baby and is closest to his mother. From about age three to six, he starts to become aware of his sex organ, indulges in fondling himself, and even creates a fantasy life. He begins to take a sexual interest in his mother. And he grows jealous of his father, fearing that that parent will castrate him because he is a rival for his mother's love (the castration complex). Referring again to the illustration, as the boy grows older he becomes more independent of his mother and identifies increasingly with his father. By the time he is a grown man he should, in psychological terms, be at an equal distance from both mother and father.

But the birdmen had a double meaning. When Freud thought about it, he remembered that they brought to mind a precocious boy he had known, who had taught him the German slang word for sexual intercourse. It is *vögeln*: the German word for bird is *Vogel*. He was not anxious because his mother was, in the dream, dead. His anxiety came from the concealed sexual craving. Anxiety is different from sorrow.

Incestuous Love

He quotes another example, this time from his medical work. He had been treating an old lady for years, giving her a daily morphine injection and some eye drops. The treatment had become automatic. But one day, he noticed, just in time, that he had filled the eye dropper with morphine. He was "greatly frightened." And yet, there was no need for that much fear. After all, he had not actually put the morphine into the eye, and even if he had, it would be harmless. And in any case, what could it have to do with the Oedipus feeling? The woman was over 90, and surely no one could be sexually attracted to an old invalid.

But one of the odd things about the actual story of Oedipus is that his mother must have been at least middle-aged before he married her. And in real life it is not really possible to imagine marrying one's own mother, because of the age gap. But the story and the imagination of the child ignore this gap, and the trace left in the mind as the Oedipus complex concerns the young, attractive mother. There is a second point. It so happens that the German verb "to make a mistake" is the same as "to commit a violent act," i.e. to rape her. Freud's unreasonable fear was explained because in his mind he had been raping an old lady who represented his mother.

No list of examples proves that we at one time wanted to kill one parent and marry the other. The fact that children go through a stage where they strongly prefer the parent of the opposite sex is evidence but not proof. The fact that neurotic patients were cured when Freud showed how the Oedipus complex lay at the root of their problems is again only evidence.

And when you consider it, does anyone actually feel a lust for incest? But then, as Freud says, if nobody wants to commit incest, is it not odd that so many countries and so many religions go to the trouble of prohibiting it?

The Legend

The story of Oedipus springs from Greek mythology and began when the goddess Hera cursed Aphrodite and all her family.

A long time later Laius, King of Thebes and descendant of Aphrodite, gave a feast to celebrate his marriage to Jocasta. As was customary, the Oracle was consulted to see what the future held. Doom and despair were the only firm promise, and Laius was told he would die by the hand of his son.

When eventually a boy was born, Laius ordered that he be killed. But Jocasta instructed a servant to abandon him instead. However, he was discovered by a shepherd whose master, King Polybus of Corinth, gave the infant to his childless wife Queen Periboea to rear as his heir. She named the boy Oedipus.

Oedipus grew to be greatly admired by all except a jealous courtier who spread the hitherto closely guarded story of his early existence. Oedipus determined to seek the truth from the Oracle.

But instead of answering his questions directly, the Oracle told Oedipus that he would murder his father and become his mother's lover. Oedipus then decided to go far away. On the journey he and his followers met another party of travelers in a narrow gorge. Neither group would give way so Oedipus killed the opposing leader. He was Laius. The first part of the prophecy had been fulfilled.

Laius had been on his way to ask the Oracle how he could rid his kingdom of the Sphinx, a monstrous creature with a woman's head and lion's body. When Creon, brother of Laius, assumed the role of Regent of the Kingdom he promised the throne and the widowed Jocasta in marriage to whoever could drive the Sphinx from Thebes.

The Sphinx ordered all who confronted her to answer a riddle. She strangled those who failed. On his arrival Oedipus challenged the creature and answered correctly. He was proclaimed King of Thebes and husband of Jocasta—thus completing the Oracle's prediction.

Some years later, while Thebes suffered from a plague, the Oracle forecast that it would continue until the murderer of Laius was found. Oedipus immediately set up a commission of enquiry and after years of search the devastating truth was revealed.

Doomed to exile for his country's sake and destroyed by grief, Oedipus put out both his eyes and was led to a sacred grove at Colonus where the earth opened up and received him.

Oedipus challenging the Sphinx, which had the head of a woman and the body of a lion. She terrorized the Kingdom of Thebes, and strangled all those who could not answer her riddle. The Greeks believed that Oedipus was a victim of his own pride in thinking he could outsmart the Oracle, the Sphinx, the very gods. Though sufferers of the Oedipus complex may meet with a less-drastic end, they have no conscious control at all over their situation.

Mansell

The key to skill

Every minute of every day our minds absorb a constant stream of information. Yet, thanks to a remarkably efficient filtering system, only a fraction actually reaches our consciousness. And even when it does the chances of remembering it for more than a few days at a time are about 100-1 against. The rest is forgotten almost instantly.

Man as we know him today would not exist if he had no powers of memory. It is the ability to remember that enables him to rectify his past mistakes and profit from his past successes.

Without memory, man would be permanently in the starting blocks of life. Every situation he faced would appear strange, even if he had encountered it a hundred times before. Language, thought, art and science would be impossible. Nor could man project from his past experience what is likely to happen in the future and prepare himself to cope with events which have not yet occurred.

Similarly, as the capacity of the brain to store memories is limited, man would find himself in the same predicament if he lacked the power to be selective about the vast amount of experiences and thoughts with which he is bombarded, day in and day out.

If all of these experiences and thoughts were stored away indiscriminately, man's brain would reach a point at which it was full to the brim. It would not be possible for him to absorb any new experiences.

In fact, man is equipped with a highly efficient filtering system. Only a tiny fraction of the information which floods in upon him actually reaches his consciousness. Even if he becomes consciously aware of something, the chances are worse than

The human has two kinds of memory, the recalling of past experience and the retention of abstract ideas. Someone may easily remember his wedding especially when recall is triggered off by a photo of the event. Abstract information like the distance between the earth and the moon is not based on experience.

100-1 against being able to remember it for as long as a few days. Most of the information impinging on our consciousness is consigned to oblivion within a few seconds or, at most, minutes.

Short-term Memory

One common example of this short-term—or, as psychologists term it, primary—memory arises when someone wants to make a telephone call but does not know the number. He looks it up, dials the number, and, as a rule, has forgotten the number again by the time he has finished his conversation. If he wishes to call again later the same day, he usually has to look the number up a second time.

It is only when he finds himself in the position of having to call regularly, or by making a deliberate effort at learning it, that he can commit the number to his long-term (secondary)

Zip Art

Barnaby's

Associated Press

Associated Press

Above: We learn to ignore recurring sounds, which in our noisy world is vital. This is known as the Bowery El Phenomenon — after a railway that disturbed local residents only when it was closed down. The silence did it! Left: Motor skills like tennis and golf may become rusty, but once learned they are never forgotten.

memory. This secondary memory is the one in which man stores the meaningful thoughts and experiences from his past.

In view of its importance, it is not surprising that the nature of memory exercised the mind of man as long as two thousand years ago. Then the Greek philosopher Plato believed that the soul possessed a faculty that, like wax, received impressions through the senses and the intellect. His pupil Aristotle also likened memory with wax.

He made a distinction, however, between memory, a faculty of the senses, and recollection, a function of the soul involving a kind of "hunting process" by which man recalls— brings into the actual memory—a past experience. Aristotle also took the view that many animals besides man possess memory although very few can recollect. Aristotle's opinions were accepted, and elaborated upon, by Christian philosophers.

The approach of modern psychologists—and, more recently, biologists—to memory is on a more practical level. They try, with the aid

273

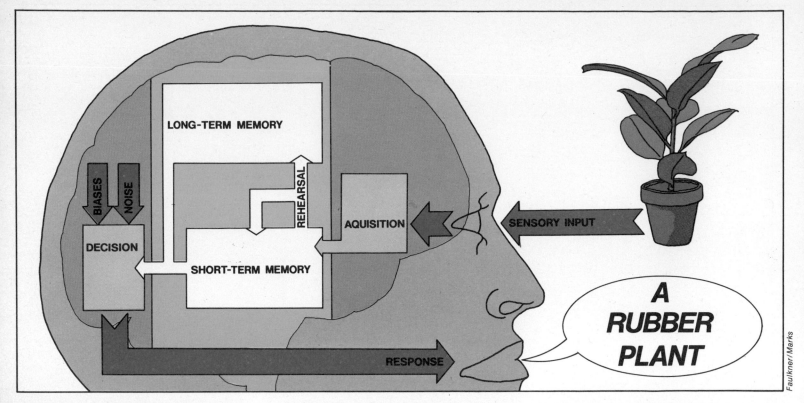

Faulkner/Marks

Memory is of two kinds. Short-term memory is the ability to remember a telephone number for as long as it takes to make the call. For material to pass from there to the long-term memory requires rehearsal. Decisions are made from material drawn from the memory but are subject to existing bias and outside interference — like noise.

of laboratory experiments, to establish precisely how thoughts and experiences are fixed in, retained in and recalled to the mind. They would agree with Aristotle that some types of memory are common to both man and the lower animals.

One of these is habituation, or, in more concrete terms, adapting to the same stimulus when exposed to it over and over again. The effect is that, because the stimulus is recurrent, we quickly come to ignore it. This is something man shares with simple creatures of only one cell.

Noise Filter

It is also one of the means he employs to shut out a large amount of the trivial information with which he is bombarded daily but which is not necessary for his — using the word in its broadest sense — survival.

Habituation explains why someone who moves to the country after living in the center of a bustling town finds himself unable to sleep: he has grown used to the noise of traffic at night and ceased to notice it. Now, however, the stimulus has changed from traffic

noise to the silence of the countryside, broken occasionally by the song of a nightingale. The silence is so "deafening" that he cannot sleep.

The same sequence of events is illustrated by what has been called the "Bowery El Phenomenon." Trains on New York's elevated railroad used to make a tremendous noise at night, but families living nearby slept through it quite happily. When the line was taken down, however, they started to wake up at the times when the trains used to rumble by. They missed the expected noise.

Probably most people have heard of the Russian scientist Pavlov's experiments in what is known as "classic conditioning" of dogs.

Briefly, a bell was rung as food was presented to the dogs. Saliva formed in their mouths at the sight of the food. Each time they were fed the bell was rung and, eventually, the sound of the bell alone was sufficient to make them salivate.

Man, too, can be made the subject of classic conditioning with similar results to those brought about with Pavlov's dogs. If you puff air at one of his eyes, he will blink. Experiments have shown that, when puffing of the air is paired with some other effect such as, say, pressing a buzzer, the man will eventually blink at the sound of the buzzer alone.

Another experiment on the same lines involved making a sudden noise, which had the effect of sending a man's heartbeat up, and at the same time shining a light. In the end the light

by itself was sufficient to increase the rate of the man's heartbeats.

The ability to learn and remember what we call motor skills is another form of memory which man shares with other creatures. The circus seal, for example, can be taught to balance a ball on the end of its nose. In the same way, man can teach himself such "unnatural" skills as standing on his head, riding a bicycle, swimming, playing golf.

Skilled for Life

Once learned, these skills are never forgotten. In the case of sports such as golf and tennis, of course, you will get rusty if you cease to play for a time, but the basic skill remains and you quickly recapture your previous peak of performance once you take up the game again. But such motor skills as riding a bicycle or swimming, once acquired, remain with you all your life.

An interesting sidelight on this is the fact that it seems likely that such diverse personalities as Little Mo Connolly, Pavlova, Jack Nicklaus and Paderewski share something in addition to eminence. That is an efficient cerebellum, sometimes called "the little brain," located at the back of the head and below the main brain.

When we are learning something like tennis, ballet dancing, golf or playing the piano, in which there is a large degree of repetitive, technical skill involved, the main brain is in charge of the operation at the outset in the usual way. It is largely a visual exercise in the sense that we have a

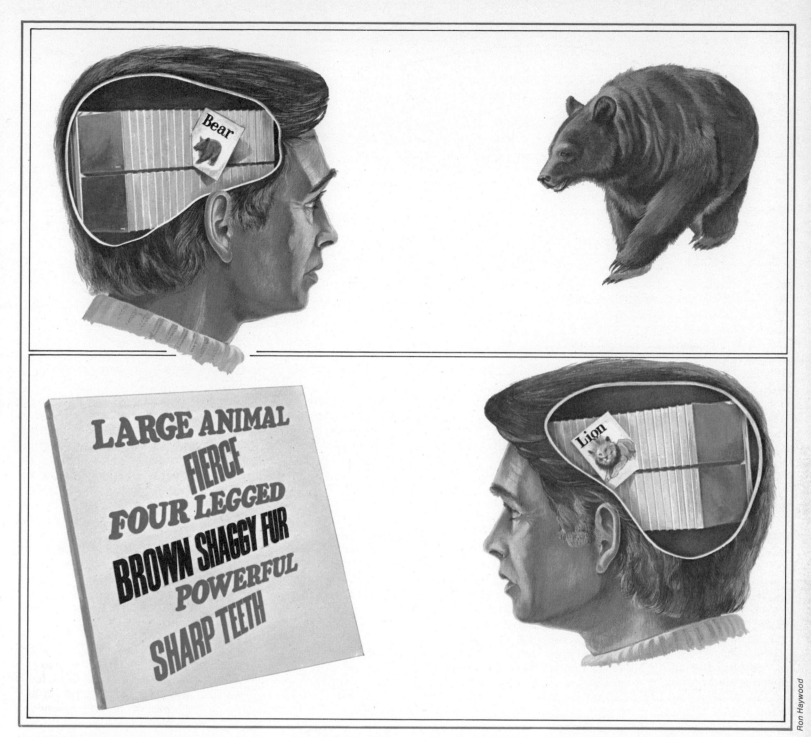

Ron Haywood

picture in our minds of what we want to do and the main brain plans how we are going to do it and also issues the necessary orders to our muscles.

There is now evidence, however, that, once the technical skills have been mastered by constant repetition, the main brain bows out, leaving the cerebellum to control these repetitive skills. It has been found that, in cases where one half of the cerebellum is damaged, the corresponding half of the body loses much of its efficiency at performing skilled movements.

The main brain has the ability to process only a limited amount of information at any given time. Being able to start the mechanical movements going by issuing just one order

to the cerebellum therefore frees the main brain to deal with other things.

The classical concert pianist, for example, can concentrate on expression without having to bother about fingering: the great tennis player can concentrate on such tactical matters as wrong-footing an opponent or luring him to the net rather than on merely hitting the ball. It is, indeed, arguable that one of the main differences between the great and mediocre players, whether of the piano or tennis, lies in the type of cerebellum they possess.

In addition to the types of memory which man shares in common with the lower animals, he also possesses two types of memory which are unique to

The word "remember" describes different processes that occur within the brain — for instance, what psychologists know as "recall" and "recognition." When a man sees a bear he immediately *recognizes* it. This depends on the fact that he has some previous experience of bears. When only data concerning the bear is presented, his mind sifts through copious filing systems to *recall* the correct image. This is analogous to the workings of a computer and explains some computer errors, for if the information is not sufficient a number of answers may fit the bill. In this case, a lion springs to mind, as it, too, suits the description.

him. Firstly, he can recall his past experience, reconstruct his past life. Secondly, he is able to form abstract memories, and this second type of memory is very much bound up with language ability.

Simple examples will demonstrate the distinction between these two kinds of memory. If we think about our wedding day we have a mental picture of ourselves, the church, the wedding reception, going away on honeymoon afterwards: we recall the whole experience of getting married.

On the other hand our powers of abstract memory enable us to recall such information as the fact that the moon is a quarter of a million miles from the earth or that the angles at the base of an isosceles triangle are equal. In this case we recall the knowledge but not, as a rule, the experience of acquiring it. We do not remember the moment when we first read, or were told, the facts.

Three-Tiered System

It is quite clear that "memory" can have a wide range of meanings. One man may have what we call a "photographic memory": he can read a page of a book and reproduce it at once perfectly.

Another, like contestants in TV quiz programs, may have stored away a vast amount of information about history, sport, geography or some other favorite subject.

A third, when he says he has "an excellent memory," may mean he has a vivid recollection of a large part of his distant childhood, or, although he has not played for some years, is still a useful performer at chess, or can recognize and name a great range of tunes played to him on the piano.

No matter what kind of long-term human memory we are considering, however, it can be divided into three phases. The first phase involves some experience or activity. A man goes to watch a football game or learns to ride a bicycle.

In the second phase the experience of watching the football game or learning to ride a bicycle passes from his conscious mind into his long-term memory where it is retained.

The last phase, occurring perhaps weeks or months later, comes when the man describes to a friend what the football game was like or hops on a bicycle and pedals away.

During the second phase, the memory is latent. We cannot look at the man and notice anything which would prompt us to say, "That man was at such-and-such a football game," or,

"That man knows how to ride a bicycle." Yet, once he starts to describe the game in detail we can infer that he was there; once he rides off on the bicycle we can infer that he must have acquired the skill of riding a bicycle at some time.

It is thus true to say that, when we speak of somebody's memory, we are nearly always emphasizing some relationship between his past and present activities.

Nevertheless, we do not recall past experience in the same sense that a concert tape reproduces exactly the performance of the orchestra. The nonduplicative nature of recalling is illustrated by the fact that no actor, no matter how well he knows his part, ever gives two performances which are identical.

The fact that, instead of being duplicative, recalling involves selection and construction can easily be demonstrated by learning experiments. Ian M. L. Hunter, for example, gives an account in his book *Memory* of an experiment in which two hundred students were given a minute to learn the following "magic square" (the digits in any column or diagonal add up to the same total):

$$\begin{array}{ccc} 4 & 9 & 2 \\ 3 & 5 & 7 \\ 8 & 1 & 6 \end{array}$$

He reports: "With only one minute spent in learning, some 90 percent of students correctly reproduce the array one hour later. When students are asked afterwards to report as much as they can about what they did while learning and remembering the array, their reports strikingly bring out three points relevant to the constructive nature of recalling.

Memories are Made of This

"The first point concerns individual differences; very few students proceed by what appears to be sheer rote repetition, that is, repeating the nine digits over and over again. . . . The great majority, even though they use repetition, do not recite digits without noting relationships between them.

"In some cases, these noted relationships are simple, e.g. that 4, 9, 2 are the last three digits of the year Columbus landed in America. In other cases, these relations are more complex, e.g. the even sequence 2, 4, 6, 8 fills up the four corners in the order top-to-bottom and right-to-left, while the odd sequence 1, 3, 5, 7, 9 fills up the remaining gaps in the order bottom-to-top and left-to-right.

"Some students note that the array is a magic square; some do not. The

main point is that, even in this simple learning task, hardly any two students carry through their learning activity in quite the same fashion. This point warns us against assuming that when two people learn the same lesson they necessarily learn it in the same way.

"The second point which emerges from the reports concerns *effort after meaning*. Despite individual differences between one student and the next, no learner passively absorbs the array. Rather, he proceeds by, so to speak, making of the material what sense he can.

Active Acquisition

"He attempts to impose pattern, to interpret the array in terms of relationships which are familiar to him, to recast the material into familiar molds. He elaborates relationships which coordinate one part of the array with another: a few examples of such relationships were cited above . . .

"So learning is not a matter of passive registration. It is active and selective, and effort after meaning plays a conspicuous part. The reports also reveal that the particular coordinating relationships elaborated during learning later play a role in subsequent recall. And this brings us to the third, and last, point brought out by the reports.

"The third point directly concerns the constructive characterization of past events. Each individual student shows similarity between the way he went about learning the array and the way he goes about reproducing it."

Clearly, memory is one of the most significant parts of man's make-up. It enables him, throughout his life, to profit from his past experience, to acquire new skills, to grow in knowledge and understanding. Each day, because he can remember what happened and what he learned, makes him more "at home" in the world. Not only can he profit from his own past experience but, because of the form of memory known as language, from other men's experience as well. These lessons determine his future.

Yet, although we all have a memory and recognize in broad terms how it works, it is an intangible. It is not like a nose or a foot. We can observe it in operation when someone recites a poem or plays tennis, but we cannot reach out and touch it. For more than half a century psychologists and biologists have been studying this wonderful and complex faculty which has played such a vital role in the story of man and his civilization.

Keystone

Colin Curwood

The signal box

Although we now understand enough of memory to know that it works in different ways, we are still a long way from discovering the reasons why it functions as it does. Solving this mystery is one of the greatest challenges facing twentieth century scientists. If and when they find the answer we shall be a lot nearer to grasping the enigma of man himself.

How does the human memory actually work? Even after more than half a century of precise research and experiment, this remains to a considerable degree a mystery. There is a certain amount we can be sure about. After that we are in territory dotted with controversies and contradictions.

The memory functions through the brain. Most biologists regard the brain as a complex machine which processes, stores and retrieves sensory information. It also directs our actions.

As you look at this complex machine,

it appears to consist of four parts. At the top, under the skull, is the main brain, made up of two symmetrical cerebral hemispheres, linked by a system of nerves. At the back are two

Chronic alcoholism induces severe amnesia but research seems to show that it is not the memory itself that is impaired but rather the ability to retrieve information from it that suffers a breakdown. The filing cabinets are fully stocked but the only filing clerk who understands the system has left the office — permanently!

smaller—and again symmetrical and linked—hemispheres known as the cerebellum, or, more colloquially, "the little brain."

One distinction between their functions can be illustrated by the case of the top-class tennis player. Initially, the main brain dictates the process of learning to play the game. Once the mechanics of serving, volleying and so on have been mastered, however, the cerebellum (because it has automatically stored the "memory" of how to do these actions) takes over control of these repetitive movements—or motor skills, as they are technically known—leaving the main brain, which has a limited capacity for dealing with information, free to deal with such important, nonrepetitive elements of the sport as tactics.

The main brain consists of a series of tissue masses piled on top of each other. At the bottom they are linked with the spinal cord and the two hemispheres are wrapped in a wrinkled sheet called the cerebral cortex.

Parts of the brain are creamy white, parts a kind of gray. The white parts are tens of millions of nerve fibers. Each is basically a microscopic cable insulated from all the other cables by a sheath of white fat. The cables link all the different sections of the brain and transmit messages electrically between every section.

Memory Bank

The gray parts of the brain are made up of somewhere in the region of ten billion nerve cells, connected to the white cables. Without becoming too technical about it, a cell may not only receive messages along the white cables. It can also send out its own signals—along a nerve fiber called an axon—in the form of a minute 0.1 volt electric impulse. Each nerve cell is linked with several thousand other cells across tiny gaps called synapses. Communication takes place only in one direction by one cell releasing transmitter substances, which travel across the tiny gap so that they excite or inhibit the other cell.

It is therefore clear that the wiring system of the human brain is far more complex than even the computers and other sophisticated space age equipment at the Kennedy Space Center in Florida.

Messages are received from the senses—hearing, seeing, smelling, touching—as well as from inside the body itself. They are evaluated against past experience stored in the memory. If action is called for, the required messages are transmitted the same way they were received—from the nerve cell along an axon to the appropriate muscles.

For example, a person who had never seen or heard of such a thing as a telephone would immediately be confused if he found himself in a room with one that started to ring. He would not know what to do. Once the function of the telephone and the significance of the ringing had been explained to him, however, he would store the information in his memory. The next time he found himself in the

same situation, his ears would transmit the sound of the ringing to his brain, his brain would evaluate it against past experience (memory), and it would then issue the instruction: "Get up, walk to the telephone, pick up the receiver, speak."

But how does this complex machine we call the brain go about storing certain thoughts and experiences, thus enabling us to make constructive use of them in the future, while it rejects (forgets) others altogether or, at best, remembers them for only a fraction of time?

It is possible to distinguish two basic types of memory—short-term (primary) and long-term (secondary). The most useful illustration of short-term memory is having to refer constantly to an unfamiliar recipe. As a rule each step of the recipe remains in our consciousness only as long as it takes us to perform it: then it is forgotten. It will almost certainly be eliminated from our memory if someone breaks our concentration by, say, asking a question before we have finished.

Remembrance of Things Past

Long-term memory is quite different. We can recall things we learned, or experiences that happened to us, more than half a century ago. Sometimes we remember because we want to, as in the case of someone who, visiting Mexico after an absence of

Above: Some of the most complex equipment in the world at Kennedy Space Center, Florida, which navigated Apollo 11 to the moon. This equipment is a pale comparison next to the intricacy of a human brain. Right: We know that motor information entering the brain is selected and stored in the cerebellum and that this information becomes second nature to us. A good tennis player thus has a good storage system in his cerebellum which automatically supplies him with a full range of strokes leaving the rest of his brain free to dictate the tactics of his game.

many years and finding himself thirsty, will hunt around in his memory for the Mexican word for beer. Sometimes a memory seems to spring unbidden to the mind. On other occasions the memory can be triggered off by some sensory experience.

Odors, in particular, seem to have the power to bring to mind past experiences with almost hallucinatory clarity. A whiff of oil can make you recall, almost as if living it again, a weekend spent at a remote farmhouse lit only by oil lamps. Proust, the celebrated French writer, had a similar experience with a cup of tea and a special kind of cake called *madeleine*.

He recalls in his massive work *Remembrance of Things Past* that,

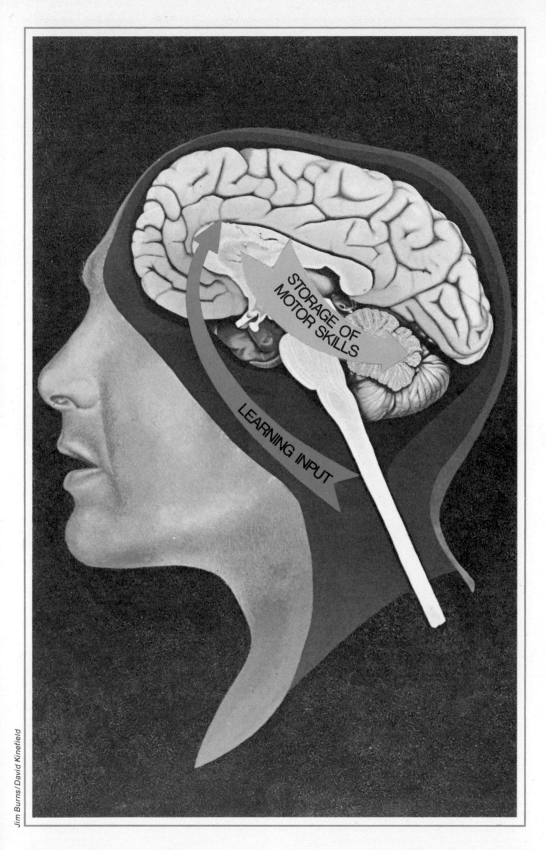

STORAGE OF MOTOR SKILLS

LEARNING INPUT

electric current was passed briefly across their brain.

Nowadays, however, the theory that short-term memory depends on electrical activity and can be wiped out if this electrical activity is interfered with—by, for instance, passing a current across the brain—has been exposed to considerable doubt. More precise tests have shown that the amnesia is more apparent than real in many cases. This view has been backed up by a number of recent experiments with animals.

If, for example, you place a rat on a platform, its natural instinct is to get down from this exposed position and scuttle around in search of a hiding place. Supposing you punish it as soon as it gets down by an electric shock through its feet. It has been shown that just one punishment of this kind is sufficient to teach the animal the lesson of not leaving the platform.

Permanent Impression

The next step is to introduce a new element into the experiment by passing an electric current across the rat's brain *immediately* after it has learned that punishment will result if it climbs down from the platform. From the theory outlined above it would follow that interfering with the brain's natural electrical activity would cause the lesson to be forgotten and have to be learned again later. Yet, in fact, memory of the lesson survives or, if forgotten, returns after an interval in a significant number of cases.

Partly to cope with such difficulties it had been suggested recently that memory shortly after learning may be based on changes in the shape of critical molecules such as proteins. It would therefore seem that the electric activity of the brain is not as important in short-term memory as used to be thought—but, in fairness, it must be said that this is still a matter of controversy and debate.

We are on firmer ground in dealing with long-term memory. Electricity plays its part here as well, of course, in the sense that messages to and from the various parts of the brain are electrically transmitted. In the case of long-term memory, however, there is no argument about whether interfering with the natural electrical activity of the brain causes temporary or total amnesia.

It does not. It has been shown, in man and in animals, that long-term memory is not destroyed even if the brain's electrical activity is radically altered and decreased by electro-

as he grew up, he retained only a very weak memory of his boyhood. One day, returning home tired, he had tea and *madeleine* cake. Their smell and taste, evocative of times he drank and ate them in his youth, brought back his early life with such clarity that he was able almost to relive it.

The accepted theory until fairly recently was that short-term memory was a purely electrical function and long-term memory a chemical one, in-

volving structural changes in the brain. This belief originated largely in treatments involving passing currents across the human brain. This is standard therapy for many depressive illnesses. It does not merely alleviate the depression: psycholgists found it also appeared to cause amnesia for recent memory. Although their long-term memory remained unaffected, patients seemed unable to recall anything that had happened immediately before the

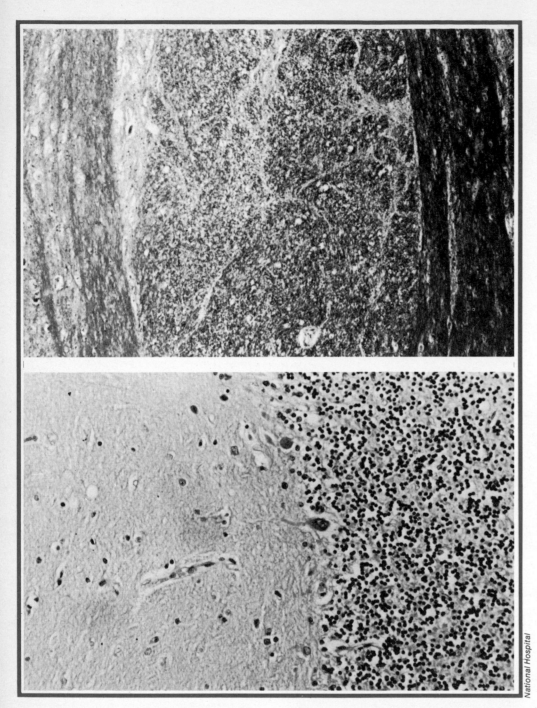

These photographs show two cells in the human brain. Above: A cell in the brain stem—the cross grain in the picture shows nerve fibers which run from the brain to the limbs and trunk for the control of all movement. Below: A cell in the cerebellum. This is the part of the brain that dicates posture—one-third of it helping to maintain balance (this is responsible for sea sickness), the other two-thirds coordinating muscular movement in response to information entering from the sense organs.

to the actual or potential synapses where they alter the interconnections of the nerves. This, at least, is the theory of many researchers.

In contrast to the limited effects resulting from interfering with the electrical activity of the brain, it has been found that animals' memory can be profoundly disturbed if learning is followed shortly by treatments that severely disrupt protein production in the brain. Similar disturbances seem to occur in humans who are kept, for therapeutic reasons, on diets likely to cause protein deficiency.

Drink Breaks the Link

This line of thinking used to be put forward to explain the condition of Korsakov patients (so called after the eminent nineteenth century Russian physician who diagnosed their condition), who apparently suffer from total amnesia as a result of chronic alcoholism. There are thousands of them in mental hospitals. They appear not to be able to remember anything from one moment to the next. They do not seem to recognize the doctors who attend to them every day.

It has been argued that chronic addiction to alcohol causes a severe vitamin B deficiency in these cases, resulting in the brain's inability to form long-term memories. And yet, illustrating how far we still have to go in understanding the human brain's complexity, more recent tests indicate that Korsakov patients *are* able to form long-term memories. What really suffers is their ability to retrieve those memories when they need them.

We are in controversial country again when it comes to the question of what parts of the brain memories are stored in and how we retrieve those memories. Early experiments in paring away increasingly large areas of animals' brains seemed to suggest that the various parts of the brain tend to overlap, with any particular memory

convulsive shock, epileptic seizures, cooling or temporary "death." Indeed, it is hard to devise any means of physically ill-treating our brains that causes a permanent loss of memory without also damaging most of our other faculties.

It seems highly likely that lasting memories do depend on structural changes in nerve cells that alter the brain's electrical circuit. There is increasingly strong evidence that experience causes such phenomena as growth and disappearance of synapses—the gaps across which individual cells communicate with each other—as well as alterations in the sizes and efficiency of synapses that were present before learning took place. This means that it takes less time to make the appropriate response, whether

verbal or motor, for the route the message travels through the nerve cells has become so well-worn with time it is automatically "remembered."

Furthermore, it is probable that these structural changes between nerves are caused by chemical changes that take place between the cells. All cells are chemical factories, and nerve cells are the most active factories of all.

Protein Power

One of the most important classes of substance that cells produce is proteins. Each kind of protein has a specific function. One group is concerned with the structure of the synapses of brain cells. Such proteins are produced by certain nerves as a result of learning and are then transported

Paul Popper Ltd.

being stored in several regions simultaneously. Karl Lashley, the leading psychologist, concluded, in fact, that each part of the cerebral cortex was equally important in storing complex memories.

Once again, however, more recent research has indicated that, in man and the apes, memory is much more localized than was thought. There is substantial evidence, for instance, that the left side of the human brain is concerned with storing largely verbal information while the right side occupies itself with visual images, music and spatial details such as the way streets are laid out in a town. This has been established by beaming information to the brain through the eyes in cases where the links between the two halves of someone's brain have been absent from birth or severed as the result of surgery.

Blank Mind

Experiments on animals have limited value, of course, in contributing to our knowledge of human memory. Animals do not share our ability to recall past life or our abstract memory. At the same time, we cannot go around cutting chunks out of human brains to see what effect the operation has on the owner. For what practical knowledge exists we have to rely on cases where a brain operation has been carried out for some other rea-

Concert pianists like Arthur Rubinstein can concentrate on technique and expression because they have the necessary basic motor skills at their finger tips.

son and loss of memory has resulted in the process.

One important part of the machinery for implanting and storing memory is the hippocampus, situated just inside the temple and under the eaves of the temporal lobes. In 1953, a 27-year-old American, well known in the case-books, underwent a brain operation for severe epilepsy.

The surgeon removed parts of the temporal lobes, in the process greatly damaging the memory-implanting apparatus on both sides of the head. In the light of what happened afterwards, no such operation would be performed today.

His personality was virtually destroyed. Since 1953, he has lived from minute to minute. He can remember his life more or less up to the time of his operation, but—at least, so it seemed for 15 years—nothing since, except for a few minutes at a stretch.

He is intelligent, well-behaved and normal to the casual observer. He does well in tests of short-term memory. But if he encounters someone introduced to him a few hours earlier, he has no recollection of having met them. He will read the same copy of a

magazine repeatedly, with evident fresh interest each time. He will assemble the same jigsaw puzzle over again with no sign of improvement or familiarity.

Brenda Milner of the Montreal Neurological Institute, who has followed his case very closely, quotes him as saying to her rather anxiously one day: "Right now I'm wondering, 'Have I done or said anything amiss?' You see, at this moment everything looks clear to me, but what happened just before? That's what worries me. It's like waking from a dream. I just don't remember."

Yet, even in his case, the complex functions of the brain produce their mystery. It seemed beyond doubt that his power of long-term memory had been totally destroyed by his operation. Nevertheless, in 1968, he picked up a half-dollar coin, looked at the head on it, and said: "That's President Kennedy. He was assassinated." The assassination took place ten years after the 1953 operation.

One of the greatest challenges facing twentieth century scientists —and biologists in particular—is unraveling the mystery of how memory works. There can be no single solution because memory itself is not one phenomenon but many. What can we make, for instance, of the man who found it almost impossible to forget?

Associated Press

Keystone

Michael Boys

Visual memory

It is November 22, 1963. In Dallas, Texas, President John F. Kennedy slumps down in the back seat of his car. Assassination! But what were you doing when you heard the news? If you were sitting down to a meal, the chances are you will remember this but not what you ate. What then decides what you remember and how does it happen? Here are some memorable answers.

One of the most remarkable memories the world has known belonged to a failed Russian musician and journalist named Shereshevskii.

Shereshevskii, virtually without effort, could memorize elaborate tables of numbers, poetry in a language he did not know, strings of nonsense words, complex mathematical formulae—and, equally effortlessly, could reproduce them perfectly years later. Alexander Luria, the Russian psychologist who spent thirty years studying Shereshevskii, records in his book entitled *The Mind of a Mnemonist*: "As the experimenter I soon found myself in a state verging on utter confusion....

"I simply had to admit that the capacity of his memory *had no distinct limits. . . .* I arranged a second and then a third session with S. These were followed by a series of sessions, some of them days and weeks apart, others separated by a period of several years.

"But these later sessions only further complicated my position as experimenter, for it appeared that there was no limit either to the *capacity* of S.'s memory or to the *durabi-*

lity of the traces he retained. Experiments indicated that he had no difficulty in reproducing any lengthy series of words whatever, even though these had originally been presented to him a week, a month, a year, or even many years earlier.

Memory Unlimited

"In fact, some of these experiments designed to test his retention were performed (without his being given any warning) fifteen or sixteen years after the session in which he had originally recalled the words. Yet invariably they were successful. During these test sessions S. would sit with his eyes closed, pause, then comment: 'Yes, yes. . . . This is a series you gave me once when we were in your apartment. . . . You were sitting at the table and I in the rocking chair. . . . You were wearing a gray suit and you looked at me like this. . . . Now, then, I can see you saying. . . .' And with that he would reel off the series precisely as I had given it to him at the earlier session."

S.'s fantastic powers of recall were visual. He did not memorize in the normal way: he simply registered

an impression, which then remained imprinted on his mind. Asked to recall a series of numbers, he could *see* the series written on a blackboard in his own hand. Asked to commit a list of words to memory, he converted them into visual images. His usual method was to take a mental walk along some familiar street, like Gorky Street in Moscow, distributing the images at houses, gates, walls and store windows. Asked to recall the words, he simply took the mental walk again, picking out the items as he went along.

But that was only the start of the peculiarities of S.'s memory. He also possessed to a marked degree the phenomenon known as synesthesia. Every sound he heard was converted in his mind to light and color, even taste and a sense of touch.

If, for example, there was a sudden noise when he was recalling a series of numbers, the noise was converted immediately into "puffs of steam" or "splashes" which obscured the figures. He had to move his mental blackboard sideways before continuing.

He saw the letter A as "something white and long." The figure 3 was "a pointed segment which rotates," while 8 "somehow has a naive quality, it's milky blue like lime. . . ." Asked to listen to a sound pitched at 50 cycles per second and a volume of 100 decibels, S. reported: "I saw a brown strip against a dark background that had red, tongue-like edges. The sense of taste I experienced was like that of sweet and sour borscht, a sensation that gripped my entire tongue."

Most of us have a small degree of synesthesia in our make-up. We may, for example, think of brown as a "warm" color and light blue as a "cold" one. But for S. there was virtually no dividing line between vision and hearing, or hearing and the sense of touch or taste.

"What a crumbly, yellow voice you have," he once said to a leading Russian psychologist. Riding on a streetcar was agony: "I can feel the clanging it makes in my teeth." The lack of a clear dividing line between vision and his sense of taste also made it difficult for him to read while he was eating. "If I read when I eat," he explained on one occasion, "I have a hard time understanding what I'm reading. The taste of the food drowns out the sense of the words."

Mind Over Matter

S.'s imagery was so powerful that he could increase his pulse rate from its normal 70-72 to 100 at will. He could also reduce it to 64-66. He explained: "I simply see myself running after a train that has started to pull out. I have to catch up with the last car if I'm to make it. Is it any wonder, then, that my heartbeat increases? After that, I saw myself lying in bed, perfectly still, trying to fall asleep. . . . I could see myself begin to drop off . . . my breathing became regular, my heart started to beat more slowly and evenly."

He could simultaneously raise the temperature of one hand ("I saw myself put it on a hot stove") and lower the temperature of the other ("I saw myself holding a piece of ice and started to squeeze it"). At the dentist's, he never felt pain: "I'd sit in the chair but imagine it wasn't really me but someone else. I, S., would merely stand by and observe 'him' getting his teeth drilled. Let 'him' feel the pain. It doesn't hurt me, you understand, but 'him'. I just don't feel any pain."

S.'s powers were similar to, but not the same as, the phenomenon colloquially known as "photographic memory." This is eidetic (identical or duplicative) imagery. It is a pheno-

menon found in around one child in ten and only rarely survives into adulthood.

In an article published in the *British Journal of Psychology* in 1924, the Cambridge psychologist Allport described some typical experiments with a group of 11-year-old children. He placed a series of pictures, rich in detail, on a dark gray mat set up at normal reading distance. Each child was allowed to study a picture for 35 seconds.

The children were then asked to look at the gray mat and report on what they saw. In about half the cases it was as if they were still looking at the picture. Their recall of what they had seen was almost photographic. The picture was not within their heads, as a normal afterimage is, but appeared to be projected on the mat. If the mat was bent, the picture bent as well.

If the mat was removed, the eidetic image, too, disappeared. Children could then still recall the pictures, but in nothing like the same detail: they had to rely on their ordinary powers of memory. Once the mat was restored again, however, they switched back to the eidetic image and, despite having seen the original picture for only 35 seconds, could describe accurately such tiny details as the number of buttons on someone's jacket and the number of whiskers on a cat's lip.

The astonishing amount of detail that could be "read off" the eidetic image on the dark gray mat is perhaps best demonstrated by the fact that one picture of a German street scene had the word *Gartenwirtschaft* written over the door of an inn in the background. None of the children knew German. Yet of thirty with strong eidetic imagery in the group, three spelled the word without error, seven reproduced it with not more than two errors and only five failed to identify at least five letters.

Young Tongues

The question is sometimes asked: Would it not be a good idea to try to cultivate this gift instead of allowing it to die out as a child grows up? It can be argued, however, that this is only one of several ways that children are different from adults. Between the age of two and four, for instance, they seem to be particularly adapted for learning languages. They learn in an entirely different way from adults and the theory is that, physiologically, the brain of a child is in a special state at that time of its development. It has

been suggested, in fact, that, if a child did not learn a language between the age of two and four, it might find it impossible to learn one later on.

Similarly, this strong visual imagery in childhood gives way with the passing years to the kind of logical, abstract memory which enables us to remember complex information for many years. The result, if strong visual imagery persists into adulthood, can bring a variety of day-to-day difficulties and, in particular, problems over the kind of logical organization that is an integral part of the process of learning for ordinary people.

Forget Me Not

As Alexander Luria puts it in his book about S., he suffered from "a distinct type of dissociation that S. and other people with highly developed capacities for figurative memory exhibit: a tendency to rely exclusively on images and to overlook any possibility of using logical means of recall."

One example was when S. was asked to learn a table of numbers which began:

$$
\begin{array}{cccc}
1 & 2 & 3 & 4 \\
2 & 3 & 4 & 5 \\
3 & 4 & 5 & 6 \\
4 & 5 & 6 & 7 \\
\end{array}
$$

He learned it by his usual method of visual recall without noticing that the series progressed in a simple, logical order. He confessed later, "If I had been given the letters of the alphabet arranged in a similar order, I wouldn't have noticed their arrangement."

S.'s gift of spontaneous recall and the strength of his visual imagery also made it almost impossible for him to forget. He tried writing down things he did not want to remember, he even burned the pieces of paper on which he had written them. Neither course did any good. This was a particular torment when he began to make his living as a professional mnemonist, or memory man, and found himself in perpetual fear that series of numbers he had memorized at one performance would pop up in his mind at the next one.

Reading was another difficulty, particularly if he tried to read quickly. The ready images collided with each other and became distorted and confused. As he explained once, "Someone read me a sentence beginning, 'N. was leaning up against a tree. . . .' I saw a slim, young man dressed in a dark blue suit. He was standing near a big linden tree with grass and woods all around.

Graham Dean/Photo: Novosti Press

"But then the sentence went on, '. . . and was peering into a shop window.' Now how do you like that? It means the scene isn't set in the woods, or in a garden, but he's standing on the street—and I have to start the whole sentence over from the beginning."

Poetry, in which somebody else's images are used to cloak ideas, was especially difficult for him. It left him, he said on one occasion, with "an impression rather like you would get if you accidentally overheard a conversation—fragments of images that made no sense."

Abstract ideas such as "nothing," "infinity" and "eternity" also posed virtually insoluble problems. The ordinary process for anyone growing up is to reach a stage of development at which they cease to think in graphic images and develop the power to use words and logic. S., however, continued to see even abstract concepts

A street could look like this to Russian mnemonist Shereshevskii, who had one of the most remarkable memories ever known. Asked to commit a list of words to memory, he converted them into visual images. His usual method was to take a mental walk along some familiar street, like Gorky Street in Moscow, distributing the images at places like buildings, gates, walls and store windows. Asked to recall the words, he simply took the mental walk again, picking out the items as he went along.

in the form of tangible images.

"What pointless images come up on account of a single word," he once complained. "Take the word 'something', for example. For me this is a dense cloud of steam that has the color of smoke. When I hear the word 'nothing' I also see a cloud, but one that is thinner, completely trans-

parent. And when I try to seize a particle of this 'nothing,' I get the most minute particles of nothing."

Luria was content to record S. in fascinating detail without constructing any special theories around him. Jerome Bruner of Harvard University, however, has tentatively described S. as suffering from two disorders. The immediate fading of memory, found in normal persons, was defective in S. with the result that images normally lost within a second or two haunted him for hours. He was also apparently unable to organize his memory and draw general conclusions from particular experiences.

S. was a freak. His case serves to remind us, however, of the everyday mental mechanisms we take for granted and on which our patterns of civilization and creative human thought depend. If everyone, like S., had an inner compulsion to transform abstract concepts into concrete images, science and philosophy would not progress at all.

The range of his memory, however, leads logically to the question: Do we possess the power of total recall? That is, might it be that we—or at least some of us—have implanted in our memories everything we have learned in the course of our lives and everything that has happened to us?

Brain Box

It used to be argued that we did have all this information stored away although, for some unknown reason, we were unable to retrieve it. This belief was based largely on the work of physicians like Wilder Penfield. In brain operations such as those to remove scar tissue after epilepsy, it is the normal practice to explore the brain electrically beforehand to ensure no damage will be done to the patient's memory or language capacity. Penfield found these probes produced what at first appeared to be hallucinations but on investigation proved to be "forgotten" memories.

Supporters of total recall generalized from this, claiming that if we had the right technique we could retrieve everything. It is true that there is more information and experience stored in our memories than we are aware of. At the same time, more recent thinking discounts the notion that we remember *everything*.

A great deal of the experience and information reaching us daily, for instance, is screened off from our consciousness and therefore cannot enter our long-term memory. Furthermore, arguments based on the number of cells in the brain maintain it has a limited storage capacity.

This is supported by empirical information suggesting, among other things, that nobody can store and speak more than ten languages—it seems to be impossible to learn more than that number. Language is quite a significant example because we know roughly how much information we have to store in the memory in order to speak one. Language capacity probably takes up about one-tenth of the cortex.

It is also possible to work out the capacity of the rest of the brain. From this it has been deduced that if we stored every fact and experience from the time we were born the capacity of the brain would probably be exhausted by the late teens and we would be unable to remember anything else unless we could get rid of old information.

This, allied with the selective nature of memory, suggests that the idea of total recall is a myth. We recall, for example, something which had a high degree of significance for us when it happened, like the assassination of President Kennedy, but we do not necessarily remember what we were doing when we heard the news. Or we may remember we were just sitting down to a meal when the announcement came over the radio, yet have no recollection about what we ate.

Over and above the natural process of "forgetting" information because we do not consider it significant enough to be worth storing, there is the malfunctioning condition of the memory called amnesia.

There are two kinds—retrograde, stretching backward in time, and anterograde, stretching forward in time —and, according to the initial cause, they may affect both short-term and long-term memory.

Why Mr. S. Was Always Late
As a boy, S. found it difficult to distinguish between what was real and what he could "see." Even his vision of himself was virtually another person. This led to confused experiences like the following.

"It's morning... I can't stay in bed. I start to get angry for I have to go to school. . . . But why shouldn't 'he' go? No, I won't go. He'll get up and get dressed. There he is, he's getting his coat and cap, putting on his galoshes. Now he's gone. So everything's as it should be. I stay home, and he goes off. But suddenly my father walks in and says: 'It's so late, and you haven't left for school yet.'"

S. also found time-keeping difficult for another reason: "I'd look at a clock and for a long while continue to see the hands fixed just as they were, and not realize time had passed . . . That's why I'm often late."

There is some evidence that amnesia can be induced by an act of the will: we forget because we want to forget. It can also be the involuntary result of a severe shock: avid movie fans will be familiar with the married hero whose memory is wiped out entirely by some traumatic experience, and who assumes a new identity and marries again, creating a tricky and tearful situation resolved in the final reel.

More prosaically, amnesia in everyday life is caused by a blow on the head which causes damage to the nerve cells of the brain and concussion. After he has recovered from the concussion and is apparently normal again, the patient may find a considerable period of his life before the accident is a blank. His memory of this period gradually returns, although the minutes or seconds immediately before the accident usually remain a total blank forever.

While he is suffering from this retrograde amnesia, he also as a rule suffers from anterograde amnesia in the form of an inability to lay down new long-term memories. This disability normally disappears when his memory of events before the accident returns. The process is illustrated by the following case history, taken from *Brain, Memory, Learning* by W. R. Russell:

"A green-keeper, aged 22, was thrown from his motorcycle in August, 1933. There was a bruise in the left frontal region and slight bleeding from the left ear, but no fracture was seen on X-ray examination. A week after the accident he was able to converse sensibly, and the nursing staff considered he had fully recovered consciousness.

"When questioned, however, he said the date was February, 1922, and that he was a schoolboy. He had no recollection of five years spent in Australia, and two years in this country working on a golf course. Two weeks after the injury he remembered the five years spent in Australia, and remembered returning to this country. The last two years, however, were a complete blank.

Forgotten Past

"Three weeks after the injury he returned to the village where he had been working for two years. Everything looked strange, and he had no recollection of ever having been there before. He lost his way on more than one occasion. Still feeling a stranger to the district he returned to work. He was able to do his work satisfactorily, but had difficulty in remembering what he had done during the day.

"About ten weeks after the accident the events of the last two years were gradually recollected and finally he was able to remember everything up to within a few minutes of the accident."

The study of these various defects is important for practical as well as theoretical reasons. Practically, greater knowledge helps us to help the sufferer. Theoretically, study of the abnormal can often throw greater light on the functioning of the normal —and much of the way memory works is still a mystery.

Keystone

Training memory

Memory is like a muscle—flex it and it will grow. But few people make a conscious effort to improve their powers of recall—like the German "memory man," Bruno Furst. With a little effort the most ordinary memories can be transformed into highly efficient recording devices.

Is it possible to transfer memories from a dead creature to a living one? Research in the last ten years suggests that this is indeed feasible in a wide range of creatures including flatworms, rats, mice and goldfish.

Flatworms are extremely primitive creatures, with virtually no brain at all, who live in water. In the early 1960s the American psychologist McConnell carried out classical conditioning experiments with them. They were subjected to electric shocks paired with a shining light. Eventually, after hundreds of repetitions (flatworms are not very bright), they reacted in the same way to the light alone—

by contracting—as they had to the electric shock and light combined.

If you cut a flatworm in half, both halves survive. Experiments also showed that both halves retained the classic conditioning response. The next stage was to kill some of the conditioned flatworms and feed them to other flatworms. These cannibal worms subsequently proved much more sensitive to the shock-light conditioning than totally naive flatworms which had not been fed the bodies of their dead colleagues.

This finding was backed up by experiments, mainly with rats and mice, by the psychologist Georges

Ungar. It is natural for these animals to seek out dark places but, in Ungar's experiments, they were punished with electric shocks when they did so. After several days of intensive training they were killed, and purified protein and polypeptides (small protein molecules forming part of the basic molecule in human and other bodies) were extracted from their brains.

Inherited Memory

These extracts were injected into the bodies of other rats and mice. The effect appeared greatly to enhance their ability to learn to avoid the dark. Similar results were obtained in further experiments involving such tasks as learning how to approach laboratory devices in which food was concealed.

Ungar claims to have identified the particular polypeptide involved in dark-avoidance learning, and to have produced it synthetically in the laboratory. In fact, independent experiments have indicated that his claim is justified and even animals which have had the synthetic polypeptide injected into their stomachs or bloodstreams are much more adept at learning to avoid the dark.

What significance do experiments of this kind have? They help to throw more light on the belief that long-term memory involves structural changes in the connection between brain cells. They may enable us to say eventually that it is not just proteins that are important in these changes, but a particular type of protein.

In this case we may have isolated the particular polypeptide which changes the cell connections in dark-avoidance learning. It must be said, however, that any particular polypeptide would affect only a small range of memory phenomena—and it seems unlikely that we shall find one which, alone, can improve the unique human gift of abstract learning.

Flex Your Memory

As a schoolboy in the German town of Metz, Bruno Furst had, he confesses, an atrocious memory. At ten, he was still struggling with the alphabet, multiplication tables, history, geography and everything else in which learning and remembering played an important part.

"I could remember nothing," he recalled later. "My classmates were way ahead of me. My teachers said I would never amount to anything. That was before I learned that the memory could be trained like a muscle."

By 1946, however, when he was the subject of a profile in the *New Yorker* magazine, Dr. (of law) Furst was a changed person. He had his own memory school in New York and was, said the magazine, "probably the greatest all-round mental athlete of the century....

"He has developed his powers of concentration so well that he can devote his attention to the head of a pin for five or six minutes. By sheer mental effort, he can regulate the beat of his heart, increasing and decreasing the tempo as he wishes. He can relax his mind so completely that he is able to suspend thought altogether and fix or meditate on infinite nothing-

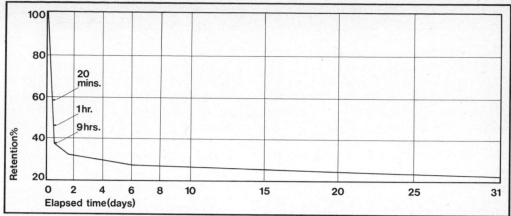

How much does the average person remember? To some extent, of course, it depends upon how interesting or important is the material to be learned. The graph (above) shows the memory retention of someone who learned a series of nonsense syllables. Forgetting was rapid at first, then much slower.

ness for several minutes at a time.

"He is a chess player of tournament rank and a first-class performer in every kind of quiz and card game. He enjoys bridge and would be a champion if people would play with him. Few do, on the reasonable ground that his mnemonic systems (memory aids) and his highly developed extra-sensory perceptions would enable him not only to communicate with his partners but to know what cards everyone held....

"He has devised a method for learning the International Morse Code in fifteen minutes. One of his favorite tricks is to fan out a deck of freshly shuffled cards, study it for a few moments and tell the sequence to the audience from memory. He can do two decks in slightly more than a minute. It generally takes him no more than a day to forget the card sequence.

"When he was practicing law in pre-Hitler Germany, he memorized the entire German Civil Code, which then comprised 2,385 paragraphs of legal language. Today, he can cite the law in any given paragraph of it or, given a law, cite its paragraph number.

Memory Game

"He has also stored up six languages, thousands of telephone numbers and street addresses, hundreds of poems, dozens of plays and a score of novels. He likes to point out that, for a man with an educated memory, being caught on a train ride or a dull weekend visit without anything to read is no problem. When Dr. Furst, whose lecturing involves a lot of tedious

travel, finds himself on a long journey without a good book, he remembers one. He can recline in his seat, close his eyes and enjoy Goethe, Heine, Thomas Mann or any of the other authors in his large portable library.

"He is greatly interested in geography, and can instantaneously recall most of the vital and geographical statistics about the earth. He knows to the mile how far it is from Murmansk to Mozambique, what mountains and bodies of water lie in between, how high the mountains are and how deep the waters, and the names and populations of all principal way stations."

Most countries have, or have had, their celebrated memory men. Britain, for instance, has been mesmerized for more than a quarter of a century by Leslie Welch, as remarkable in his way as Dr. Furst although he plows a narrower furrow.

His specialty is sport. He has stored away in his head all the important facts about 37 first-class sports, from bullfighting to badminton, and his ability to answer obscure questions about them has made him the veteran of eight Royal Command vaudeville performances, twelve films, five hundred TV shows and more than four thousand radio programs.

Ask him the result of a football game played half a century ago and he will not only tell you the score but the names of the scorers. As likely as not he will also recite the names of the members of both teams and, for good measure, the name of the referee. The most difficult question he was ever asked, he says, was shortly after Little Mo Connolly won Wimbledon for the first time in 1953 at the age of 17.

"Who is the youngest player ever to win Wimbledon?" he was asked by a frail, elderly woman on one of his programs. "I was tempted to answer Little Mo," he confesses, "but it suddenly struck me that would be too obvious. I groped around in my memory and finally came up with the answer—Lottie Dodd, aged 15, in

1887. 'Quite right, young man,' said the old lady who had posed the question. 'I'm Lottie Dodd.' "

Like Dr. Furst, Leslie Welch is an excellent bridge player and has difficulty finding opponents. "I can remember all the cards that have been played and, after a few tricks, work out what everyone has." Also like Dr. Furst, he believes "memory is a muscle. It screams out for exercise. People probably don't use more than a fifth of the capacity of their memories because early in life they get into the habit of writing things down." This view is borne out by the fact that foreign waiters who are unable to read or write appear to have no difficulty in remembering a complex order from half a dozen customers at a time in a busy restaurant.

To evaluate the highly trained memories of Dr. Furst and Leslie Welch, it is important to grasp that our ability to remember complex information is determined by two factors.

Filing Systems

The first is physiological retentivity, the physical capacity of the brain to absorb and retain information. We do not know a great deal about this. It is, however, something we are born with: it depends on the efficiency of the electrical and chemical processes that occur in brain regions such as the hippocampus and cerebral cortex. This efficiency declines with age, although there is reason to hope that chemical treatments will eventually enable us to boost it. Our memory for material learned by rote is probably largely determined by our powers of physiological retentivity.

The second factor is our ability to organize complex information when we are learning it. This factor has a positive connection with intelligence. It has been shown that good memory for meaningful material, such as the plots of novels and scientific information, depends on our level of general intelligence, our verbal ability and our interest in what we are learning.

These individual qualities cannot be readily increased. However, if we are trained to organize what we learn more effectively, our memory for meaningful material—and even non-meaningful material such as telephone numbers—can be substantially increased. In fact, it can be said that memory is all about organization. You can store masses and masses of material, but the big problem in the long term is: How do I get it out again? Unless you have an efficient system of retrieval, it is rather like having an enormous library in which the books are stacked higgledy-piggledy and there is no cataloguing system. You might as well not have the library.

Mnemonic devices, the basis of Dr. Furst's prodigious memory, help by providing artificial organizing principles. Even people not familiar with the word "mnemonic" make use of simple mnemonic devices. One is the rhyme for remembering the number of days in each month which begins with "Thirty days hath September . . ."

The notes which occupy the spaces and lines of the treble clef in music are conventionally recalled by the word FACE and the sentence (E)very (G)ood (B)oy (D)oes (F)ine. Similarly, the six common French nouns which end in -age but are feminine in gender (*rage, image, plage, cage, nage, page*) can have their initial letter brought to mind by the offbeat sentence (R)est (I)n (P)eace, (C)ats (N)ot (P)ermitted.

To remember numbers, Dr. Furst devised a code in which each number from zero to nine is represented by a consonant sound (that is, although the number eight is represented by the letter "k" he is free, if it is convenient, to replace "k" with a hard "c"). Vowels are then dropped in between the consonants to make up suitable words.

For example, he had a friend, a lung specialist named Dr. Goldberg, whose telephone number was BU8-7878. Dr. Furst remembered it as "Buf-cough-cough." This was arrived at by adding "f" (the symbol for eight) to BU; using the hard sound of "c" for each of the sevens; and using the soft "gh" sound instead of "f" for the second and third eights. The flexibility of the system can be shown by the fact that, had Dr. Goldberg been a tailor, the number could have equally well been remembered as "Buf-cuff-cuff."

Mnemonics—the Name of the Game

The basis of all mnemonic devices is association, and they can be highly useful when used in conjunction with visual images. Our visual memory is much more efficient than our verbal memory. We can, for instance, glance only briefly at a picture, yet, quite effortlessly, absorb and retain a great deal of information about it. In contrast, learning and retaining verbal information is hard work. It requires concentration and rehearsal. This probably has an evolutionary explanation in the sense that we had sight for millions of years before we developed the facility of language.

The kind of mnemonic known as a visual-symbol system (as opposed to Dr. Furst's digit-letter system for remembering telephone numbers) is not new. It is supposed to have occurred originally to the Greek poet Simonides around the year 500 B.C. The story goes that, after giving a recitation at a banquet for an Olympic Games wrestler, Simonides was called from the room to speak to someone outside. No sooner had he left than the roof of the banqueting hall fell in, killing the host and all his guests.

When asked to help identify the crushed and mutilated bodies, Simonides found the simplest method was to visualize where each of the guests had been sitting. Thinking about it later, he came to the conclusion that, if the system worked for places and people, it should work equally well for names, objects and ideas. He therefore developed a successful registration system furnishing an imaginary room with vivid images of as many items as he wished to recall later.

Tricks that Stick

An even simpler process is the successive-comparison system, based on the fact that, if two simple ideas are blended vividly in the mind, recalling one of them will automatically lead to the recall of the other.

Supposing, for example, you have a series of words to learn beginning "tiger, milk, canoe." You have to commit "tiger" to memory as your starting point. You then associate "tiger" and "milk" together in an extravagant image, perhaps of an enormous tiger lapping away at a bathtub full of milk. Now you dismiss this image from your mind and form a similarly extravagant association between "milk" and "canoe," perhaps a canoe loaded with painted warriors shooting rapids of foaming milk. This process continues down the list. To recall the list, you simply think of "tiger." This recalls "milk." Then you think of "milk," which recalls "canoe," and so on.

This system works so successfully because it breaks down both the learning and recalling processes into simpler subtasks. Of course, anyone thinking of becoming involved with mnemonics should first consider how relevant they are to the learning tasks they wish to undertake. The mnemonic can sometimes be more complicated than the thing to be remembered! Nevertheless, for anyone who genuinely wishes to improve their memory there is a vast amount of practical help available both in the form of books and courses.

Quartet

The value of mnemonics employing a vivid image can be demonstrated by learning two lists of words, A and B, one with a mnemonic, one without.

Here is list A:

Table
Sky
Duck
Piano
Book
Gun
Lawn
Candle
Duster
Apple

This list should be learned by repeating it over and over to yourself until you can reproduce it faultlessly. This is rote learning. Time how long this takes you.

Now here is list B set alongside a mnemonic device:

Mnemonic	List B
One is a bun	Spear
Two is a shoe	Pig
Three is a tree	House
Four is a door	Radio
Five is a hive	Car
Six are sticks	Window
Seven is heaven	Ladder
Eight is a gate	Ball
Nine is a line	Plate
Ten is a hen	Paper

You should be able to learn the mnemonic rhyme by reading it through once. Then link the first item in list B with the first line of the rhyme in a vivid image (a cannibal spearing a bun, for instance). Do the same for each word and corresponding rhyme in turn. Time how long this takes.

Try not to practice either list until you test yourself a day later. You should find you can recall more items from list B than list A.

All right! You know it's a tiger. But supposing you didn't. Having seen one for the first time, how many of its characteristics would you be likely to remember? Studies indicate there would be about a 50% chance of recalling its name and the general outline of most of its features (far right). The most notable markings — in this case the stripes — would tend to be accentuated at the expense of subtler highlights and tones. One or two features would almost certainly be wholly wrong. Compare, for example, the shape of the ears in the two drawings. What this reveals, above all, is that the mind is likely to invent when it is unable to remember. This is one of the major problems experienced by the police when trying to obtain accurate descriptions of suspects from imaginative witnesses.

Faulkner/Marks

TIGER   TIGER

All you want to know about...
SEXUAL BEHAVIOR

Camera Press

Q WHY DO PEOPLE GET HANG-UPS ABOUT SEX?

A The main reason why people have hang-ups about sex is because they are suffering from a conflict between mind and body. The essence of all sexual behavior is a gigantic physical drive aimed at perpetuating the species. Its machinery is set in motion by physical signs from members of the opposite sex indicating a willingness to mate, and by internal triggers basically related to the distribution of hormones in the body. Although this is an over-simplification, it will do as a description of sexual motivation in animals. But man's role as an animal has been changed by his acquisition of language and this includes the ability to think about sex, to speak about it, to write about it, to describe it in stories and pictures, and (to complicate matters) to get worried and muddled about it. The trouble is that the great biological sex drive frequently finds itself in conflict with the requirements of society and with the individual's psychology, and a large

number of sexual hang-ups arise from this conflict. Freud in particular recognized the reality of this situation, and in psychoanalysis and psychotherapy today the assault on sexual insecurity begins with an attempt at resolving these conflicts. Often the problem is one of ignorance—a man may believe that what he wants to do as part and parcel of his sex life is somehow socially wrong (he may consider oral sex to be a perversion, for example) or physically wrong (he may believe that birth control is physiologically harmful). Both these are simple yet very common examples which lie at the root of many sexual hang-ups. Unfortunately the nature of man is such that he is unlikely ever to be free of them totally for he has structured his world in such a way that he must behave sometimes as an animal and sometimes as a man. It is a difficult balance to strike, and there are penalties for attempting it. The acquisition of language and conscious control over our sexual activities naturally poses all kinds of problems. On the other hand there are some huge advantages. Few human beings would wish to be able to emancipate themselves totally from all

sexual conflicts if it meant returning to the mechanistic love life which is all that nonhuman animals can experience.

WHAT IS HOMOSEXUALITY?

Homosexuality is sexual attraction or sexual intercourse between members of the same sex. This, incidentally, includes sexual relationships between women, which has the popular name of lesbianism. Its rather widespread existence in all societies and all historical times suggests that it may have some practical or psychological advantages—perhaps in channeling sex drives to prevent a population explosion in economically difficult times or to relieve frustration and tension when men or women are deprived of each other for long periods of time, as in wars. Its existence is also a reminder that the sexual drive is initially diffuse and only becomes attached to particular behavior patterns as the result of learning. It is natural, for example, for a man to feel pleasure when his sexual organs are stimulated, but the female vagina is not the only physical object which will provoke such pleasurable stimulation. Psychologists believe that homosexuality as the dominating theme in an individual's sex life may be brought about when the "traditional" course of learning and sexual education goes astray. For example, if a boy is prevented for some reason from interacting with girls during adolescence and young adulthood, his sexual appetites—at their peak at this time—will be diverted elsewhere. The role of a dominating or possessive mother may be very significant here, but of course this is not the only way in which homosexuals can be created. Nevertheless many homosexuals *do* have a basic fear or aggression towards members of the opposite sex, and if the history of their sex life is one of continued gratification with someone of their own sex, and continued withdrawal from commitment with one of the opposite sex, then the pattern may become established for life. The same applies to female homosexuals.

IS HOMOSEXUALITY HARMFUL?

An exclusively homosexual species would die out, but fortunately homosexuality, like masturbation, is held by most people as a kind of secondary substitute for the genuine article. Homosexuality really becomes harmful in two cases. One occurs when the individual is trapped within a homosexual framework of life, can only get gratification from such relationships and yet basically wishes to be bisexual —perhaps because he feels alienated from society, because he would wish to have a wife and children or for some other similar reason. Another harmful instance occurs when a homosexual, for one reason or another, seduces a younger "normal" individual—probably an adolescent—who is still in a transitional stage and whose sex drive is not yet conditioned to bisexual relationships. Homosexuals who feel a conflict within themselves over their behavior patterns often seek psychotherapy. This treatment attempts either to reeducate them by a long process of psychoanalysis to enter into the world of bisexual relationships, or to persuade them to accept their deviant behavior and restructure their life around it. But if one discounts strictly moral issues—such as the idea that homosexuality is "sinful"—then it is unlikely to be harmful except in the two instances mentioned above. Nevertheless it is fortunate for the continuity of the human race that it remains a minority pastime. Society, incidentally, recognizes the dangers of homosexual conversions taking place at critical periods in adolescence, and homosexual relationships with minors and juveniles are therefore punishable by law in most parts of the Western world.

WHAT IS A FETISH?

A fetish is an object or group of objects which, even though they are themselves not part of the biological mechanism of sex, have somehow come to be an essential part of the sex act. For example, a masochist might well not be able to get sexual gratification unless a whip or punishing instrument features in the sex ritual. At a less dramatic level, a man may be unable to achieve an erection or have an orgasm unless his partner is wearing some particular article of clothing. In both cases, the fetish has become a symbol of sexual gratification, an essential link in the chain which leads from sexual arousal through intercourse to orgasm. Most human beings in fact have some degree of fetishism—it may be long hair, a suntanned body, flimsy underwear, particular perfumes, etc.—and these are acquired over the years when the sex drive is converted from its infantile diffuse state to its final adjustment in an adult. In the course of growing up and maturing certain things, for one reason or another, come to *mean* sex and when they are seen, heard, smelled or touched sexual arousal takes place. From this end of the continuum, present in everyone, we proceed to more extreme fetishism and to a more strict definition within the understanding of abnormal psychology. This is where sexual satisfaction is not just enhanced but *can only be obtained* when the fetish is present. If the fetish is a simple one of the flimsy underwear variety, then this is hardly a problem for most people. When some bizarre dress or behavior pattern—which may perhaps be ludicrous or even objectionable to the partner—is involved then the fetish acquires a dominating role which often needs to be removed in psychotherapy.

WHAT IS A NYMPHOMANIAC?

This is a greatly misused word which refers to a woman with uncontrolled or insatiable sexual appetites. It is often carelessly employed to describe promiscuous women or those with a high interest in sex. True nymphomania is in fact extremely rare, and contrary to general belief women obsessed with sex to this degree are the last people to say that their sex life is agreeable. It might be described as *active*, but that would be about the best that could be said about it. Curiously enough even this hyperactivity does not necessarily imply a genuine interest in sex. More often the woman is seeking in sex a solution to all her problems, and as such she is doomed to more or less perpetual dissatisfaction. There is no cure for nymphomania apart from psychotherapy, which attempts to prove to her that sex—while a vital and exciting facet of life—is only part and not the whole of existence.

IS THERE A MALE EQUIVALENT TO NYMPHOMANIA?

There is, and it has the name of satyriasis (or satyromania). Once again there should be no confusion between this abnormal condition and that of the man who leads a usually dynamic and active sex life and who merely represents one end of the scale of normal sexual behavior. In satyriasis the man is either out to repress his anxieties and problems by an obsessive preoccupation with sex, or he is out to prove to himself that his sexual adequacy or potency (which he secretly doubts) is "as good as any man's." This is often known as a "Don Juan" complex, and by an ironic twist, many of the most aggressively "oversexed" males often turn out (when they finally trot in to a psychologist) to be latent homosexuals, desperately attempting to prove the opposite to themselves. Occasionally males and females of this type get together, when the sparks really fly; such matches are rarely successful however, for satyromaniacs and nymphomaniacs tend to have one thing in common—they want everything from the sex act but give very little.

IS PORNOGRAPHY HARMFUL?

Clearly it depends on the nature of the pornographic material. If by its nature it incites people to indulge in sexual behavior which is perverse to the extent that it violates the rules of society or the freedom and well-being of another individual, then it *is* harmful. Psychologists and lawyers alike are very uncertain as to what constitutes pornography of this kind, and evidence that even the most extreme pornographic materials operate in this way is hard to come by. There is some suggestion that some of the more sadistically sexual murderers were enflamed to some degree by reading sadistically oriented material, but it is hardly certain that they would not have committed their appalling crimes anyway. On the other hand it could be argued that pornography of this kind, by serving as, say, an aid to masturbation, diverts otherwise antisocial drives into harmless channels. As for pornography which avoids what are generally accepted to be sexual perversities, many psychologists believe that its effect is beneficial rather than harmful. This material—straightforward, imaginative and openly frank varieties of erotic art, which after all only serve to depict the richness and subtleties of human love-play—is often recommended by psychologists to patients suffering from inhibited and repressed attitudes to sex. Ignorance of the potential of love as recreation is still one of the principal barriers that psychologists encounter when being consulted by "sexually incompatible" or "inadequate" couples. This, incidentally, is principally a hang-up of modern Western society. In Asia techniques of love-making and erotica are supposed to be required reading for all young married couples, and a profusely illustrated "pornographic" book is often given as a wedding present.

IS PROSTITUTION HARMFUL?

There is good reason why prostitution is known as the "oldest profession." It is clear that the enormous potency of the sex drive will require humans to seek an outlet of some kind if they are unable for one reason or another to find a regular mating partner. Masturbation serves as one outlet and prostitution another. Most civilized societies, since the dawn of history, have accepted prostitution as a necessary part of life, and only rarely do they legislate vigorously against it. In many modern societies brothels, staffed by medically inspected and licensed prostitutes, exist quite openly and operate in the same professional role as filling stations, supermarkets and all the other essentials of modern living. Male brothels where homosexuals congregate and even establishments offering sexual services to women are becoming increasingly common. The arguments pro and con are unusually complicated. Some people hold that the offering of sexual favors for sale is an offense to the dignity of human beings, but that is taking a rather high-flown view of mankind and perhaps misunderstanding the meaning of "dignity." Others argue that prostitution, legal or otherwise, encourages sexual promiscuity, but this probably underestimates the strength of the human sex drive. Other questions concern whether or not venereal disease tends to be spread or reduced by the presence of brothels. Casual prostitution may certainly help to spread disease, but brothels because of medical inspection may actually be helping to eliminate it. In the long run the question, like so many others, can only be answered in terms of how society and the individual view the practice. If the rights or wishes of society or of individuals are seriously violated by prostitution, then it is harmful. If not it is probably best considered just as part of the way in which human beings choose to live together in their complex and regrettably imperfect society.

ARE THERE ANY TIMES WHEN YOU SHOULD NOT HAVE SEXUAL INTERCOURSE?

The simplest answer to this is—Any time you do not want it. Apart from this apparently obvious rule—which is ignored to a surprising extent by couples who often go through the motions of a sex act because, for some reason or another, they feel they "ought to"—the only other occasions are when you are advised not to for medical reasons. Contrary to what many people believe, a woman may lead a full sex life right through pregnancy until at least a week or so before labor is likely to begin. The baby in the womb is remarkably well cushioned against interference and will *not* be damaged by the penis. Sexual intercourse after pregnancy may be resumed almost immediately, just as soon as the woman feels in the mood for it. The most common medical reason for advising couples not to have sexual intercourse is when the doctor believes that the woman is in danger of miscarrying. The reason for this, incidentally, is that a miscarriage may be induced in certain women by orgasm. This therefore unfortunately means a rather total prohibition on all forms of marital sex—including masturbation and oral sex.

CAN WE EXIST WITHOUT SEX ALTOGETHER?

As human beings we are equipped with sexual organs and with many instinctive drives to use them. For this reason we are stuck with sex whether we like it or not—and fortunately we mostly like it! But there are vast numbers of people who for one reason or another find themselves without opportunities for leading complete and total sex lives, and some who are obliged to do without sex with another person altogether. Think, for example, of astronauts on extended space flights, scientists or explorers living apart from the rest of society, people confined to prisons or hospitals for long periods, or such other voluntary social exiles as monks, nuns, creative people concentrating on writing, painting, composing, and so on. For most people in these groups, masturbation will often serve as a satisfactory and healthy sexual outlet for their powerful and ever-present sexual drives. Where this is not acceptable for some reason, involuntary sexual relief is often achieved by dreams during which orgasm occurs. About 70 percent of men and women have had such dreams at one time or another in their lives, though they are more common among men. However the question "Can we do without sex?" generally implies "Can we lead happy and productive lives without having a regular sexual partner?" The answer to this is Yes. The psychic energy which is involved as part of the sex drive can often be channeled into other activities, many of which are creative, productive and satisfying to the individual. No life devoid of sex could of course be a completely full one, but it could still be happy and successful.

IS IT RIGHT TO HAVE SEX WITHOUT LOVE?

For human beings sex can take three forms and have three functions. It can serve as a means of producing children and ensuring the continuity of life; it can serve as an expression of love and the deep affection which people who live closely together will generally feel for each other; it can serve as a magnificent form of recreation and enjoyment, in which the body's remarkable sensory apparatus and the exquisite sensations it can generate are exploited to the full. To this extent it is certainly possible to have sex without love. A casual attraction between two people may lead to a brief but contented sexual relationship based primarily on the third facet of sex. When there is no more to it than that, the relationship often dissolves. Miraculously and magically, however, as one facet is explored, other facets often come into play and when all three are in harmony we speak of sexual happiness and fulfillment.

Improve your reading skills

The speed-reading industry has grown enormously in the last decade and shows signs of expanding into schools and colleges. Many people need to improve their reading skills, to cope with the tidal wave of paperwork engulfing their jobs.

But is speed everything? Speed readers claim to absorb as much meaning from their material as they did at much slower speeds, and laboratory tests show that "naturally" fast readers do tend to have better comprehension than plodders, but recent investigations hint that some loss of understanding can occur at very high speeds.

There is not a lot of gain if mechanical reading, or mere skimming, gives insufficient data or poor memory for what has been read, so most educators think that improving comprehension should precede the building of faster reading.

How good is your comprehension and retention of reading matter?

We read different kinds of material for very different reasons; there is no need to remember every word of a detective story read to pass the time, but it could be vital to remember a recipe or information from a first aid manual. In the same way as you adjust your speed of reading—slow for difficult, unfamiliar or closely written matter, fast for easy, relaxing texts—you need to have some idea of how much you want to learn and remember.

Before You Start to Read

What kind of reading is in front of you? What do you want to get out of it? Let us say it is factual information. How much do you know already about the subject? What are your own ideas about it? This advance organization, even if it takes up a few moments, will direct your efforts ACTIVELY.

Reading is not a matter of passing print before your eyes; your brain is involved, sifting, commenting, attaching the new information to already existing structures. If possible, start out with specific questions in mind and see if they are answered, but do not let your initial questions stop new ones from arising as you go along.

While You Read

Continue your active search for meaning. Usually, there will be important clues to look out for—headings, for example, or markers like "The first important point is . . ." Most writers center a paragraph around one or two major ideas with some illustrative material. All the time you should be asking, "What is the real point here? What is he really getting at?"

Let your mind think as you go; you will agree, disagree or reserve judgment. You may not be convinced by the arguments or examples. Be careful, though, not to let your thoughts expand too far, or your attention may wander and lose the thread.

We have all had the experience of getting to the end of a page, or chapter, and not really knowing what it was all about. That usually means fatigue—time to put the book down. Active reading demands concentration and when that goes, it is better to rest for a time. Nothing more will be learned by driving the eyes once more over the same meaningless print. After a rest, your efficiency will be improved and you can make up for lost time. If you are trying to assimilate a long piece of work, it is better to jot down notes of the major points.

The surest way to remember the information you have just read is to rehearse it in some way. Say it aloud if you like (and if your family will put up with you), write it down or go through it mentally. Practice summing up the main theme in a few sentences, one if possible. Keeping these suggestions in mind, try the passages below. Do not time yourself, but read at whatever speed you find most comfortable.

The Human Zoo

"In any organized group of mammals, no matter how cooperative, there is always a struggle for social dominance. As he pursues this struggle, each adult individual acquires a particular social rank, giving him his position or status, in the group hierarchy. The situation never remains stable for long, largely because all the status strugglers are growing older. When the overlords or 'top dogs' become senile, their seniority is challenged and they are overthrown by their immediate subordinates. There is then renewed dominance squabbling as

Barnaby's Library

everyone moves a little farther up the social ladder. At the other end of the scale, the younger members of the group are maturing rapidly, keeping up the pressure from below. In addition, certain members of the group may suddenly be struck down by disease or accidental death, leaving gaps in the hierarchy that have to be quickly filled.

"The general result is a constant condition of *status tension.* Under natural conditions, this tension remains tolerable because of the limited size of the social groupings. If, however, in the artificial environment of captivity, the group size becomes too big, or the space available too small, then the status 'rat race' soon gets out of hand, dominance battles rage uncontrollably, and the leaders of the packs, prides, colonies or tribes come under severe strain. When this happens, the weakest members of the group are frequently hounded to their deaths, as the restrained rituals of display and counter-display degenerate into bloody violence.

"There are further repercussions. So much time has to be spent sorting out the unnaturally complex status relationships that other aspects of social life, such as parental care, become seriously and damagingly neglected.

"If the settling of dominance disputes creates difficulties for the moderately crowded inmates of the animal zoo, then it is obviously going to provide an even greater dilemma for the vastly overgrown super-tribes of the human zoo. The essential feature of the status struggle in nature is that it is based on the *personal* relationships of the individuals inside the social group. For the primitive human tribesman the problem therefore was a comparatively simple one, but when the tribes grew into super-tribes and relationships became increasingly impersonal, the problem of status rapidly expanded into the nightmare of super-status."

Desmond Morris, *The Human Zoo*

What Have You Read?

1. The main theme in this passage is that
a. animals do not live natural lives in a zoo b. status-seeking is a bad thing c. humans, like other mammals, are forced to overemphasize status struggles in crowded conditions.
2. What two reasons are given for *status tension*?
3. In what conditions is *status tension* tolerable?
4. Name two results of overcrowding in social groups.
5. What is different about the status struggle in primitive tribes?

Your first clue was in the title; you may perhaps have heard of Desmond Morris and so had some expectation of what was to come. If you had read other articles on territory and aggression you might have been familiar with the concepts of dominance and "rituals of display and counter-display." The first sentence states the theme of the opening paragraph, and "*status tension*" is the second clue.

Freud's Lectures

"First and foremost we have found out one thing. Psychoanalytic research traces back the symptoms of patients' illnesses with surprising regularity to impressions from their erotic lives. It forces us to suppose that among the influences leading to the illness the predominant significance must be assigned to erotic disturbances, and that this is the case in both sexes.

"I am aware that this assertion of mine will not be willingly believed. Even workers who are ready to follow my psychological studies are inclined to think that I overestimate the part played by sexual factors; they meet me with the question why other mental excitations should not lead to the phenomena I have described of repression and the formation of substitutes. I can only answer that I do not know why they should not, and that I should have no objection to their

doing so; but experience shows that they do not carry this weight.

"A conviction of the correctness of this thesis was not precisely made easier by the behavior of patients. Instead of willingly presenting us with information about their sexual lives, they try to conceal it by every means in their power. People are in general not candid over sexual matters. They do not show their sexuality freely, but to conceal it they wear a heavy overcoat woven of a tissue of lies, as though the weather were bad in the world of sexuality. Nor are they mistaken. It is a fact that the sun and wind are not favorable to sexual activity in this civilized world of ours; none of us can reveal his eroticism freely to others. But when your patients discover that they can feel quite easy about it while they are under your treatment, they discard this veil of lies, and only then are you in a position to form a judgment on this debatable question. Unluckily even doctors are not preferred above other human creatures in their personal relation to questions of sexual life, and many of them are under the spell of the combination of prudery and prurience which governs the attitude of most 'civilized people' in matters of sexuality."

Test yourself

1. Can you pick out in the first paragraph the key sentence?
2. What was Freud's answer to those who accused him of overemphasizing sexual factors in neurosis?
3. Were his patients eager to reveal details of their sexual lives?
4. What objection does Freud make to the attitudes of some other doctors?
5. Are you convinced by this passage?

You should be improving your comprehension with every exercise. The more you read, the more practice you will get in organizing your mind beforehand, actively thinking and evaluating while you read, and summarizing afterwards.

Answers

The Human Zoo

1. c. With super-tribes comes the battle for super-status.
2. Aging of older members, growing up of younger ones, and the incidence of death and disease.
3. Where the group is not too big.
4. Battles between leaders are more violent; leaders come under severe strain; weaker members are killed; parental care becomes neglected.
5. The struggle is based on personal relationships.

Freud's Lectures

1. The second sentence.
2. That that is what he has found among his patients.
3. No—not until they felt confident.
4. That they too are prey to the same mixed attitudes towards sexuality as other people are.
5. No right answer here! If you have followed the argument you are the only person who can decide.

If you are reading properly, you will find that you increase your comprehension *and* your speed as well, because your mind does not wander passively but concentrates and moves quickly ahead.

All you want to know about...

Mary Evans

Q WHAT EXACTLY IS MEANT BY HYPNOSIS?

A The first thing to establish about hypnosis is what it is *not*! Hypnosis is *not* a magical power of some kind possessed by certain individuals which emanates from their eyes or brain like a mystical radar and which allows them to influence people at a distance. It may seem odd that one has to spend time dismissing this image of hypnosis, but it is one that is very strongly welded into most people's minds as the result of the influence of a combination of comic books, TV serials and assorted old wives' tales. This peculiar image in fact goes back to its

early origins as "Mesmerism," and it is responsible for that vague feeling of suspicion and uneasiness with which most people approach the topic. Actually hypnosis, while still rather poorly understood, is a much less dramatic phenomenon than any of the folklore implies, but the first tip to understanding it comes when one realizes that it is not a *power* but an *attitude* of mind. How then does a hypnotic state differ from a "normal" one? First, the hypnotized person differs from the unhypnotized one in the following two ways: his attention is focused dramatically on one individual—the hypnotist—largely to the exclusion of information coming from all other sources, and he is in a state

of extreme suggestibility as regards any statements or commands made to him by the hypnotist (and only the hypnotist). Suggestibility in this context means that he effectively agrees with all statements made to him by the hypnotist *whenever it is possible for him to do so.* Hypnosis therefore is looked upon not as something which is switched on and off like electricity, but rather as a continuum or sliding scale of "agreement" which begins as soon as one human being *pays attention to* and *accepts a suggestion from* another. This may seem far removed from the popular conception of hypnosis, but it nevertheless represents the most recent psychological view of the phenomenon. Despite this rather prosaic approach it is true that hypnosis may induce marked changes in behavior and can be accompanied by curious psychological and physiological phenomena.

WHO WAS THE FIRST PERSON TO USE HYPNOSIS MEDICALLY?

James Braid, who gave the subject its name, was also one of the first people to use it medically and performed some minor surgical operations in London with the subjects in a state of hypnotic sleep. The most sensational use however (and it has never been used more sensationally since) was by a British army surgeon named James Esdaile, who performed literally hundreds of apparently painless surgical operations (on unsuspecting Indian patients) in the early part of the nineteenth century. Esdaile's specialty was the removal of giant tumors, the most spectacular of which was one with a circumference of seven feet and weighing over a hundred pounds. His young Indian patient, who was more than delighted to be rid of the tumor (which he had to bring to the operation in a wheelbarrow), stated that he felt little if any pain during the surgery. Reports of Esdaile's work filtered back to England, but before they could be repeated to everyone's satisfaction something occurred which gave hypnosis a setback from which it has never recovered. This was the discovery of general anesthetics—ether and nitrous oxide in particular—which induced instant and controlled unconsciousness in any patient and allowed reliably painless surgery.

IS HYPNOSIS USED MUCH IN SURGERY TODAY?

No, apart from occasional experimental sessions, hypnosis is rarely used in major surgery. There are a number of reasons for this. Firstly, it is enormously unreliable and can be induced only in those subjects who have a complete belief in the phenomenon and who have more or less absolute trust in the hypnotist's power. Secondly, it takes time to induce, and even excellent hypnotic subjects may sometimes not respond to the hypnotic commands. Thirdly, a certain amount of special training is needed to practice hypnosis and thus it is not generally available in a hospital setting. Fourthly, existing general anesthetics are vastly more reliable, longer lasting, more controllable and may be administered by

any physician on any patient. There are however areas where hypnosis appears to have some value. Many women, for example, have been assisted through a difficult childbirth by the technique, and some dentists employ it to help treatment in the case of highly nervous patients or those who are likely to respond unfavorably (because of a heart condition, say) to general anesthesia. But it is significant that all such applications work only when the patient totally accepts the reality of hypnosis and the power of the hypnotist to induce it.

Mary Evans

At first called mesmerism after Viennese physician Franz Mesmer, hypnotism (from the Greek *hypnos*, sleep) received its more usual name from Dr. James Braid (above) who was one of the first people to use hypnotism medically.

IS HYPNOSIS USEFUL IN PSYCHOTHERAPY?

It appears to have some limited use. Freud was one of the first people to experiment with it in this role. At first he was enormously enthusiastic for he found that patients with "hysterical" or psychosomatic illnesses could often be apparently cured after treatment with hypnotherapy. Unfortunately he found that these "cures" were often very temporary and that the patient would, after a month or so, return with the same or a slight variation of the original complaint. After abandoning this approach, Freud then turned his

attention to the use of hypnosis to induce patients in psychotherapy to recall painful memories which had been repressed by the unconscious mind, and which were at the root of their mental distress. Once again, Freud found this unsatisfactory and soon began to doubt whether the "memories" that the patients were dredging up really were memories or just peculiar fantasies which he himself was unconsciously suggesting to them. Psychotherapists today rarely pay much attention to "repressed memories" unearthed during hypnosis for this reason, but occasionally they use the technique as an aid to relaxation and to removing some of the surface inhibitions which prevent the patient from speaking freely about emotionally unsettling topics. Even in this setting only a small number of patients respond.

WHAT ARE THE TECHNIQUES OF INDUCING HYPNOSIS?

These rely on inducing a suggestible state in another person—which means persuading him to agree with a series of statements which are made about his psychological and physical state. Traditionally this begins with statements of the "Your eyes are feeling tired" and "Your arm is feeling heavy" variety with which, after a number of repetitions, it is almost impossible not to agree! From then on the statements requiring agreement become progressively more ambitious until the hypnotized person agrees that he is "asleep," "paralyzed," can only hear the hypnotist's voice, and so on. He may even be told to hallucinate or to perform some unusual act and he will do so as long as he is prepared to accept the hypnotist's suggestions *and no longer*. The limits of hypnosis are reached at precisely the moment the subject reaches his "limits of agreement."

ARE HYPNOTIZED PEOPLE JUST "PLAY ACTING"?

This is too simple a view and it does little justice to the enormous complexities of human consciousness and personality. It also fails to account for some of the weirder phenomena of hypnotism—the apparent insensitivity to pain, the apparent sharpening of memory, the apparent rejection of "bad habits," the apparent cures of many minor psychological complaints. Even more at odds are such quite remarkable phenomena, rare though medically attested, in which blisters may appear on the skin when a deeply hypnotized subject is told that he has been burned. However strange these phenomena may seem, it must be realized that all human beings appear to have some intrinsic ability to control pain and that this is a matter of psychology rather than physiology. On one end of the continuum, for example, a brave man sufficiently well motivated will endure appalling physical torture rather than betray, say, his country or his comrades; at the other end of the scale a neurotic hysterical person may experience agonies from a condition which should only cause a "minor headache." As far as changes in the external appearance of the body are concerned, it has long been known that the condition of the skin, to take the most obvious example, can be changed rapidly—blushing, rashes,

meditation, participating in a physically exhausting dance or ritual or occasionally eating certain foods containing stimulating or hallucinogenic drugs. In all such states the common characteristic is that the individual's mental powers appear to be altered in some curious way. For example, he may believe that he is resistant to pain, that he is cured or can cure other people of illnesses, or even that he can see the future or demonstrate some other form of extrasensory ability. Until the latter part of the eighteenth century, such states were generally classed as "religious" or "mystical" and no attempt was made to investigate them scientifically. Perhaps the first person to do so however and the first person who believed that he had pinned down the secret of at least one aspect of these phenomena was the Viennese phy-

etc.—with mental stress. The point here is that all the phenomena experienced in the hypnotic state are phenomena which the individual *could* achieve or create if he were really prepared to set his mind to it. Memory may be improved, but not to the point of perfect recall; pain may be relieved, but not totally eliminated and in any case no more so than as the consequences of a placebo drug; hysterical blindness or paralysis may be alleviated, but hypnosis cannot restore sight to a damaged retina or to a wasted muscle. Hypnosis does *not* induce telepathy, levitation, an increase in intelligence, an abnormal life span, greater fertility or any other attribute of which the individual is not inherently capable. What hypnosis does seem to do is to steer the individual, as the result of a series of "agreements" with the hypnotist, to exploit some of his *normal* potential and it is here that its limited benefits are most obvious.

Trancelike states have been recorded from ancient times. The Oracle at Delphi (top) may have used hypnotic trances for divining purposes. Mesmer (above), discoverer of hypnotism for modern times, was not held in such esteem. Fame brought him into conflict with the French Academy. Lavoisier (left) and Benjamin Franklin (right) were two investigators on the commission that caused his downfall.

WHO DISCOVERED HYPNOSIS?

The fact that certain human beings are prone to peculiar detached states of mind or "trances" has been known throughout recorded history, from the Oracle at Delphi in ancient Greece to the witch doctors of primitive societies and the spiritualist mediums of today. Traditionally these weird states are achieved either through some religious exercise, a prolonged period of

sician Franz Mesmer, whose experiments and demonstrations in Paris just before the French Revolution made him world famous. Mesmer, like many intellectuals of the time, believed that the universe was permeated with a mysterious force, rather like gravity and yet which was an essential aspect of all living things. This force, he believed, was very close to or probably identical with magnetism, and from here it was only a short step before he was believing that bathing people in a magnetic field would be bound to have beneficial effects. His consulting room therefore contained a huge vat of magnetized iron filings, around which his patients would stand, and he would add to the "treatment" by touching wounds or the sites of diseases with a special magnetic wand. He also found that by pointing the wand at the heads of mentally sick people, or alternatively making mystical passes in their direction, he could often apparently cure them. The word "apparently" should be stressed here, for "cures" associated with hypnosis from Mesmer's time right up to the present day tend to be of an unfortunately temporary kind. Nevertheless Mesmer was on to something even though it was not quite what he thought, and his strange phenomena were given the name "mesmerism." To this extent, by being the first person to realize that these mental states obeyed some basic rules and therefore were potentially *useful*, Mesmer can be stated as being the man who "discovered" hypnosis.

HOW DOES MESMERISM DIFFER FROM HYPNOSIS?

Probably not at all. Hypnosis was simply a name given to the phenomena when it was rechristened long after Mesmer had gone into disgrace and died. Mesmer's downfall, incidentally, came as the result of his growing fame. The French Academy of Sciences had naturally been very curious at the strange tales of miracle cures that had come from Mesmer's consulting room. As a result they set up a commission of inquiry—it included such famous names as the French chemist Lavoisier, the great American scientist Benjamin Franklin and an interesting character by the name of Dr. Guillotine (who was later to become famous in quite another context). They immediately set out to conduct a series of experiments, and Mesmer, who was absolutely convinced that "animal magnetism" was at the root of everything, was only too pleased to assist them. The commission conducted experiments with and without magnets, and while they were puzzled to find that Mesmer did seem to be effecting cures without using the established medical techniques of the time, they discovered that these were not related in any way to the presence of a magnetic field. In fact they appeared to be much more dependent upon the patient's *belief* in Mesmer and his apparatus, and they summed it all up in their report by saying "magnetism minus imagination is nothing." Mesmer was staggered by this finding, which rather unfairly led to his persecution, and he left Paris to die penniless and in obscurity. His "cures" however were still sufficiently interesting to keep the topic alive in people's minds and before long other people began to get interested. Fifty years later a skeptical English physician by the name of James Braid, who had been watching a demonstration of mesmerism, decided to try it out on his wife. He found that by asking her to fixate with her eyes on a luminous object held above her head he could induce in her a kind of dozy trance state. He immediately jumped to the conclusion that mesmeric phenomena were in fact a kind of variation on sleep and thus he rechristened it hypnosis—from the Greek *hypnos* (sleep).

CAN SOMEONE BE HYPNOTIZED AGAINST HIS WILL?

No. In a hypnotized state the individual merely responds readily to suggestions put to him by the hypnotist, provided that these are acceptable to him in principle and in practice. All hypnotists are aware of the fact that even the best hypnotized subjects have "suggestibility blocks" where presumably issues of moral or ethical significance are involved. A hypnotist may induce a person to do something strange or even make a fool of himself before a group, but he will not be able to do this with anyone who does not have a prior inclination of this kind, and while he might well persuade a person to touch a piece of hot metal by convincing him that the metal is cool, he would not be able to persuade anyone to put his hand into a fire. It is also quite untrue that a hypnotized individual could be ordered to kill or even commit a crime against his will.

HOW CAN YOU TELL WHEN SOMEONE IS HYPNOTIZED?

The hypnotic state begins the moment that the first agreement with the hypnotist's statement is made. A skilled practitioner of the art, given a group of subjects, will give a few simple commands and as there is considerable human variability in responsiveness, for a number of reasons, he will soon be able to tell who are likely to be the most productive individuals. In a public demonstration he will eliminate those showing resistance and concentrate on one or two of his "best" subjects, who within a matter of minutes will be in a hypnotic trance or behaving in an eccentric fashion at his request. The sole criterion for establishing the existence or depth of the hypnotic state is how readily the individual agrees to the hypnotist's requests.

Mesmer's consulting room contained a vat of magnetized iron filings (called "Mesmer's tub") since he believed that magnetism might have healing qualities.

Mary Evans/Quartet

Do you never forget a face?

The human face is particularly compelling to our attention. Most people find some difficulty in remembering the names of newly introduced acquaintances, but can recognize their faces even after some time. A newborn infant's vision has a fixed focal distance of about eight inches, so that he sees his mother's face from the normal feeding position much more clearly than anything else. Fantz, an American psychologist, showed that infants will respond with interest and prolonged looking at even a mask approximating a face. It is interesting to speculate what could be made of an adult's response.

Consciously or not, we study other people's faces in communicating with them, reacting to minute differences of expression. Yet this very interest can be an obstacle to remembering faces when it really matters—as in giving evidence about identification. Studies in the United States and elsewhere indicate that fewer mistaken convictions are made on circumstantial evidence than on direct but inaccurate eyewitness accounts.

Test out your memory by glancing at the faces below for 45 seconds only. Then turn to the "identikit" pictures overleaf and see if you can assemble the parts correctly.

Easy? Or more difficult than you thought? As a further experiment, try to match the identikit parts in a week's time, WITHOUT LOOKING BACK AT THE PICTURES. If possible, base your

judgment entirely on your memory of the pictures, not on your memory of the right answers. With time, accurate remembering becomes more difficult.

Why Memory Fails

Before anything can be remembered, it has to be "seen." At any one time, there is a limit to how much we can take in. The most ordinary scene presents a huge battery of stimuli; our systems would be rapidly overloaded if we attended to each detail, and we would be paralyzed for action. We could not even walk along a road if we had to pay attention to everything we are capable of seeing.

Luckily, our perceptual systems are geared to selection of significant details. To a great extent we see what

A.

B.

C.

D.

E.

F.

Paul Popper Ltd.

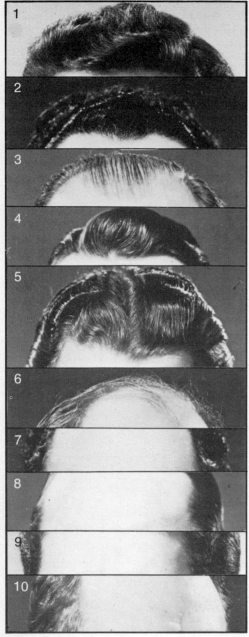

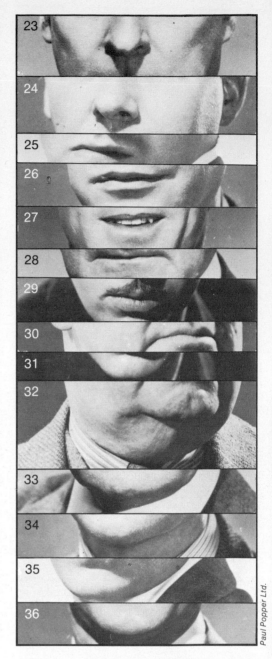

Paul Popper Ltd.

we expect to see, picking up a handful of cues and filling in the rest from memory and habit. Attention is also influenced by internal states. Hungry people pick up cues about food more readily than people who are sated.

If you are looking deliberately for something, you will be more alert to signals—scanning the telephone directory for R. S. Brown will help you to ignore all the Browns with initials from A to Q. When you looked at the faces here, your attention was focused, but in real life, you are often preoccupied with thoughts that take attention away from external stimuli.

Even if you have been attending, memory changes your perception in subtle ways. Outstanding features become exaggerated. Look briefly at the previous pictures, then draw them after an interval of five minutes. (You can vary the time—the longer it is the more likely the effects will appear.)

Leaving aside technical competence, what do you notice about the drawings? Outstanding features become exaggerated. The nose and bushy eyebrows are usually remembered as larger than life. Slight irregularities on the other hand tend to become more regular.

Test this out by making a sketch map of the area around your home—our mental "maps" have more symmetry than reality, or, if there is a distinctive feature like a sharp curve, it becomes even more curved.

Often, a stranger reminds us of someone else. If we see them seldom, the memory tends to exaggerate the resemblance. What probably happens is that we reconstruct our memories of people, rather than retain a single clear impression. Language plays a crucial part in such reconstruction.

Think back to your first study of the faces. Was it entirely a visual experi-

ence, or did some labeling words float into your mind?

Language provides easy storage; a word like "young" sums up a whole cluster of different experiences. But this has its drawbacks. A labeling word can stereotype our perceptions and our memories. "He's just a guy" is a label that stops us from seeing someone as an individual. Witnesses often, maddeningly, describe someone as "kind of average."

Good witnesses, in a legal sense, are sure about what they have seen. But with a knowledge of perception and its uncertainties, which of us can be so definite?

Answers

A. 5, 11, 18, 21, 29, 31. B. 4, 8, 13, 24, 26, 34. C. 6, 10, 17, 20, 30, 32. D. 2, 7, 15, 22, 27, 36. E. 1, 9, 16, 19, 25, 35. F. 3, 12, 14, 23, 28, 33.

Sherrington's reflexes

Touch a red-hot point and you will snatch your finger away before you feel anything. Trip while walking and you will automatically regain your balance. These are called reflex actions and much of our knowledge of them is based on the behavioral experiments of Charles Sherrington.

Charles Scott Sherrington was a visionary English neurologist who, at the beginning of this century, first described reflex actions as a "coin-in-the-slot" process. He removed the "thinking" part of the brain from cats and dogs and demonstrated that even in these mindless animals certain stimuli could still provoke certain predictable reactions.

It was a concept that seemed to reduce a wide range of animal and human behavior to the clunk-click nature of a fundamental piece of machinery. This was hardly flattering to the complex creation we fondly imagine ourselves to be. But Sherrington's experiments and conclusions proved immensely valuable in helping us understand how we function, how we relate to the outside world and just how complex we really are.

The unconditioned behavior that Sherrington studied had its contemporary parallel in the researches into conditioned behavior for which Pavlov is renowned. Conditioned behavior implied "learning." Unconditioned behavior implied behavior patterns that occurred without any apparent control.

In the uncontrolled or mindless animal, whose brain had been removed, Sherrington observed, "If a foot treads on a thorn that foot is held up from the ground while the others limp away. Milk placed in the mouth

Charles Scott Sherrington (left) whose researches into reflex actions appeared to reduce many human functions to the level of a machine. Sherrington removed part of the brain of a cat and showed how the cat (now rigid) would automatically adjust its balance. Sherrington was influenced by Jean Fernel (right), a sixteenth century physician.

301

is swallowed; acid solution is rejected. Let fall, inverted, the reflex cat alights on its feet. The dog shakes its coat dry after immersion in water. A fly settling on the ear is instantly flung off by the ear."

We all experience examples of reflex behavior every day. A finger touches a red-hot point. The finger is snatched away even before the pain is felt. The animal with its "mind" surgically removed does not feel pain but it removes its foot just as quickly.

Trip as you walk and you will catch your balance without thinking how to place your feet or position your arms or body in order to regain control. That is a reflex action. An object approaches your eye suddenly, someone's finger or the twig of a branch. It is very difficult, even when you try to exert your mind, to stop yourself from blinking instinctively.

Action-Reaction

The list of similar actions is almost endless. Sherrington was concerned with how these reflexes occurred, and how they tied in with what was already known and being learned about the nervous system.

Although he regarded himself preeminently as a student of animal behavior, Sherrington hoped to understand that behavior through this sort of meticulous study. He knew the nervous system relays messages to the muscles so they can cope with the sort of immediate crises that call forth a reflex action.

And he knew that within the nervous system there is a constant tug-of-war, as each message attempts to override or "inhibit" weaker messages. It is a complex and brilliant self-defense mechanism.

To demonstrate this tug-of-war, Sherrington, using an artificial electric "flea," made a dog with its cerebrum removed scratch itself. Then he knocked the dog off balance. It is not difficult to imagine the resultant consternation in the nervous system. Priorities were immediately readjusted and the dog stopped scratching in order to regain its balance, even though the source of irritation continued.

Sherrington's most remarkable experiment involved a decerebrate cat, or "cat-without-a-brain."

When the upper section of the cat's brain was removed—the part that provided memory, thought and feeling and which could control the reflex actions of the central nervous system—the animal became absolutely rigid. Its head was held up, its tail curved up and over its back, and its body and legs were stiff and outstretched. Sherrington called this state "exaggerated standing."

Exaggerated standing was an unconscious reflex action, which enabled the animal to maintain balance and equilibrium. If the cat was knocked off balance while in this rigid position, it would automatically adjust itself in the same way as the scratching dog had done, to regain its balance. If the head was moved to one side, the eyeballs moved in the opposite direction to compensate and maintain a "straight-ahead" posture. Sherrington suggested that this sense of alert balance, vital to humans as much as to animals, was largely the responsibility of the *proprioceptors*, or "deep receivers" which pick up information about the body's internal state and the pressures applied to it.

He drew an example from Greek medicine, where the healthy tautness that our muscles keep, even when we are not moving, was compared to a taut string and spoken of as "tone." This tone distinguishes the living from the dead, and is responsible, during our waking hours, for the maintenance of posture and a general state of vigilance.

Tone is also evident in a simple experiment that every doctor has used for centuries to test the health of his patients. Everyone, at some stage or other, has been lightly tapped on the knee by a hammer or a hand, and watched their knee jerk helplessly in reaction to it.

Knee Tapper

This automatic knee jerk was once regarded as a purely muscular reaction. But Sherrington proved conclusively that it was a reflex action involving the nerves. In order for the body to retain its equilibrium at all times and of its own accord, the nerves are so arranged that as soon as the message of a stretching effect on one extensor muscle (in this case, the hammer tap) has reached the appropriate nerve, a decision is made to overrule that effect with an automatic contraction of an opposing flexor muscle. The result is that a tap produces a kick. It sounds like that old axiom, action and reaction are equal and opposite.

The doctor understands that the nervous system is integrated throughout the patient's body. The message caused by the tap contacts thousands of other nerves. If the patient is not healthy, the reaction to the tap will be delayed noticeably. It is one of the simplest and best gauges of the alertness of your body.

Sherrington received the Nobel Prize for medicine in 1932. The presentation speech stated: "Of fundamental importance for our knowledge of the workings of the nervous system was the discovery that an external stimulus can, without the cooperation of the will, call forth a definite response, such as the contraction of certain muscles. A well-known example is presented by the involuntary blinking at a loud and unexpected noise. The external influence is, so to speak, thrown back, or reflected, from which the phenomenon received the name 'reflex.'"

Scholar Poet

He had first presented his case in 1904 and two years later, at the age of 49, he published his famous book, *The Integrative Action of the Nervous System.*

He was born in 1857. His father died when Sherrington was quite young and he was brought up by his stepfather, Dr. Caleb Rose. It was Dr. Rose who first influenced Sherrington to study medicine.

After going to a well-established grammar school, he went on to Cambridge University where, though shy, he proved himself an energetic rugby player and became a Science Scholar. He left with a first class degree.

When he had finished at Cambridge, Sherrington traveled in Europe for a few years. Then, in 1891, he made his decision to concentrate his work on the spinal cord and the study of its related reflexes.

He returned to Cambridge as a Fellow for a number of years and then went to Liverpool University, where, as Holt Professor of Physiology from 1895 to 1913, he did much of his best work. He then moved to Oxford University where he became Waynflete Professor of Physiology and a Fellow of Magdelen College.

His working life spanned nearly 70 years. When he died in 1952, at the age of 95, still active and alert, he had received a knighthood and the esteem of several generations of colleagues and students.

He was described in one obituary as "short in stature, about 5 feet 6 inches, very precise and neat in all his movements, and he tended to peer through rimless spectacles though not severely shortsighted. He had lively, humorous, gray eyes and a light, easy, friendly manner. He was one of the mildest men I have ever known, rarely being vexed and at most saying, 'Dear me' or 'That is most annoying.'"

If that sounds like the archetypal abstracted professor, this image was contradicted by the meticulousness of his work, his eager questioning of assumed judgments and a sensitive and intellectual nature. He was always excited by new ideas, read widely and was a confirmed humanist.

He found time to write a great many papers and several books. One of these was *The Endeavor of Jean Fernel*, a deep and complex study of the sixteenth century physician and philosopher, on whom Sherrington based many of his own intellectual ideas. He also wrote a collection of poems, *The Assaying of Brabantius and Other Verses*. One reviewer remarked that he would welcome more verse from "Miss Sherrington." This implied sentimentality seems a little unfair. The lines are often intricately worked and the style revels in complicated simile.

Bird Brain

In 1940 he published *Man on His Nature,* a remarkable combination of science and philosophy, in which he let slip a glimpse of his inner passion and his wonder at the ultimately inexplicable nature of the mind.

In this book, he distinguished carefully between the reflex "urge-to-live" and the "zest-for-life" of the mind. He saw mind as a product of evolution, not concerned with the muscle and gland activation of most animals but with aim and control. His sense of wonder was combined with an equally wondering humility:

"If, as is sometimes said, history is the tracing of past purposes, here (in the evolution of the mind) is a history which might, while telling of past purposes, whisper to us of future purpose. It would seem to whisper to us that we have been Earth's purpose. We must not let that flatter us too far."

If Sherrington owed a debt in his philosophy to Jean Fernel, he also owed other debts in his physiological studies. Early work on the nervous system had of necessity been partly guesswork, largely based on practical anatomical experiment. Sherrington's cats were not the first animals to have their brains removed and live. Everyone knows that a chicken will continue to run around without its head. There have even been stories of people who have been executed and then stood up and walked. But this is not precise scientific study.

The French philosopher René Descartes compared the working of man's body first with a clock and then with a water fountain in a fairground. He discussed the theory of reflex action from a purely philosophical angle, in order to distinguish between the automatic control of the soulless animal and the voluntary behavior of human beings.

Others also had recognized the existence of reflex actions. Among these was an English physician called Marshall Hall, who stated firmly, after experiments with a decapitated chicken, that its spinal brain was a good deal more alert than its real brain.

Flesh on Facts

Even so, when Sherrington was born, four years after Hall's death, reflexology was not an accurate science. It was his luck that he appeared on the scene at the right time.

His greatest debt was to Santiago Ramon y Cajal, the Spaniard whose microscopic work first established the nerve cells as separate units. It was Sherrington's achievement that he recognized the importance of this and translated anatomical detail into action. His mind was capable of bridging the gap between the microscope and the patterns of behavior. He put flesh on the facts.

The flesh is not always as dramatic as some of the achievements of other fellow scientists such as Pavlov or Delgado. Sherrington was not inclined to statements or experiments that aroused public or professional antagonism. He did not make any extravagant claims that would disrupt fondly held religious beliefs.

His contribution to knowledge was that he stated clearly how reflexes worked and tied reflex action directly to microscopic study. This work served as a stepping stone to even more detailed analysis. The steady analytical steps that Sherrington took were considered of immense value by his contemporaries and those of his students who themselves achieved distinction in their own right.

All or Nothing

In his long working life he saw many aspects of his work taken up by others who supplemented or extended his researches. His Nobel Prize was shared with Lord Adrian, whose work on amplification enabled Sherrington to trace the messages through the nerves more closely. Adrian also proved that nerve cells fire their messages on an all-or-none basis. That is, if the message comes through powerfully enough, the neuron transmits it wholeheartedly. Otherwise it is completely ignored. No half measures. This helped to explain how messages built up to cause a sudden reflex.

Twelve years after Sherrington and Adrian received the Nobel Prize, two other scientists shared it for their work on the different speeds at which the messages traveled. In time, thanks to his early work, the neuron itself was seen in greater and greater detail.

One final aspect of Sherrington's work was a small part of what did develop into a major field of study. Scientists such as Herrick, Child and Coghill demonstrated that reflexes were more complex than had been thought. They proved that even simple reflexes were, over a long period of time, subject to some sort of ecological adjustment.

Adrian had hinted that reflexes could adapt, that nerve ends would get used to hot water so long as it did not cause actual pain. We have all experienced that. The extension of the argument was that many reflexes, if not all our reflex actions, are specialized environmental adaptations which have been developed gradually and have their origin in some far distant mass behavior. So, when Sherrington wrote about the evolutionary nature of reflex energy and the mind, he was reflecting a current line of thought.

Adaptability

This process of evolution or adaptation seems to suppose that the so-called unconditioned reflex can, in a fashion, learn, as the conditioned reflex can. Sherrington had seen this when he experimented with electrical stimulation of the brain in apes. By surgically removing the relevant portion of the motor cortex of the brain, he was able to incapacitate the animal's leg. When the ape woke from the anesthetic it found, when it tried to move, that it could not use the leg properly. Several attempts were made before the ape realized that the leg would not do as it wanted. Over a longer period of time, the ape then learned to reuse the leg, adapting its brain to the purpose.

Sherrington had high hopes for mankind. Writing in the years just before World War II, with a brilliant career behind him and time to reflect, Sherrington's mind jumped far beyond his laboratory experiments.

Man is on test, he said, with our unnatural ethics and our hopes based on the passions of altruism. We are an extraordinary evolutionary experiment that, to survive, must always be prepared to adapt.

David Levin

The frigid wife

There are few things more damaging to a marriage than a frigid wife. Whatever the cause the effect is devastating. The woman begins to think she is unfeminine and the husband resents her failure to appreciate him. But with proper understanding and outside help a couple can usually overcome their difficulties and renew the sexual bond.

A man and a woman who satisfy each other sexually have the basis of a strong relationship. Problems in other areas may be serious, but there are no hidden undercurrents that can sweep the relationship away. When sex itself becomes a problem, nothing is firm. The marriage may last, but small differences threaten to grow until nothing holds the relationship together. A wife's frigidity can be one such problem.

Sexuality has two components: psychological and physical. When making love, a woman who can fully respond to enjoyable psychological

and physical stimulation follows a well-charted route to sexual climax. She passes through stages of excitement and slowly increasing sexual tension to the emotional and physical release of orgasm. Then there is the final sexual relaxation.

Sex Duties

Put simply, the woman who is frigid does not reach orgasm—although a husband may call his wife frigid because she does not wish to make love whenever he demands. The reasons may be complex and vary widely from woman to woman—and

so do the effects on the relationship. One woman may think sex is distasteful or believe that to enjoy sex is sinful; another may find the situation, or her lover, uncongenial; another may reach orgasm when masturbating but not through sexual intercourse.

Janet had been brought up in a convent school after her mother's death, had worn the dowdy clothes her father demanded, and kept her face clear of make-up. She took a course in teacher training at the university her father selected and after a year met Anthony, a young

Marshall Cavendish

A frigid woman is understandably a frustrated woman as well. This tension often finds an outlet in senseless bursts of anger at the equally agitated husband. Frigidity can often be successfully treated by psychotherapy but a major obstacle is that the frigid woman may react against any attempt to discuss her problem.

about it, of course, and eventually we both began to enjoy sex as much as before—we even make love with the light on now—but it was a painful experience.''

The influences that lead to frigidity seem to form a list almost as long as the number of women affected. There are women who cannot admit to themselves that sex is enjoyable, or who have never learned it; women who cannot let themselves go, who cannot face the loss of control they believe orgasm brings; women who believe a husband will be disgusted if a wife climaxes; women who separate sex from all other areas of the relationship.

Religion, Rape, Rancor

There are those who fear old wives' tales of exploding; who are scared of pregnancy or disease; who have suffered painful sexual intercourse; who are ill or physically out of condition, perhaps when the pelvic muscles have lost their tone after a number of births; or are tired, drunk or drugged; women who find their partner boring, or lacking consideration; or are worried over money or the husband's confession of an extra-marital affair.

Whatever the specific reasons, and whether they are linked to long-term withdrawal or coolness in a particular situation, these causes tend to group themselves under the three Rs of frigidity: Religion, Rape and Rancor.

Religion links sex to sin. Parents themselves inhibited—and this is one way Victorian repression can affect society today—are unable to talk freely to their children about sexual matters. Authoritarian ministers of religion thunder against the evils of the body, against the temptations represented by sex. Women, they imply, should sublimate their sexuality.

A girl raised against this background may grow into a woman who represses every sexual feeling, who allows her husband to use her body but sees no possibility of returning his caresses. Some women claim this state to be desirable—"I don't feel

student from a background as restricted as her own.

They kissed for the first time at the formal party Janet's father held to celebrate their engagement. And they made love for the first time on their wedding night after Janet had undressed in the darkness of the bathroom and slipped into bed wearing a new nightgown. Their love-making was not disastrous, but it was painful for Janet and embarrassing for both of them. Neither knew what would please the other—nor even realized they could give and gain pleasure. Sex was a duty.

Switch Off

Without a mother to talk to, Janet had little opportunity to learn what it is to be a woman. With Anthony as a husband, this opportunity might never come. Additionally, the people they mixed with held the traditional view that a wife should care for her husband and bear his children. Women were for breeding, not for sexuality.

A psychosocial background of this

kind could make it difficult for a woman to enjoy even compassionate and skillful love-making. Physical causes, too, such as a serious illness or some abnormality might make it impossible for her to respond fully.

In other cases, however, a woman's lack of response might be the result of a specific situation. Although normally she enjoys sex, in this particular context she cannot.

David and Sylvia had been married for several years. They had two growing children and a pleasant house. "I enjoyed our love-making," said Sylvia. "I suppose it was fairly mundane but we like each other and over the years we gave each other a lot of pleasure. Then, one night David reached over and switched on the light while we were making love—I still don't know why he did it without warning me. I just went cold.

"David tried, he tried very hard, but I just couldn't seem to respond. It was like that for two weeks. I didn't trust David somehow, and he couldn't understand how one little thing had caused such a problem. We talked anything," they almost boast. Diatribes against masturbation, too, may give the impression that all sex is wrong.

If sex is evil, sex is also dirty. Making love with an unwashed partner can be unpleasant for anyone, but a delicately reared girl may have difficulty accepting the stickiness and apparent lack of hygiene of real love-making. She would prefer the cool romanticism of a cheek kissed by a scented Hussar to the enjoyment of sexual intercourse with her unshaven husband—the odor of sanctity becomes more gratifying than the sharp smell of sexual passion.

Frigidity—Why?

Rape, and virtually any other form of sexual assault, can lead to emotional difficulties and frigidity. When incest is involved, a sexual assault is particularly likely to be disturbing. The experience of rape can leave a fear of bodily harm or mutilation that makes sexual intercourse impossible to enjoy. Trusting a male, any male, takes emotional strength after a frightening and probably painful attack.

After taking a secretarial course, Carol left her small-town home to move to a city about a hundred miles away. She wanted to be independent for a while and have some time to think about her relationship with Robert, her childhood sweetheart. Everything went well in the city—she found a job, an apartment, friends—until she went to a party with one of the girls she had met at the office.

Carol danced with several men and towards the end of the party accepted when Paul, a slightly older man than the others, offered to drive her home. He made a joke of driving into the alley behind her apartment block and then leaned over and kissed her. Carol tried to get out of the car, but Paul dragged her back, forced her down on to the floor of the car and tried to have sexual intercourse with her.

Carol finally escaped and ran sobbing up to the apartment, too ashamed to tell the girl she shared it with. Next day she returned home but felt she could not explain to her parents what had happened and just let them assume she had become lonely.

Time went by and she married Robert. But on their honeymoon, as he began to make love to her, she stiffened up and held herself away from him. It took several days of patient coaxing by Robert before they were able to make love fully, and much longer until the memory of Paul's attack ceased to affect her enjoyment of sex.

Rancor is the last of the three Rs, and the widest in range. It covers the woman whose hatred of life itself makes any enjoyment impossible, through one who resents some aspect of her husband's personality, to a wife who takes a momentary dislike to the surroundings.

A woman who believes that life has not been good to her may withdraw into fantasy—it is not her husband who makes love to her but a prince or movie star—and by withdrawing prevents herself from sharing the enjoyment of orgasm.

Possibly she may remember an earlier love and by some twisted logic keeps herself pure for his memory by frustrating her husband's efforts to bring her to climax. Closer to an everyday situation may be the woman who is frigid with her husband but reaches orgasm with her excitingly forbidden lover.

A woman's resentment of her husband can have very real causes. His financial recklessness or unattractive drunkenness may be matters she feels she cannot talk about and so she uses the one form of protest available —passivity. Unconsciously she criticizes his activities by demeaning his sexual prowess. Boredom, too, can lead to frigidity: couples who do not stimulate each other during the day can hardly expect to excite each other by night. Some husbands, for example, close themselves off, perhaps bringing work home, or concentrating on a hobby, and paying little attention to their wives.

Be Bold Not Cold

The most debilitating causes, however, are those that are directly sexual. A tendency to homosexuality in either partner, for example, may make orgasm difficult for a wife to attain. And a sexually inadequate husband may virtually drive his wife into frigidity.

An unsophisticated husband may think that since caressing his wife's vulva excites her, caressing it harder will excite her further. He does not realize that the clitoris, the center of a woman's sexual feeling, becomes irritated when rubbed continually. If his wife is unable to tell him what she feels, they will quickly reduce each other to a state of frustration.

Alternatively, the husband may make a sudden move to a form of stimulation he thinks more exciting still—perhaps oral sex—which his wife believes is near perversion. This worry may inhibit her from enjoying their love-making.

A husband who is partially impotent, who suffers from premature ejaculation—or who is just so selfish or ignorant that he makes no attempt to give his wife pleasure—allows her little alternative to frigidity. To reach orgasm, a woman needs a confident expectation of enjoyable love-making. If the husband repeatedly brings his wife to a halfway stage of excitement only to disappoint her, she will soon learn to hold herself back, to expect little—to become frigid. In addition, she may come to resent her husband "using" her sexually.

"I wasn't a virgin when I married," said Donna. "But Ed was. I wasn't what you might call experienced, but I'd enjoyed making love and reached orgasm nearly every time—I thought that with Ed, once we were married, it would be even better.

All Talk and No . . .

"But things didn't work out that way. The honeymoon was fine. We lay in each other's arms and talked a lot. But when we got back Ed was flung into a demanding job and just seemed to get more and more tired. At night we'd go to bed, kiss and then he'd roll on top of me and almost as soon as we'd starting making love he'd be finished. Then he'd fall asleep and I'd stare at the ceiling.

"We took a holiday at one point— but that was almost worse. Ed was a lot more relaxed and he really tried to please me. But whatever he did I couldn't reach a climax. It was almost as if I didn't want to. When we came home again, Ed's love-making went right back to what it had been. I don't think he realizes what I feel at all."

In a marriage, a wife's frigidity, whatever the cause, is likely to affect the relationship in many ways. Purely physical symptoms can result when sexual excitement is not followed by the release of orgasm: sleeplessness, headaches and tension, backache and a sense of fullness are some of the

Mirror, mirror on the floor who is the coldest of them all? Undoubtedly, the frigid woman, frosty Ice Queen peering through a glass darkly, fearful that she should see herself as she really is. Beneath that cloak of frigidity she is a hot-bed of naked fears and hang-ups covered over by a cool and oh so brittle exterior.

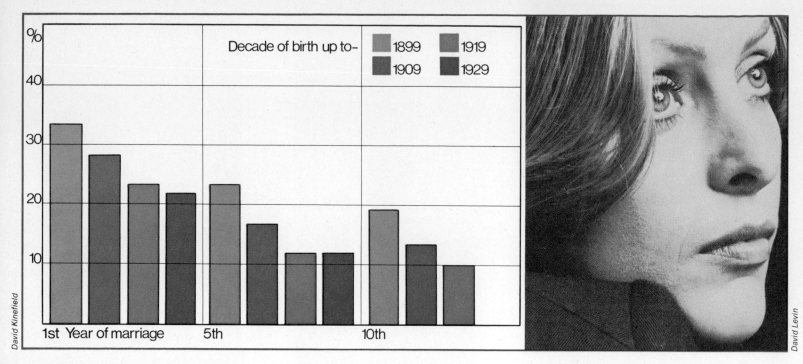

David Kinefield

David Levin

potential ill effects. And these can lead to short-tempered irritability that soon has husband and wife snapping at each other and leaves them further than ever from sexual compatibility.

Psychologically, frigidity may cause deep and growing unhappiness. The wife may worry that she is unfeminine or that her husband lacks masculinity. The husband may become dissatisfied because he sees it as a failure to appreciate his efforts. These rifts can deepen until the marriage splits apart. Paradoxically, the frigidity that causes the rift can be an attempt at communication—please love me more, the wife is saying unconsciously, do not take me for granted.

In some cases, husband and wife may sublimate their sexual energies or find sexual release elsewhere while preserving the social arrangements of marriage. A wife may concentrate on her role as a mother, or begin a creative feminine pastime such as embroidery, while the husband discreetly finds a lover. Or making the worst of a bad job, the wife may use her own distaste of sex to bargain with her husband, rationing his use of her body to his compliance with her other demands.

Two's Company

Overcoming frigidity requires the cooperation of husband and wife— indeed, one of the causes may be just this lack of cooperation. With cooperation, and help from marriage counseling or other professional guidance, a couple can identify the roots of their sexual difficulties and establish a more rewarding sexual relationship.

The Kinsey Report showed how frigidity among women had declined since the turn of the century and that there was a higher percentage of frigidity among women born before 1900 than for subsequent decades. The chart above shows that a third of the married women born before 1900 failed to have orgasm during the first year of marriage, though for all women this figure decreased significantly after ten years of marriage. Kinsey's report hinted that frigidity might be induced by the morality of society as a whole. In 1900, Victorian notions inhibited a woman's natural reactions, while the permissive "Roaring Twenties" loosened the chains on her mind—and body.

Where fear, anxiety and anger have become involved with sex, both husband and wife must try to substitute reassurance and unselfishness. They share the responsibility for helping each other find happiness in sex.

One simple step is to lessen the sources of worry. If fear of pregnancy holds a woman back from the full enjoyment of sex, a family planning clinic can suggest effective forms of contraception. A medical checkup can reveal physical causes of tiredness or pain during intercourse that may be easily cured. And the doctor can explain to a woman who thinks she has lost her sexual responsiveness after pregnancy that it will return. If she is afraid that the neighbors, in-laws or her children may hear their love-making, perhaps rearranging the bedrooms will help.

Learning to enjoy sex and under-

standing the reaction of their own bodies can be a shared experience. Love, and help from professional counselors, can point a way out of despair. Tact and relaxation are the keys and, as a husband and wife begin to communicate, they will learn that neither is to blame, but both are involved.

The well-known sex researchers, Dr. William Masters and Virginia Johnson, see this mutual involvement as most important. In their intensive two-week program aimed to bring a couple who have experienced sexual difficulties to the point of enjoying sexual intercourse to orgasm, they call the couple a marital unit. And the principles behind their course apply to many situations where a couple seek to improve their love-making.

Both husband and wife need tolerance and understanding of each other's sexual nature. Then both can develop an unforced enjoyment of sexuality. Perhaps it begins with affectionate touching—but touching that takes account of the other's wishes. Then affection moves to sexual stimulation—but stimulation that does not press immediately for sexual intercourse.

Husband and wife gradually explore the reactions of each other's body and learn to appreciate their own sexual excitement. And then they progress to sexual intercourse—but intercourse in which they now communicate and can move towards orgasm together.

A loving response between husband and wife is the key point. If a couple enjoy each other sexually, whether they experience orgasm or not, then they can find sexual satisfaction.

Mary Evans

Pleasure & pain

It seems that nearly everyone enjoys a little pain from time to time—if lovingly inflicted. There is a great difference between this, however, and the behavior of those ignoble noblemen, the Marquis de Sade and Chevalier Leopold von Sacher-Masoch, or the masochist who begged, "Hit me, hit me," and the sadist who replied, "No I won't."

Sadism is the word generally used to describe sexual excitement derived from the infliction of pain; masochism is the reverse side of the coin—the desire to receive pain and the tendency to be stimulated by it.

The words were coined after the Marquis de Sade and the Chevalier Leopold von Sacher-Masoch, two minor aristocrats whose prolific writings were laden with graphic details of their sexual tastes. Their most celebrated books are still to be found wrapped in discreet covers on the shelves of pornographic book stores and are certainly read by far more people than is generally supposed.

Even more significant is the wealth of literature which has sprung from their works. It ranges from the hardest of hard-core pornography to mild fantasies in popular magazines, stories with a sado-masochistic content that are churned out in increasing numbers. Most of us buy them in one form or another, read them and are aroused by them. Sometimes we go a stage further and act out, either in masturbation fantasies or with a

309

sexual partner, some kind of dominant or submissive role which probably has sado-masochistic overtones.

This is not to say that the entire human race is made up of perverts. It simply means that there is an element of sado-masochism in everyone. Only in their extreme forms can sadism and masochism be considered as deviations. Exactly where the dividing line occurs between "normal behavior" and perversion is still a matter of considerable argument among psychologists.

Me Tarzan — You Jane

Members of highly civilized societies often find such facts difficult to accept. The Christian belief that love is synonymous with self-sacrifice and gentleness has been taken up with distressing frequency by so-called advanced sex manuals. They devote whole chapters to instructing husbands to "be careful" and to avoid hurting their wives by what is described as "clumsiness." In reality, a certain level of aggression involving pain may be just what both partners secretly long for. Similarly, unmarried people of both sexes, in search of a mate, may find themselves behaving in ways quite contrary to their innermost desires.

Most men in Western society have fantasies at some time about the delights of ravishing a beauty who has caught their eye and it is a fact that more erotic literature exists in which women are bound, beaten and rendered helpless than any other single type of pornography. Conversely, the idea of being seized and carried off by a brutal male and then subsequently being forced to submit to his every wish is intensely exciting to most women, particularly during the early part of their active sexual lives.

Film and pop stars who have acquired "ruthless" images like Mick Jagger and Steve McQueen, fictional seducers like Rhett Butler and even monsters of the King Kong variety owe some of their appeal to the thrill of fear combined with hidden erotic arousal which they evoke in fascinated female audiences. Thus the nervous or excessively polite young businessman and the overly demure young

The Chevalier Leopold von Sacher-Masoch, who gave his name to an extreme sexual deviation known as masochism. Sacher-Masoch went so far as to consider having his lover behead him. The plan had to be shelved owing to its unfortunate side effects!

secretary may well be subconsciously suppressing their natural sexual roles simply as a result of their "civilized" education. The cartoon ape-man wielding a club in one hand and dragging a delectable girl by the hair with the other is still a sufficiently accurate reflection of sexual behavior to have retained its relevance as a popular joke. This is because, in an amusing and exaggerated form, it reflects fantasies experienced by many people of both sexes.

Many men enjoy the idea of dominating a woman and having the power to inflict pain on her—even if they choose not to exercise it. Most girls have, at some time or another, been excited by thoughts of being dominated and thus "forced" to give way to a man's wishes. Women's Liberation finds such observations highly unpalatable despite the fact that they are supported by the findings of most psychologists. This is probably because they tend to confuse sexual roles with concepts of superiority and inferiority.

The truth is, of course, that no sexual roles between members of the opposite sex are possible without the consent of both partners. Only a view of human history which sees man's development—even the development of his subconscious—as an accident, a kind of cosmic error, could defend a theory which requires women, in general, to dream of dominating men. There are such women, of course, and there are plenty of men who wish to be dominated; but they are unquestionably a minority and are *generally* considered to be abnormal.

Love Comes in Little Bites

In bed, the desire to hurt and be hurt, within certain though undefined limitations, is accepted as a normal aspect of sexual relations. In fact, many couples derive extreme excitement from the mutual infliction of pain both before and during intercourse. Even vicious and violent rows between husbands and wives can be, and often are, intensely stimulating. Such rows may become horribly painful mentally even if no physical violence is involved, yet they frequently lead to passionate love-making. Why? Simply because the couple are playing an elaborate game.

A wife who desires to be dominated may have to provoke a mild husband into losing his temper before he will assert himself over her; or conversely a man may wish his wife to dominate him and thus deliberately sets out to infuriate her. The ensuing row estab-

Mary Evans

Aubrey Beardsley's design for a frontispiece to "Earl Lavender" is based on a sado-masochistic appeal.

lishes sexual roles according to the fantasies of the two players. In some cases the more they provoke each other the greater will be the intensity of their sexual passion.

Reactions to extreme pain and extreme pleasure are remarkably similar and, almost certainly, interrelated. The *Kama Sutra*, the Persian "love manual," recommends the enthusiastic use of scratches and bites to heighten sexual pleasure and in certain primitive societies the "marks of passion" on a man or woman are seen as evidence of skill in love-making.

Kinsey's work on human sexual behavior went even further. Not only did he confirm the "normality" of pain infliction in sexual intercourse but he noticed that the movements and facial expressions of people in the throes of orgasm are practically indistinguishable from those of people suffering the severe agonies of physical torture. It is rare, but not unknown, for people with masochistic tendencies to endure quite serious physical injuries. Sacher-Masoch once genuinely considered the possibility of allowing one of his domineering lovers to behead him, a proposal which eventually had to be shelved owing to its inconvenient side effects. He was not, of course, interested in suicide, merely in submitting himself entirely to the will of his mistress.

Clearly, the domination-submission theme is all important in sado-masochistic behavior and almost all human beings are stimulated to some extent by the manipulation of pain. At what point then does such behavior become deviant?

This is a much more difficult question to answer than it may seem. Above all it is important to realize that everyone has within him the seeds of perversion and that a combination of circumstance and suggestion can turn the most apparently harmless individual into a monster. At the extreme end of the sadistic scale, for example, can be placed the mass torture and extermination of the Jews during World War II. And it was not only a grim, perverted Nazi hierarchy that was involved. Common, ordinary, perfectly conventional soldiers also played their part and many apparently enjoyed what they were doing.

Marquis de Sade

Some psychologists have referred to such savagery in terms of a reversion to primeval instincts, claiming that, on the whole, man is becoming increasingly "civilized" and is therefore less likely to inflict cruelties on his own kind. It is a poor argument. Modern man is the only animal which indulges in these wholesale acts of destruction and, as the anthropologist Margaret Mead has pointed out, many primitive societies are extremely tolerant and gentle.

Just as, especially in wartime, groups of men are capable of appalling acts of cruelty, so too are single individuals within a society. Battle-scarred soldiers have the right, so it seems, to murder, rape and torture. In peacetime, to perform such acts is to behave like a criminal. This should serve to remind us that sexual criminals are not different beings; they are simply lacking in control over basic impulses which we all share. War, because it establishes murder and savagery as norms of behavior, releases our control system, which Freud referred to as the super ego, and thus unleashes the forces of cruelty normally held in check.

Fortunately, in peacetime at least, sadistic murderers are extremely rare. A very large number of people, however, are excited not only by the idea but by the act of beating or being beaten.

There have been no better exponents of these sexual tastes than de Sade and Sacher-Masoch themselves. De Sade's books, of which the most justly celebrated is *The 120 Days of*

Sodom, are veritable catalogues of sexual perversions in which male dominance is supreme. Women are "weak and fettered creatures fated only to serve our lusts . . ." and are consequently reviled, flogged, tortured and unmercifully humiliated. Furthermore, it is clear that de Sade practiced what he preached, as a result of which he spent a great deal of his active life in prison. His degradation of women led, in other words, to a degradation of himself. He wallowed, as a prey to his own passions, in the luxuriant undergrowth of what he would have called "evil." "There may be no hint of delicacy in crime as there is in virtue," he once wrote, "yet is it not more imposing, doesn't it always have a sort of grandeur and nobleness about it which will forever attract us more than the dull idea of being good?"

Essentially, to de Sade, the truly enjoyable aspects of sex were forbidden and had to be forbidden in order to preserve their charm. His dream was literally impossible to realize since it would require not only excessive pliancy on the part of his female partner but also constant, miraculous recovery from the wounds inflicted the night before so that she would be ready to begin again. Frustration characterizes de Sade's work just as it characterizes the sexual plight of those whose demands are only met in fantasy by reading his books.

The same applies to Sacher-Masoch, whose most widely read publication, *Venus in Furs*, sells as many copies now as it did when first published in 1870. The heroine of *Venus in Furs* is a passionate and highly domineering young woman who reduces her male lover to the status of a slave and gets pleasure from humiliating him. The lover responds to this treatment with undisguised adoration which both demeans him and stimulates him to the heights of sexual excitement.

Many of Sacher-Masoch's contemporaries recognized their own tastes in these literary fantasies. Women, in particular, were avid readers of his work and this may well be a reflection of the subservient position of European women at that time. Their reaction was to dwell in their thoughts on a total reversal of sexual roles, to break the stranglehold of conventional mores and give free rein to their passions. What could be a better symbol of revolt than the idea of dominating men?

As it turned out, few of the women who met Sacher-Masoch found themselves excited by the possibility of turning fantasy into reality. Most flatly rejected his proposals for action. Occasionally, however, he met someone who would comply with his wishes and often this would result in the drawing up of a formal document setting out the rules of the game.

The wording of these documents provides a fascinating insight into the masochistic mind: "Herr Leopold von Sacher-Masoch gives his word of honor to Frau Pistor to become her slave and to comply unreservedly with every one of her desires and demands. . . . The mistress has the right to punish her slave in any way she thinks fit for all errors, carelessness or treacherous crimes on his part. . . . He must be totally obedient to his mistress and accept as a delicious condescension any favorable treatment she may give him. At the same time he recognizes that he has no claim upon her love and he renounces any of the rights over her normally enjoyed by a lover. . . ." Legally worthless as it may have been, the contract was signed and sealed as part of the elaborate ritual Sacher-Masoch required for the satisfaction of his sexuality.

Like de Sade, however, he was not really concerned, when he enacted a fantasy, with any kind of mature emotional relationship with his partner. On the contrary, one of the things we notice about sado-masochistic deviancy is that it requires alienation from the feelings of the other person. There is no question of giving pleasure, only of receiving it by whatever means are necessary. Sexual partners are thus reduced to the level of mere instruments. Sacher-Masoch once admitted this in a letter to one of his "lovers": "My ideal cruel woman is for me simply the instrument with which I terrorize myself."

Pleasing Pain

Because of this, the sado-masochist tends to degrade human sexuality and to immerse himself in the criminality of his behavior. Here lies a further difference between the use of pain in normal relationships and its use in relationships which are generally accepted as abnormal. The ordinary pair of lovers, whose sexual excitement is intensified, perhaps, by following some of the precepts of the *Kama Sutra* with regard to inflicting pain, are motivated by the idea of giving pleasure to their partner. The man who sees his wife or girlfriend writhe with excitement when he nibbles various parts of her body is himself thrilled by her reaction. This is not true of the real sado-masochist whose mounting excitement is totally egocentric and may well depend on the degradation of his partner. He wants her to enjoy the situation, but only in his own terms and according to his own desires.

Perhaps the true hallmark of a sado-masochistic sexual deviant is his *dependence* upon giving or receiving pain in order to obtain any kind of sexual satisfaction. For most lovers, pain, if used at all as a stimulant, remains secondary in importance to the sexual act itself. It adds excitement but is not essential. Rather it performs the same kind of function as a good bottle of wine with a meal: delightful especially when shared.

Sex Games

The sado-masochist, on the other hand, cannot do without pain. It becomes an addictive drug. Furthermore, pain for him is not a stimulant in itself, it is merely the expression of basic, overwhelming impulses to dominate or submit to domination. Absolute power against absolute helplessness, imperiousness against total submission are the basic driving forces behind deviant sado-masochism.

Why then are people plagued by such desires? Are we born with certain inherent sexual leanings, or are these acquired by childhood experiences? Surprisingly, perhaps, attempts have been made to show that there is a physical difference between sado-masochists and normal people. One survey provided evidence that certain male psychopaths have an extra chromosome in their physiological make-up, though to what extent this is also to be found among the population in general remains unanswered. The theory which asserts that sado-masochism is a reflection of arrested childhood development is more credible.

Aggression is the basis of cruelty and the desire to dominate, but it is also essential to normal, healthy development. A child comes into the world utterly helpless and completely dependent on its parents. Without an aggressive urge which leads him to establish his own identity as an independent being he would remain in this primitive state forever. The fantasy life of children is characterized above all by a desire to be master of the situation, to be big, strong and powerful, and it goes hand in hand, especially in the first few years of life, with savage bouts of temper and intensely destructive impulses.

At the same time, all children ex-

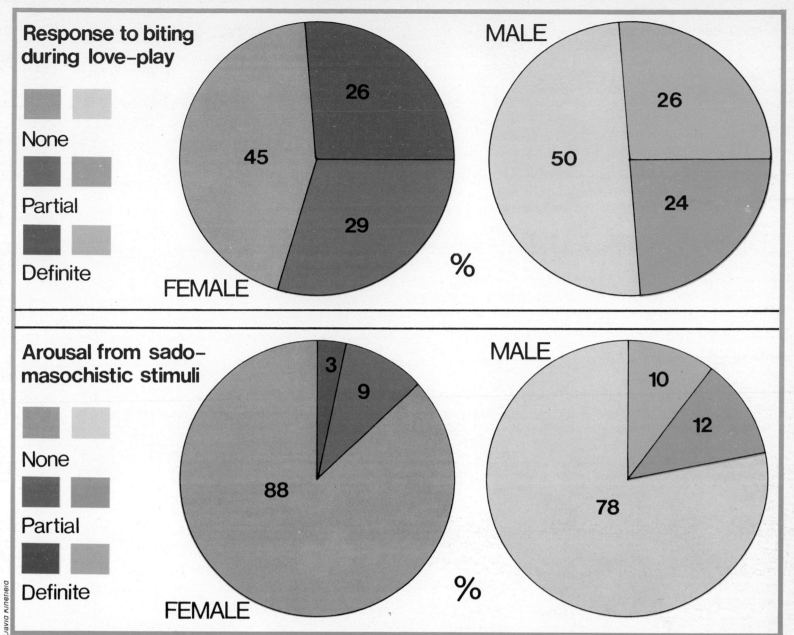

Response to biting during love-play

None
Partial
Definite

MALE

26
50
24

FEMALE

26
45
29

%

Arousal from sado-masochistic stimuli

None
Partial
Definite

MALE

10
12
78

FEMALE

3
9
88

%

David Kineriela

Can pain give pleasure? This chart which is in two parts shows (top) male and female response to biting during love-play: 55% of women display an active response to biting as opposed to 50% of men. The second part (bottom) shows male and female arousal by sado-masochistic stimuli. Here 12% of women show a response as opposed to 22% of men.

perience the conflicting desire to to be loved, cherished and protected from the hostility of the outside world. The result is an ambivalence from which no adult is entirely free. In fact, in adult sexual relationships nearly all stable couples find that, at different times, they alternate between the two poles. Each partner takes turns at being dominant and protective while the other is subordinate and childlike. Total independence is, of course, just as impossible and undesirable for a

normal person as is total helplessness.

The sado-masochist, however, has usually failed to develop this fine balance and remains either excessively aggressive or excessively dependent or both. In other words, the childhood pattern is repeated and is exaggerated particularly in the most intimate and revealing human activity: sexual behavior. Prostitutes armed with an assortment of whips, corsets, chains and minor torture devices, and underground booksellers who specialize in "flagellation," have made a great deal of money out of this unfortunately widespread failure to develop. But we should not imagine that normal people are not affected. Clearly they are. Paperback publishers and skillful advertising agencies have used the average person's susceptibility to sado-masochistic stimuli to great effect.

Nor should we overlook the sexual games we play in our own lives. The pretty girl who dresses in skin-tight

blouses and pants is subconsciously accepting a masochistic role akin to the lurid fantasies of bondage and flogging of the true sado-masochist. Few girls would argue that such clothes are actually comfortable.

On a slightly different level, the teasing and withdrawal games enjoyed by so many couples as a preliminary to love-making have their roots in the same impulses which dominated the thoughts and writings of Sacher-Masoch and de Sade. The question is not basically one of kind but of degree. What really separates the sado-masochist from the normal person is not, essentially, his impulses but his alienation both from reality in general and from his partner in particular. Most of us, under normal circumstances, are incapable of alienating ourselves completely from the feelings of a sexual partner. Sexual deviation is, in the last analysis, sex without any kind of love, or the possibility of love.

Luck on the stage

You would be hard pressed to find a more superstitious group of people than actors and actresses. If they stumble over their lines during the first rehearsal it signals impending doom; shoes placed on a dressing room table invite death; green is an unlucky color and disaster always attends a production of *Macbeth.* But once on stage the play's the thing.

The professional European and American stage is probably governed by more taboos than any other sphere of civilized twentieth century activity; torn between the unreal glitter of the footlights and the grim reality of his often underpaid existence, the actor relies on "magic" to bolster himself just as much today as he ever did.

Shakespeare, with his plethora of ghosts, fairies and omens, was steeped in theatrical superstition, but he was building on foundations stretching back to the early Greek tragedies and beyond; perhaps because it is a world of fantasy, the theater has attracted superstitions which were once widespread, and kept them alive.

Fame and Fortune

The "magic" begins with personal tokens of success; if something brings luck the first time around, then it should be effective again and again. An English actor who went into politics in the late sixties was given a ring which had been worn, he was assured, by the great Edmund Kean as a prop in a Shakespeare tragedy. He has worn it ever since, both on the stage and in the House of Commons. "If my role demands that I don't wear a ring, I hide it about my person. In one performance where I appeared stripped to the waist I put the blasted thing in my underpants."

The same idea has obsessed many other artists, and in some cases film stars have worn the same "prop" in every film they have made. James Stewart, for instance, has worn the same battered cowboy hat in all his Western films, and on a recent British TV show he explained a great deal about casual superstition when he told the audience, "I would feel kinda uncomfortable without it."

An ex-Broadway British actor feels

similarly uncomfortable without his vast collection of teddy bears around him in his dressing room. Despite his now international fame he also wears his "lucky tie" whenever he goes for an audition. "It's never failed me yet," he says. "I wore it for my first audition and passed. Since then I have lent it to numerous friends in the business for their auditions, and it has never ceased to come up trumps."

This particular actor is also notable for the fact that he seems to have made a successful deal with God. "I was in a big success in Britain which later had a long Broadway run. It was based on a religious figure. I was having trouble with a long speech I had to make, and I swore, literally, to God that if He allowed me to make the speech flawlessly, I would give up smoking. I went on stage and delivered it without a single mistake for the whole run of the play, and true to my bargain I haven't smoked since."

Self-hypnosis? Probably. But almost every actor, however exalted or obscure, can tell a similar story; lucky jewelry, clothes and, in the case of actresses, scent, have been treasured over the years. One highly successful comedy script writer even carries a piece of back-cloth, from the first production for which he ever wrote, in a Jewish "mazzuzah" holder—although Jewish by birth he is not orthodox.

Curtain Custom

These, of course, are personal quirks. Much of theatrical superstition, however, runs like a vein through the body of the profession as an entity, and embraces everything from rehearsal to the closedown of a particular play. For instance, some actors, stumbling over their first reading, feel that their ineptitude is an omen of bad luck; if they manage the reading at the second try the bad luck is washed out. If they are "name" actors and yet still somehow manage to bungle their second reading, their subordinates consider that the play is jinxed—understandably enough, perhaps.

Once on stage and into rehearsal "the play's the thing" and even superstition takes second place, although two rules are adhered to by even the most down-to-earth directors: the curtain is never completely lowered at a rehearsal, and the last line of the play is never spoken. According to one veteran, these two customs at least have not been broken in the British theater since the turn of the century—for fear, presumably, that the performance be brought to an untimely, "magical" end. Another odd superstition also concerns rehearsals; in the south of England, a cat running across the stage during rehearsal means certain success, while in the north the opposite applies. In both cases the color of the cat is immaterial, and no one seems to know the origin of either belief.

An III Wind

During the run of a performance, each actor virtually lives in his dressing room, and around this often scruffy sanctum several rites and traditions have grown up. On the first night of a play good luck telegrams are hoarded carefully; first they are stuck up around the dressing room mirror for the run of the play and afterwards they are taken down and preserved—if the play is a success. Favorable press reviews often get the same treatment, and experienced actors seem to believe that luck is a commodity which can be stored for further use; the telegrams and press clippings often share the limelight in an old trouper's "memory box" with bits of soap and stubs of grease paint associated with past triumphs.

The dressing room seems to bring out strong territorial feelings in its occupier. Hollywood romanticism has popularized the idea of the "star" on the door of a successful actor, but the notion is much older than motion pictures. The "number one" performer is master in his dressing room, his cabinet of secrets, and he guards his domain jealously. According to legend Charles Macklin, a famous eighteenth

Luck be a lady tonight. Actors are a notoriously superstitious breed. Peter Bull, ex-Broadway British actor, has a collection of teddy bears to ensure roars of applause when he is on the boards.

century Shakespearean, challenged and killed a colleague in a sword fight at the Drury Lane Theatre in London after his actor-opponent had persisted in looking over Macklin's shoulder at his image in the make-up mirror. Mirror superstitions, and the danger of "overshadowing" people by sharing a mirror with them, seem to have been common in ancient Greece, and to this day no actor likes to be "overshadowed" while making up—although dressers appear to be immune from this fad.

The actor in his dressing room shares at least one superstition with the sailor: neither whistles while at work. The sailor believes that whistling conjures up wind, and to an actor anyone whistling in a dressing room or on the wings of the stage summons bad luck though whistling on the stage itself—if the production calls for it—is permissible. There are, however, antidotes in both cases. At sea, the inadvertent whistler throws a small coin into the waves; in a dressing room he either curses as loudly and obscenely as possible, or leaves the dressing room, turns around three times outside, and knocks three times for readmission—the number being a powerful magical symbol.

Another seafaring and theater superstition involves shoes; neither at sea nor in a theater dressing room should anyone ever place footwear upon a table, however cramped the conditions. The most likely explanation is that in the old days corpses were laid out on tables, and the concept of "putting one's feet up" either literally, in the modern sense, or symbolically in the form of shoes is a clear invitation to death.

Tragedy Tonight

Oddly enough, in view of all these precautions against bad luck, invitations to good luck have always been anathema in the theater, and the rule also applies in films and television—one of the few examples of stage superstitions being passed into these comparatively new fields. An actor may, before stepping from the wings, request a colleague to "wish him luck" but under no circumstances should the colleague actually do so. Instead, he will wish the opposite and say "break a leg" or "do a bomb."

Folklorists claim that this practice harks back to the days when it was necessary to "fool the gods." By asking a mischievous spirit to bring disaster, you prompted his contrary nature to do just the opposite and shower you with success. One charming exception to this rule exists; a confident Shakespearean may quote *The Merchant of Venice* to a nervous colleague: "Fair thoughts and happy hours attend on you."

Assuming that a production does achieve rave notices and packed houses, the performers can relax a little and concentrate on their roles; but there is always the business of getting to the theater. Route and method of transport must be chosen with care, for reasons explained by the Teddy bear collecting actor quoted above.

"I was late for a first night," he explains, "and drove part of the way in my car before becoming involved in a traffic jam. So I parked the car and took the subway, got off at Leicester Square and walked the rest of the way. The first night was a wild success, which was rather awkward because like many of my colleagues I believe that to retain success the same route and the same transport must be taken to the theater for each night of the play's run. The show ran for nearly two years, and each night I part drove, part trained, and part walked there."

Such determination to suffer inconvenience for the sake of a superstition is not uncommon and illustrates convincingly the need for self-assurance which lies behind these apparently pointless beliefs. Interestingly enough, the two most ingrained of all theater fads—and possibly the two most famous among the general public—are both of fairly recent origin and sprang not from a distortion of mythology but from very practical considerations. One is the *Macbeth* myth, and the other is the refusal—infuriating to costume designers—of many actors to wear green on stage.

No actor with very much experience will happily talk about *Macbeth.* From drama school onwards he learns to refer to it as "that play" or even "that cursed play." Those who have to perform in it for financial or other reasons go on stage loaded down with lucky charms and with eyes peeled for bad luck omens, and almost anyone in the theater will, with grim satisfaction, tell hair-raising stories connected with *Macbeth* productions. According to these, performers have died of heart attacks on stage, cut themselves badly in the fight scenes, been crippled by falling scenery or, on a lesser scale, merely received the worst critical notice of their careers.

Macbeth is of course one of the most melodramatic of Shakespeare's tragedies, a bloody tale of regicide,

witchcraft, and the thrice cursed Thane of Cawdor, slain by Macduff who was "from his mother's womb untimely ripp'd." Sinister stuff perhaps; but then so is *King Lear*, a play as popular with actors as the equally sinister *Hamlet*. And if bloodshed is the criterion by which "cursed" plays should be judged *Titus Andronicus* surely leads the field.

A Simple Answer

The answer to the *Macbeth* riddle is a simple one, and yet interesting because it demonstrates the functioning of a sort of folk memory among theater people. Until the beginning of the nineteenth century *Macbeth* was one of the most popular plays of all with audiences. David Garrick, the great eighteenth century English tragedian, achieved one of his most resounding successes in the lead part, and in doing so lent it wide appeal.

With the coming of the nineteenth century, touring companies of English players visited the new music halls and theaters in the provinces; these companies had a standard repertoire of plays, but usually set out from London with a new production. They were booked at each theater for a week or more, and if the new show flopped on opening night a quick replacement was hastily mounted in its stead.

More often than not the one play that every actor knew by heart, without needing rehearsal, was *Macbeth,*

Ronald Grant

Kobal

Many famous actors have superstitious quirks. James Stewart insists on wearing the same hat in every Western. Director John Ford objected to this battered stetson and tried to persuade him to wear one of John Wayne's cast-offs. Stewart refused and Ford growled, "If you ever work for me again — which I doubt — have a hat approval clause written into your contract!" Stewart took him at his word.

and gradually the play became associated with failure because it so frequently took the place of a flop. Hence the fact that, though the haphazard staging of "fill in" plays among repertory companies died out sometime in the 1870s, the smell of failure continued to hang around *Macbeth* and intensified over the years — until today "that play" is positively cursed.

A similar explanation seems likely in the case of the "wearing of green" taboo, although here the tradition is a deep-rooted one. From earliest times green has been the color of the fairies — Jack o' the Green, the Green Man and even the half-mythical Robin Hood. Actors, being superstitious folk, were loath to associate themselves with these supernatural beings.

In medieval times green was also the color of prostitutes — the song "Greensleeves" is said to have been written by Henry VIII as an ironic, rather than romantic, tribute to his ill-fated wife Anne Boleyn. At law, "strolling players" were lumped together with "thieves, rogues, vagabonds and whores" as undesirables, a classification which the players naturally resented, and their antipathy to green possibly springs from this time.

A much more likely, if less picturesque, reason for avoiding green — or for that matter light blue — stage costume followed the introduction of "limelight" in the 1820s. Prior to this period the stage was lit either by chandeliers or by candle footlights

and gas-produced limelight was a welcome innovation. It had one curious property, however — its blue green light emphasized certain colors, but caused others, notably green, to become almost invisible. Thus an actor wearing an all green outfit would literally fade into the background, a thing that no performer likes to do. And although limelight was finally replaced by electric lighting towards the end of the century, the folk memory lingered on.

Flower Power

There are other unlucky plays besides *Macbeth*, but these usually change from actor to actor; one man, for instance, swears that plays with the word "Peacock" in the title should be avoided. There are also lucky and unlucky theaters. The Theatre Royal, Drury Lane — the scene of Macklin's sword fight — is said to be haunted not only by Macklin, but by the shades of Edmund Kean and comedian Dan Leno, and yet is considered to be one of the luckiest venues for a production; perhaps the past triumphs of these great figures still cling.

Flowers, too, have their attendant superstitions. Roses, tulips and chrysanthemums are welcome in an end-

of-show bouquet, but lilies, with their funereal associations and — for some obscure reason — carnations are dreaded; a celebrated opera singer once threw back a spray of carnations which was tossed to her on stage by a French president.

Possibly because of the "make-believe" nature of a theatrical production, real jewelry is bad luck and is rarely worn by actors, however dazzling the gems might be. Douglas Fairbanks Senior is said to have had a rare tiff with his wife Mary Pickford because of this belief. Miss Pickford was playing the part of a noblewoman in a film, and her costume consisted of rich clothes, diamond tiaras, pearl necklaces and emerald and ruby rings — all imitation, of course. On her birthday, the well-meaning Fairbanks substituted real gems for the fakes: a prodigiously generous gesture, but one which was not well received.

When she realized what had happened, Mary Pickford flew into a panic-stricken rage and scattered the valuables around her dressing room floor, screaming for the return of her paste jewelry. The episode is possibly apocryphal, but nevertheless illustrates vividly the dramatic force of irrational beliefs and fears.

The Snob

He seeks it here, he seeks it there, he seeks for status everywhere. Encouraged by the breakdown of rigid class structures, snobbery has become the disease of our times. To hide his inner emptiness, the snob tries always to clamber to the top of the heap. Reality is the only price he will not pay, for he never understands that airs and graces do not make the man.

Show me a snob and I will show you a fool. A snob is a social climber, anxious to ape people he thinks are his betters. There is nothing inherently wrong in that; what makes the snob a fool is that he goes about it the wrong way.

He does not recognize the distinction of having and being. Like a man looking at the tip of an iceberg and thinking he sees the whole truth, the snob looks at those he feels are above him and imagines that their possessions make them what they are.

The snob, asked to visit Aristotle Onassis on board his yacht, invests in new slacks, a new shirt, new socks and new casual shoes. He is quite likely to find Onassis, who does not care too much what anyone thinks of him, wearing bedroom slippers, the grubbiest white slacks east of Suez and an old black shirt stained with spaghetti sauce.

Snob Value

The snob, invited on a weekend in the country, buys new tweeds, new boots and a deerstalker hat. For his wife, if his personal economy is buoyant, he buys a totally inappropriate mink jacket. For the occasion, anxious to impress, he rents a Cadillac. On similar occasions, the Queen of England, who also does not have to bother too much about what people think of her when she is off duty, dresses in rubber boots, an old coat and a headscarf, and she drives a mud-spattered station wagon.

Snobs are sunburned in the summer after a vacation at what they believe to be the right place to be seen. Nonsnobs are sunburned in winter after a vacation at what they *know* is the right place for them, whether anyone sees them or not. By the time snobs discover Miami and

To the snob status symbols are all that count, but the need to acquire yet bigger and better signs of affluence will break him in the end for outer trappings can never conceal his inner poverty.

Robin Clifford

the Costa Brava in Spain, rich non-snobs have abandoned these resorts in favor of the Seychelles.

Take the simple example of being what the world calls a gentleman. The true gentleman *is*, the snob merely *has*. If you dressed a gentleman in rags, his quality and spirit would remain. He would still, very obviously, be a gentleman. Even the snob understands this, but as a rule he misses the simple paradox that a lout in a hand-made suit is still a lout. Another distinction that can be made is that, whereas a gentleman never wittingly offends anyone, the snob unwittingly offends everyone.

The snob, easily identifiable when you meet him because his life revolves around his material possessions, makes the recurrent mistake, in fact, of trying to attain something that only comes from within. He does not grasp that the people he (or she) envies possess qualities which have nothing to do with their material possessions, and mere acquisition of similar possessions is not going to get the snob anywhere.

Of course, there are various types of snobbery and the world's vast army of snobs is made up of men and women, old and young. It would therefore be misleading to think of the snob and the true gentleman as opposing poles. It is really a question of self-deceit versus authenticity. Consequently, it is more accurate to refer to them as "the snob" and "the authentic."

Spiritual Poverty

The authentic person, the one the snob admires and stands in awe of, has a quality that comes from within. His or her assets are not perceptible to the senses. They cannot be seen like expensive clothes, cannot be touched like a diamond ring, cannot be smelled like French perfume. In contrast, the snob is a walking shop window with nothing inside. He collects material plenty but suffers from spiritual poverty.

Nowadays, sad to say, snobbery is on the increase as a result of the

breaking down of the old class system. Snobbery is possible, in fact, only when classes mingle and there is a possibility of moving from one to the other. Take, for example, the matter of clothes. In the days when the rich were rich and the poor were poor and they met only as masters and servants, fine clothes were an accepted outward sign of superiority. Higher wages and the growth of the off-the-peg clothes industry gave the snob the chance to ape his superiors in the matters of appearance.

Snobbery—Traps and Trappings

Did this worry the authentics? Not at all. They simply stopped bothering about clothes. In the case of men, patent shoes, spats, gaiters, fancy waistcoats, frock coats, top hats and other fripperies have virtually disappeared. Nowadays, in fact, the tuxedo is almost the only remaining form of formal dress for the civilian male.

Homes—like the Cadillac versus the Volkswagen—are another convenient example of how the snob misses out. While he is slaving away to try to put together the price of an elegant town house or a desirable mock-Tudor residence in the country, authentics finding themselves pushed for money are quite happily moving into humble farm cottages and doing them up.

The snob, it can be clearly seen, lives a life of constant frustration, whether he is a *nouveau riche* businessman trying to keep up with a socialite or a determined housewife trying to keep up with the wife of the manager of the neighborhood's biggest store. The snob is like an animal on a treadmill, walking round and round and getting nowhere. The authentics are always one or more steps ahead of him and, if he shows any sign of catching up, they simply change the rules of the game.

The tiny, but important, aspects of behavior that separate the authentic from the snob are perhaps nowhere better demonstrated than in Britain. As Nancy Mitford, herself a peer's daughter, pointed out in her book

Lvn Grav

Noblesse Oblige: "Today, in 1956, the English class system is essentially tripartite—there exist an upper, a middle and a lower class. It is solely by its language that the upper class is clearly marked off from the others.

"In times past [e.g. in the Victorian and Edwardian periods] this was not the case. But, today, a member of the upper class is, for instance, not necessarily better educated, cleaner or richer than someone not of this class. Nor, in general, is he likely to play a greater part in public affairs, be supported by other trades or professions, or engage in other pursuits or pastimes than his fellow in another class."

She goes on: "There are, it is true, still a few minor points of life which may serve to demarcate the upper class, but they are only minor ones. The games of real tennis and piquet, an aversion to high (cooked) tea, having one's cards engraved (not printed), not playing tennis in suspenders, and, in some cases, a dislike of comparatively modern inventions such as the telephone, the cinema and the wireless are still perhaps the marks of the upper class."

U And Non-U

But it is their use of the written and spoken language that serves to demarcate the U (upper) class from the non-U. The non-U snob wishing to be mistaken for a gentleman must therefore be prepared to abandon many of the words and expressions he has been using since childhood.

He will be exposed as an impostor immediately if he uses such words as wealthy (instead of rich), cycle (bike), home (house), ill (sick), mental (mad), toilet paper (lavatory paper), sweet (pudding), dentures (false teeth), glasses (spectacles), and bye-bye (goodbye). A similar fate awaits him if he responds to the greeting "How do you do?" in any way except repeating "How do you do?" or if he says his son is "studying for an exam" where a U would use the verb "working for." "Perhaps," says Miss Mitford, "the best known of all the linguistic class-indicators is the use of the non-U 'serviette' for the U 'table napkin.'"

It is hardly surprising to learn, therefore, that the snob lives a life of fear because he knows, subconsciously, that he is a phoney and could easily be found out. But there is a difference between the self-deceived snob and the confidence trickster pretending to be rich. The snob's fear is vague, a muddled irritant, because he truly believes in himself and does not see his snobbery for what it is. Were he able to see that, he would be capable of understanding authenticity, for it is his inability to understand authenticity that makes him an acquisitive snob, a dressed-up dummy rather than a real person. But blind though he may be to this truth, his subconscious knows it and that is where the fear stems from.

It is not just the loosening of social bonds which makes the age we live in so very much the age of the snob.

It is the vast emphasis put on material things by the consumer business. People without too much confidence in themselves, and perhaps with little understanding of themselves, are faced with a constant barrage of advertising aimed solely at turning them into snobs. The propaganda of materialism is harmful to a person's happiness if that person is vulnerable to snobbery.

Defense Mechanisms

From every section of the media people are told constantly that they are inferior unless they dress in a certain way, unless they wash their clothes in a certain type of powder, smoke a certain type of cigarette, drive a smooth car. Every advertising copywriter knows the snob and spends his life exploiting him—and there is no one easier to exploit.

The system is especially hard for the masculine snob who, after years of hammering himself into the ground to earn enough to feed the dragon of snobbery, is more than likely to be carried off with a coronary thrombosis before he reaches 50. Snobbery is, in contrast, much easier physically and emotionally on women, who can marry one of their acquisitions and then wring him physically and financially dry to acquire more.

Why is a snob a snob? It is not simply a matter of being born poor. There are snobs in all walks of life, at all income levels and in all different social environments.

One way of looking at the snob's

The snob's path is paved with perils. Determined to be one up, the snob (left) must have a wardrobe for every eventuality. Asked for a country walk, he arrives looking like a tailor's dummy straight from the store window and spends his time negotiating mud and puddles for fear of soiling his perfect gear. His host, who, like Queen Elizabeth (right), needs no uniform to prove who he or she is, is happy in old clothes and rain boots and will enjoy the walk—puddles and all —without loss of dignity.

Camera Press

motivation is that he has split his personality and subconsciously tried to kill the worthless side of himself. We all have a worthless side of our natures, of course, but for most of us it is an accepted part of ourselves.

Snobbery is also a defense. The snob suffers from a deep-seated inferiority of which, on a conscious level, he is unaware. He does not *feel* that he is inferior. The opposite, if anything, is true. But, subconsciously, he is driven to demonstrate his superiority by the acquisition of possessions.

It is also important to grasp the fact that the snob is sincere in his self-deception. His failing is that he has not reached the depth of character at which authenticity takes over. Although the dictionary will tell you that "sincere" and "authentic" both mean "genuine," psychiatrists have come to use them in this other way to indicate the difference between someone who is self-deceived and therefore "sincere" in putting forward the false image he believes to be true, and the person who actually does put forward his true image.

Inverse Snobbery

The snob *feels* like a god, but he behaves like a worm. His need to enhance his self-esteem is paramount. It can make him a difficult person to be with and, in particular, to work with, for the snob is potentially a bully. He has no compunction about shattering someone else's self-esteem in order to enhance his own.

Although snobbery is as old as life itself, inverse snobbery is a relatively modern phenomenon. The man determined to cling to an impoverished and rough image has the same root to his problems but has given his snobbery a slightly different facet. Pretending to be what he has ceased to be is as bad as pretending to be something he has never been.

The person who has fought his way

Ron Embleton

up the ladder—in business, politics or the arts—and then tenaciously sticks to a sloppy way of talking and acting when, in fact, his very mode of living has smoothed it out is the most pretentious kind of snob. There is a great difference between being proud of your background and self-consciously flaunting it. Why does the white businessman or the black politician who has risen from the slums of the city to great success and a house in the suburbs wear an undershirt to greet his guests or belch in public? You can be sure they are both canny enough to control their "image" and would not be guilty of such social lapses if they were still in the slums. What they are actually crying to those they think are above them is "See—I don't need your fancy ways. I'm as good as you are any day, no matter what I do!"

This is also the most childish form of snobbery because, apart from the normal causation of snobbery, it stems also from a petty resentment. The inverse snob is a victim of dis-

Meet Mr. Unpleasant—the inverse snob. This snob trades in bad manners and rude behavior in spite of his luxurious surroundings. He uses his uncouth habits to poke at his "equals" since he knows he cannot compete on their terms. His alienation is complete.

appointment and unreal ambition. He has chased an ambition which he has achieved, only to find it was not what he wanted, it did not turn him into the person he thought he could be or give him the esteem he expected it to bring. He feels cheated, conned out of what ought rightfully to be his.

He is perhaps the saddest type of snob because he alienates himself from others even more than the ordinary snob. He is disliked by the people among whom he was raised as much as by those he is kicking against. His pride and arrogance set him apart. His lack of authentic feeling turns his pseudoattachment to his original class or racial group into patronage, and he is often surprised

when it is resented by others.

Snobbery, like everything else, varies in degree, but to the authentic person snobs are always rather obvious once their acquaintance has been made. They might be snobbish to a high degree, collecting their status symbols with grim determination, or they may be the more subtle kind of snob, confining their snobbery to one aspect of life such as art or their job. However, snobbery is an empty sham which only impresses other snobs so it can be described as nothing more than a lifelong waste of time. Just as con men are the easiest prey for other con men, so snobs themselves are easily impressed by other snobs.

The only way to remain unsullied by the corrupting avarice of the snob is to remain free of pretension oneself. To achieve this it is necessary to know oneself and to find the intrinsic values of life in the qualities of man that come from within him, not from what he has materially produced. This is why the wise seek humility, not adoration.

B.P.C./Janet Grant

Exorcism

A prayer: *"I adjure thee, O serpent of old, by the Judge of the living and the dead; by the Creator of the world who hath power to cast into hell, that thou depart forthwith from this house. He that commands thee, accursed demon, is He that commanded the winds and the sea and the storm. Hearken then Satan and fear. Get thee gone. . . ."* Exorcism—fancy or fact?

An "unholy row" on the merits or otherwise of the film *The Exorcist* greeted its release early in 1974. Critics everywhere were vociferous in their views for and against; some showed the movie as a parable of our time, others saw it as a straight "horror" film, and yet others claimed that it was a deeply religious statement.

But all the public in-fighting about the merits or otherwise of the film were as nothing to the "holy row" the publication of the book on which it was based had caused just two and a

half years previously. The author, William Peter Blatty—subsequently the film's producer and script writer, had published his work in February, 1972. In his novel, Blatty had argued persuasively for the continued existence of the medieval Devil, and either he or one of his associates decided to test "official" opinion on the matter: they sent a copy of the book to the authoritative journal *Roman Jesuit Review*.

In the summer of 1972, the magazine's literary critic, Father Domenico

Mondrone, an influential Jesuit, published a solemn opinion. "The book is sound doctrinally," he stated, "and advisable for an initial introduction to demoniac phenomena"; it also "furnished proof" that a Christian can be possessed by the Devil. Important as they were to theologians, Father Mondrone's views would perhaps have never reached the attention of the world's press had it not been for a single important fact. One of the most avid readers of the *Roman Jesuit Review* was Pope Paul VI.

According to Vatican sources, the Pope, already cautious about the Catholic church's increasingly liberal attitude to the modern world, brooded deeply on the implications of Blatty's book and Mondrone's consideration of it. And then, in mid-November, 1972, His Holiness gave voice to his thoughts. The occasion was a general audience at the Vatican, at which principals of the Catholic church from all over the world were present.

Papal Bulwark

The Pope surprised even some of his more conservative listeners. "On the world scene," he said, "there is the invisible presence of an obscure agent and enemy, the demon . . . the evil is not only a spiritual deficiency, but an efficiency, a *live being, spiritual, perverted and perverter, a terrible reality, mysterious and fearful.*"

In effect he was claiming that the Devil—horned, hooved, red-eyed and scaly—still, as the Catholic catechism put it, "wandered through the world

for the ruin of souls." A great hollow groan went up from the ranks of more liberal Catholics and those other Christians who had felt, since the time of Pope John XXIII, that the Vatican was drawing closer to them.

But more was to follow. Later the same month, the Pope referred to a recent Vatican Council, and said that, after it, he had hoped that "a day of sun would have come for the story of the church, but a day of storms, clouds and uncertainties came instead." This was, he claimed, because "the smoke of Satan has entered the temple of God through some crack."

These Papal statements—not made *ex cathedra* and therefore not subject to the controversial "Papal infallibility" rule—undoubtedly caused a few sparks of rebellion among the younger Catholic clergy; but others regarded them as a timely warning to arm against Satan, the old arch-enemy who had been neglected for so long. Thus, indirectly, *The Exorcist* led a good number of priests to brush up

The film *The Exorcist* sparked off a storm of controversy because of its portrayal of a small girl's depravity in the grips of demonic possession. It brought home the fact that the Devil is no laughing matter and showed that exorcism may be a dangerous business— that is if you believe in it!

on their knowledge of the almost forgotten practice of exorcism, the casting out of devils. As it happened, they had centuries of tradition to go on.

The comparatively modern word has its roots in the Greek "horkos"— meaning oath—and refers to the act of expelling evil through command, ritual, or prayer. Immediately before Henry VIII's break with the Roman church, the formula for exorcising a "house troubled by an evil spirit" was long and wordy, while a hundred years later, in the middle of the seventeenth century, a Puritan parson is reported to have cut the process short. Losing his temper with the demon which

A Zar priestess in Egypt. The priestess goes into a trance to expel certain evil spirits, called zars, from her flock. Those who could combat evil were always held in reverence in primitive cultures.

possessed a young woman in his parish, he charged it with being a "ninny, a drunkard, and a sow." Upon which the apparently sensitive spirit vanished.

The literature of almost all ancient peoples records the existence of "devils"—positive menaces to the tribe or culture which were normally driven out by medicine men, witch doctors, or priests. The Old Testament has no real reference to exorcism, although by the time of Christ Hebrew law had apparently recognized the need for the practice. The Jews had, however, reflected their fears of the dark powers in the words of the 91st Psalm: "Thou shalt not be afraid for the terror by night; nor for the arrow that flieth by day; nor for the pestilence that walketh in darkness; nor for the destruction that wasteth at noonday."

Sexy Demons

Christ himself cast out devils on a number of occasions, although modern Christian thinking has it that he was merely pandering to Jewish fads —a theory which does not tie in with earlier Christian beliefs, for, almost from the beginning, the Christian Fathers were obsessed by the "real" existence of the Devil and the necessity to put him down. And the Devil's assistants were apparently just as troublesome. St. Augustine, in his fifth century *De Civitate Dei*, mentioned "incubi," sexy demons which "sought and obtained coitus" from women, while Albertus Magnus, the bishop-alchemist of the eleventh century, was complaining that things were so bad that "a man can scarcely sleep at night without a succubus (female demon) accosting him."

Presumably the idea of laying "dirty thoughts" and "wet dreams" firmly at the feet of incubi and succubi gave the consciences of the medieval holy men who suffered from them great relief; in any case if there were demons of sex, why not demons of every other "ill"? Soon there were whole regiments of evil spirits, all with names, and all carefully recorded in long lists. One demonologist claimed that they were "numerous as the sands of the desert," another that they merely amounted to 7,405,926, while a third, the occultist Binsfield, writing in 1589, named the devils which controlled the seven deadly sins themselves: Lucifer, pride; Mammon, avarice; Asmodeus, lust; Satan, anger; Beelzebub, gluttony; Leviathan, envy; and Belphegor, sloth.

Having given the powers of evil "real" personalities, theologians not unnaturally saw their influence everywhere—in crop failure, famine, war, and plague.

Chant Softly, and Carry a Big Stick

More importantly, any manifestation of abnormality in human behavior—epilepsy, for instance—must be diabolical in origin, and had to be cured at all costs. In a typical "cure" of the early days one priest beat the epileptic into insensibility, while another prayed over him.

At the time of the establishment of the great monasteries in Europe, novices aspiring to the priesthood went through several grades of initiation. First they served as doorkeeper, then as reader, and thirdly were appointed "exorcist"—the first time the term was used in anything like its modern sense. But these early exorcists were not so much Satan-fighters as male nurses, whose patients were monks suffering from what we would now recognize as mental illness.

It was considered that the hearing of Mass would benefit these unfortunates, but they could not be allowed to mingle with their "normal" colleagues; instead they were herded into side chapels, where the exorcist, sometimes armed with a stick, could keep a careful eye on them.

Lettuce Pray

Curiously enough, while the more fanatical demonologists were busy drawing up family trees for devils, more moderate elements in the church were equally active in quelling superstition. Pope Hildebrand, in 1080, claimed that women who professed to work spells through "familiar spirits" were deluded, and that to punish them would provoke the anger of God; the Synod of St. Patrick went so far as to decree excommunication for anyone *believing* in witchcraft, and even after the notorious

Inquisition was launched in 1163 by the Council of Tours a cautious attitude prevailed with regard to "possessed" persons—as opposed to actual devil worshippers and heretics.

In the middle of the twelfth century John of Salisbury pointed out that would-be exorcists must be men of extreme piety; if they approached their task flippantly or hypocritically, not only would the evil become deeper entrenched but might take hold of the exorcist too. Thomas Aquinas, who gave a great deal of thought to the problem, was of the opinion that no one could be possessed against his will—and if he had "opened his soul" to the demon, then he presented a danger to the exorcist.

Pope Urban VIII (1623-44) began to clarify the question of possession and exorcism in his *Rituale Romanum.*

First, the exorcist had to be certain that he had a genuine case of demonic possession on his hands. Demons entered the body of a victim in various ways—Gregory the Great had cited the case of a nun who had incautiously eaten a piece of lettuce without first crossing herself, unaware that a devil lay curled like a caterpillar in its folds.

Once established, the devil usually began to throw the victim around; the possessed person writhed, foamed at the mouth, twisted himself into impossible contortions or became unnaturally rigid. He also blasphemed horribly and obscenely, spoke in a language normally unknown to him, vomited pins, insects, or evil-smelling liquid, and stank of sulphur. Besides holiness, the exorcist needed the muscles of a weightlifter, for a possessed person usually showed superhuman strength and wrestled physically as well as spiritually with his would-be savior.

Different rituals emerged for dealing with cases of various kinds; Urban VIII's *Rituale* gave several, including one for dealing with poltergeists: "I adjure thee, O serpent of old, by the Judge of the living and the dead; by the Creator of the world who hath power to cast into hell, that thou depart forthwith from this house. He that commands thee, accursed demon, is He that commanded the winds and the sea and the storm. . . . He that commands thee is He that bade thee

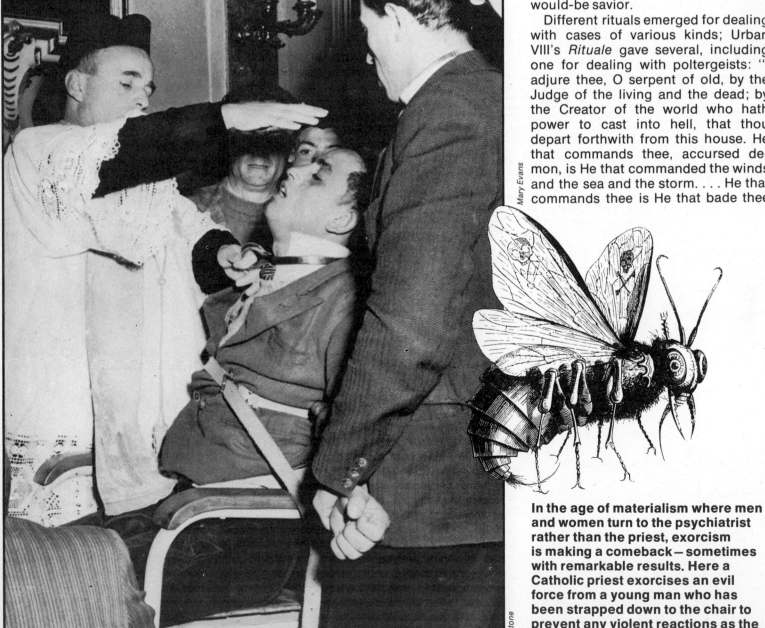

Mary Evans

Keystone

In the age of materialism where men and women turn to the psychiatrist rather than the priest, exorcism is making a comeback—sometimes with remarkable results. Here a Catholic priest exorcises an evil force from a young man who has been strapped down to the chair to prevent any violent reactions as the evil spirit is forced to leave.

depart from Him. Hearken then, Satan, and fear. Get thee gone, vanquished and cowed, when thou art bidden in the name of Our Lord Jesus Christ who will come to judge the living and the dead and all the world by fire. . . ."

Most rites against demons involved water—the ancient element opposed to fire. The "dunking" of witches in the seventeenth century was an offshoot of this idea, for if the water rejected the witch—if, in other words, she floated—she was possessed by spirit familiars. Sometimes, in their misguided enthusiasm, exorcists administered the water with fanatical cruelty, holding the victim under the surface until near-drowning occurred, or—as in the case of the "possessed" nuns of Loudon—injecting boiling water into the victim's body in the form of an enema.

Each exorcist gained his reputation by formulating his own methods, and as a breed exorcists in one form or another—often falling far short of the standard of personal holiness advocated by John of Salisbury—flourished throughout Europe for almost eight hundred years. With the coming of the "Age of Reason," however, skepticism on such matters as "possession" and the very existence of "evil powers" became more and more prominent. The Roman Catholic church began to regard the subject warily, and by the end of the nineteenth century the old "demon hunter" was a comparative rarity.

Father J. de Tonquedec, who acted as exorcist for the archdiocese of Paris between the years 1919 and 1939, dealt with hundreds of cases; of these, he said later, over 90 percent involved people in need of psychiatric treatment; the remainder *may* have been due to some paranormal cause.

Since Father de Tonquedec's time the treatment of mental illness has advanced considerably, and until recently looked as if it had put the old-fashioned exorcist out of business altogether—until, that is, the publication of the book so significantly reviewed by Father Mondrone in the *Roman Jesuit Review.* Following Pope Paul's statements in 1972, both his own church and the Church of England have blown the dust of centuries from their books of ritual: once again they have declared open war on the Great Demon.

All religions hold that if there is good there also is evil and offer their followers protection against evil influences. Thus the Papal blessing secures the safety of all.

Novosti Press Agency/Quartet

Pavlov's dogs

Pavlov's famous discovery was accidental. Feeding his dogs, Russian scientist Ivan Pavlov noticed that they began to salivate before eating. Soon Pavlov was showing the world that a dog's "learning" could be stimulated by signals other than food.

Of all the animals that have been used in scientific experiments none have achieved the distinction earned by Pavlov's dogs, which to this day remain almost better known than their master.

The term "Pavlov's dogs," apart from becoming a colloquialism, is now used as a recognized scientific shorthand to describe the elaborate psychological theory of the conditioned reflex.

But the beginnings were almost accidental. At the turn of this century the Russian physiologist Ivan Petrovitch Pavlov, already 52 and professor at the Military Medical Academy in St. Petersburg, was using dogs for his researches into digestion. During this work he noticed something which at first sight had no apparent connection with digestion. This accidental observation launched him on a series of ingenious experiments, which result-

ed in one of the most revolutionary discoveries in the history of psychology and for which he was awarded a Nobel Prize in 1904.

While presenting a plate of powdered meat to one of his dogs, Pavlov noticed that the animal began to salivate. This was to be expected once the food was in its mouth: salivation was a natural, inborn reflex action, part of the digestive process. But now the same action was being stimulated by the mere *sight* of food. Pavlov was not the first to notice, or record, that mouths watered at the sight or sound of food. But he did, profitably, investigate it.

Why, asked Pavlov, had the dog's digestive processes started to operate *before* they had come into contact with the food? It appeared that this premature salivation was not an inborn reflex action at all, but a response the dog had "learned." The

reflex had become "conditioned."

Abandoning his other work, Pavlov began experiments to discover whether the dog's "learning" could be extended so that its salivary reflexes would be stimulated by other signals which had nothing to do with food.

Conditioned Reflex

He started by using a buzzer—a sound which had no food associations for the dog. The animal was then placed in a special chamber and held in a loose harness, and the buzzer was sounded every time it was fed. Gradually the interval between the sound and the arrival of food was lengthened, yet the dog continued to anticipate the arrival of food by salivating on hearing the sound.

This reflex response—or "excitation"—was inevitable so long as the new stimulus was reinforced by the eventual presentation of food. In time, the dog's salivation on hearing the buzzer, or the ticking of a metronome, or the footsteps of an attendant, or whatever signal the dog was conditioned to recognize, became as great as its response to feeling the food actually in its mouth.

The food itself constituted what Pavlov called an "unconditioned stimulus," with the natural inborn reflex response to it (salivation) being the "unconditioned reflex." But if that same reflex was activated by a signal which had no more than an "acquired" association with food, then the unconditioned stimulus was converted into a "conditioned stimulus" and the reflex it activated became known as the "conditioned reflex."

Classical Conditioning

These principles formed the basis of what is now called "classical conditioning." Pavlov's experiments proved that a stimulus which was originally inadequate to excite a reflex can, when repeatedly associated with an effective stimulus, become sufficient itself to elicit a reflex action.

Conditioning could thus be defined as a process through which a reflex is modified so that a hitherto neutral stimulus comes to evoke a specific response and thus form the basis of new behavior.

Repetition of the experiments threw more light on how the reflexes operate. They showed that once the dog was conditioned it would salivate every time it heard the buzzer whether food was presented immediately or not, but that this conditioned state would not hold unless the stimulus was constantly "reinforced."

Pavlov found that if it was not reinforced by the arrival of food the conditioning principle operated in reverse; the animal's reflexes would become "deconditioned" in relation to that particular stimulus. The dog would dissociate the sound of the buzzer and the idea of food, and the salivary reflexes would cease to respond.

In fact, the buzzer would now become associated with the idea of "no food" and the reflex action would be extinguished. This process of "inhibition" would often leave the dog drowsy and lethargic.

The experiment showed a simple form of learning taking place, with the dog adjusting its habits in deference to new circumstances and new experiences. The association between the old and new stimulus was one which the dog made for itself; the "pairing" of the two ideas had oc-

curred in the animal's own mental processes.

Pavlov's experiments were to go far beyond the simple conditioning of dogs to perform in response to prescribed sounds, for he found they were able to achieve far more subtle feats.

He revealed that dogs were capable of sensory discrimination which enabled them to distinguish pitch in sounds, to recognize shapes, and to differentiate between edible and inedible food, by reacting to certain properties other than taste and consistency.

Pavlov recorded: "In the psychology of salivary glands, as it has displayed itself to us, we find all the elements of what we usually attribute to mental activity; sensations, choice, dispassionate consideration, judgment. . . ."

All these new-found attributes and the scope of their functions could be tested by experiment using the conditioning process. The extent of a dog's mental capacity could be measured by, first, conditioning it to respond to a new stimulus, and then modifying the stimulus until it ceased to activate the dog's reflexes. The point at which the stimulus ceases to be effective is where the dog's higher mental activity has made the distinction between the stimulus to which it was originally conditioned and this new variation of it.

A Dog's Life

In such experiments Pavlov found that when the dog's sensory discrimination failed it, the animal suffered an emotional breakdown and behaved in strange and unprecedented ways. For instance, a dog conditioned to respond to a square shape, but to ignore an elliptical shape, would become confused if the two shapes were gradually made indistinguishable. It would not know which of two conditioned reactions was required of it.

Similarly, when a dog was conditioned to attempt tasks it could not perform but could not evade, it would show all the signs of having a nervous breakdown. It would work itself into a high state of neurosis.

It followed that through the conditioning process, and by judicial manipulation of stimulus and reflex, Pavlov could create neuroses in dogs for experimental purposes. In this new facility to create prescribed mental conditions lay the true significance of Pavlov's work, for it did much to pioneer a scientific approach to mental disorders in man.

The conditioning principle provided physiologists and psychologists with a means for making contact with the innermost recesses of the psyche through the reflexes. The seat of mental activity in any organism is the cerebral cortex, which transmits the impulses that govern reflex actions.

Pavlov held that all psychic activity is mediated at this cortical level; whereas actions which do not involve higher mental activity, for instance unconditioned reflexes, are operated at subcortical level. This he could prove by removing the cerebral cortex from a dog by surgery, thereby depriving it of all psychic faculties with which it had previously been able to make distinctions and choices.

Animal Learning

In Pavlov's time, the study of the cerebral cortex was believed to be the exclusive domain of psychologists, whose approach to their work tended to be subjective, introspective, and theoretical. But Pavlov took the view that the mind was not mystical but could be studied physiologically from an objective standpoint. Theories of the mind could and should be put to the test and proved or disproved by experiment. The conditioning principle became the basis for such experiments.

Pavlov was not the first to discover the existence of reflexes, neither was he the first to apply physiological principles to psychic phenomena. He was also not the first to use experiments to test theories.

Much of the groundwork had been done by I. M. Sechenov (1829-1905), "the father of Russian physiology," who had published a work called *Reflexes of the Brain* in 1863. It was he who advanced the belief that all the activity of the mind is a matter of reflexes.

Pavlov had been aware of Sechenov's ideas for some time and had been making a detailed study of "nervism"—the idea that bodily functions are regulated by the nervous system. He was not alone. There was indeed a fairly general retreat among scientists from "dualism"—the idea that the body and the mind were isolated entities—to "monism"—the view that they were two components within a single framework.

The significance of Pavlov's discovery did not have its full impact until after his death in 1936, when the same principles were applied to the higher mental activity of man.

The experiments with dogs had done no more than show "respondent conditioning'' in operation—that is, a given stimulus eliciting a prescribed response. It was for Pavlov's successors to pioneer ''operant conditioning,'' the process whereby an animal learns to repeat a spontaneous act which is reinforced by reward.

If an animal accidentally depresses a lever and as a result food is presented, then after one or two chance meals, it will learn to operate the lever whenever it is hungry. What began as a spontaneous act becomes associated with food and that association becomes absorbed into the animal's thinking processes and determines its behavior.

Birth of Behaviorism
It was on such observations as these that many subsequent theories about the workings of the human mind were based, and out of which grew the science of ''behaviorism.'' Behaviorism is the name given to the school of psychological thought which explains all behavior purely in terms of stimulus and response—the reaction of muscles and glands to certain signals without reference to any higher mental activity.

Pavlov had also sown the seeds of a theory of learning. Learning can be described as the process of changing behavior as a result of past experience. The dogs in the Pavlov experiments had learned new behavior as a result of conditioning. In human terms the principle is the same, but the conditioning is achieved not by experiment, but by real life encounters and experiences.

A child's learning, Pavlov held, is acquired in much the same way as the dog's. If a child is presented with a furry toy but is simultaneously startled by a loud noise, he may associate the two and become frightened every time such a toy is presented. His fear he attributes to the furriness of the toy perhaps, and not the noise. This fear is a conditioned reflex, as it is not the toy itself that originally stimulates the fear but its associations which have been transferred to the new stimulus.

Operant conditioning also features in a child's learning process where spontaneous acts are reinforced by hope of reward which his past experience of a particular act has led him to expect. On the other hand certain other patterns of behavior are discouraged by their associations with punishment or pain.

Pavlov, who was born in 1849, was the eldest son of a priest, and his upbringing did much to foster the habits of a lifetime. In addition to acting as

pastor and teacher, a Russian priest was required to make his own living from the soil—a dual occupation demanding both mental and physical strength.

The call for both intellectual and physical endeavors characterized Pavlov's childhood, and he remained robust in mind and body throughout his life. Exercise gave him a feeling of what he called ''muscular joy,'' and in later years he said of himself, ''I am by nature more of a peasant than a professor.''

Although his father encouraged academic pursuits, the young Pavlov's love of hard work, his literary ability, and indeed his frugal life style were probably due to the influence of his godfather, the abbot of the monastery in Ryazan, Pavlov's home town.

A distinguished academic career began for him at the ecclesiastical seminary in Ryazan, and after four years he graduated to the science and medicine faculty of St. Petersburg University. Here he was influenced by Professor Ilya Cyon, author of the first book on experimental techniques, who persuaded him to specialize in physiology.

But it was at the military medical academy at St. Petersburg that Pavlov's life's work was to begin and end. His qualification as a doctor was considerably delayed by constant departures from the courses, while his special abilities, which were promptly recognized, were put to work on vital researches being conducted there. Notable among these were the experiments of S. P. Botkin, which were to lay the foundations of Pavlov's special physiological interest in the processes of digestion.

An Imaginative Man
It was a source of amazement to his contemporaries that this recently graduated student, who had not yet qualified as a doctor, had become director of scientific investigations at the most famous clinic of internal diseases in Russia. Pavlov eventually qualified in 1883 and was professor of pharmacology seven years later, switching to the chair of physiology in 1895.

Even early in his career he was earning a reputation as a man of high principle and scientific integrity. He was scrupulous and meticulous in all things, be it observing experiments, documenting data, performing operations, classifying drugs, or attending to everyday departmental or laboratory routines.

As an experimenter Pavlov dis-

played remarkable imagination and artistry. Experiments with dogs were not uncommon, though Pavlov's embellishments of them were highly original. Most of the experiments at this time involved surgery and ended with the animal being painlessly destroyed. Where possible Pavlov avoided this form of ''acute experiment'' in favor of ''physiological experiment''— conducted according to the rules of surgery after which the animal would come out of the anesthetic to be used again.

Foundation Stone
All experiments on the brain at this stage in Pavlov's career were performed by surgical operation, but now, with the conditioned reflex theory, here was a method of experimentation which left the brain intact.

He found the destruction of animals distasteful, and wrote: ''When I dissect and destroy a living animal I hear within myself a bitter reproach that with rough and blundering hand I am crushing an incomparable artistic mechanism, but I endure this in the interests of truth for the benefit of humanity.''

Pavlov was dedicated to his science, everything else taking subordinate positions in his scale of priorities. In appearance and manner he was every bit the ''absent-minded professor,'' with his bushy beard and the habit of talking to himself or forgetting to button up his regulation military coat —a uniform which the academy insisted should be worn by all staff.

The scrupulous care and attention which he lavished on scientific matters did not spill over into his private affairs and household considerations—an aspect of his life for which Pavlov had no relish. In this respect he was almost totally impractical, and after several errors of judgment and miscalculations he abandoned all such responsibilities to his wife, Seraphima.

Pavlov regarded his work on the conditioned reflex as his most important, although it involved deserting the fields of research with which he had previously been closely associated—the circulation of the blood and the action of digestive glands.

In fact a friend wrote to him at about the turning point in his career urging him to ''drop this fad'' of conditioned responses and return to real physiology. However, it remained the chief preoccupation until the end of his life. Through this work, Pavlov, with an impact as great as Freud's, laid the foundations of modern psychology.

All you want to know about...

HYPNOSIS

Mary Evans

Q IS HYPNOSIS A KIND OF SLEEP?

A The answer, perhaps surprisingly, is No. Psychologists and physiologists are now quite certain that whatever happens to the brain when a person is in a hypnotized state, it has practically nothing to do with sleep. By attaching electrodes to the outside of the scalp, and coupling these to an amplifier and recording apparatus, one is able to observe the complex patterns of electrical activity which take place in the brain and which probably have something to do with the firing of the thousands of millions of nerve cells in the cerebral cortex.

These patterns—the EEG or electro-encephalogram—are amazingly similar for all human beings and differ with changes in the state of alertness or mental arousal. For example, it is possible by looking at an EEG to say whether the subject was concentrating on something at the time it was taken, or whether he was relaxed. It is also possible to state whether he was taking certain kinds of drugs, whether he was an epileptic, or even whether certain types of cerebral tumors were present. With sleep the whole EEG changes, and once again an expert can, by looking at the amplified electrical signals, state not only whether the subject was asleep, but also what was the depth of his sleep, and even whether he was dreaming

or not! Now the interesting fact about the hypnotic state is that the electrical traces or brain waves of a subject in a hypnotized state are to all intents and purposes identical with those of the relaxed waking state. They are totally unlike any of the brain waves associated with sleep. Even in the so-called "deep hypnotic trance," the brain waves look much the same as those of the waking mind. This and a number of other factors have led to the modern view that hypnosis is not a special *state of consciousness*, as was once assumed, but much more an *attitude of mind*. Occasionally hypnotized subjects, if told to do so by the hypnotist or if left in a resting position for some time, will drift off into a light "genuine" sleep in which the typical sleeping EEG is observed. It is interesting to point out that when this "real sleep" occurs, rapport between hypnotist and subject is almost always lost, and the subject will have to be woken by normal means.

HOW USEFUL IS HYPNOTISM IN CURING BAD HABITS?

It appears to have some limited use in assisting people to throw off such habits as smoking, nail biting and occasionally even excessive drinking. The prerequisite however is that the individual, before the therapy can work, must really want to be rid of the habit. The task of the hypnotist is therefore to guide the individual, by a series of suggestions, to the realization that he does have it in his power to cure himself. Hypnosis has been successful on occasions in treating such trying problems as enuresis (bed wetting), but probably this is because it increases the sufferer's motivation and focuses his attention on the problem and his own inherent ability to control his bladder.

CAN ANIMALS BE HYPNOTIZED?

Not really. There are however a number of curious states which exist in animals which used to be referred to as animal hypnosis. For example, if one takes a chicken and firmly holds it in an unusual posture it will often remain apparently paralyzed for minutes or even hours. This experiment, incidentally, was first performed in 1646 by the Swiss Abbé Kircher. He actually drew a chalk line around the animals but later found that this was unnecessary. The same experiment has been tried with a number of animals, but this odd state is now generally assumed to be a kind of sham paralysis or "playing dead" which the animal employs in response to the highly threatening situation presented by the antics of the would-be hypnotist.

IS THERE SUCH A THING AS MASS HYPNOSIS?

In the popular understanding of the phrase, the answer is No. It is not possible for a man, by some hypnotic technique, to put his whole audience into a hypnotic trance or to make them all behave in a certain way by merely willing them to. There are ways however in which a clever individual, equipped with some of the techniques of hypnosis and some understanding of psychology, can lead an audience along a particular direction of thought by the skillful use of words. Professional politicians are adept at this of course (though they frequently do not realize what they are doing), and they may rouse an audience to unusually enthusiastic support for their views. It is significant however, and an important factor in understanding the limitations of the hypnotic method, that no matter how skillful the politician (or hypnotist), he is unlikely to be able to do much with an audience which is not in pretty general agreement with his views in the first place. Another example of this kind of "mass hypnosis" can be seen in the exploitation of the media by advertising agencies.

ARE WOMEN MORE EASY TO HYPNOTIZE THAN MEN?

There is some evidence that women are more suggestible than men and may be hypnotized more readily. It is also a fact that easily the majority of people practicing hypnosis are men, and this may reflect the dominant role of the male in our present society. A substantial number of women have been brought up to accept this relationship and not to question statements or commands given by men. Such a state of mind will certainly enhance the powers of the male hypnotist with female subjects. In many parts of the world—in particular the Far East—where female servility is even more deeply entrenched, there is some evidence that women are exceptionally readily hypnotized. It is also perhaps worth noting that some of the most dramatic successes of hypnosis were achieved in the early nineteenth century with British doctors working with native Indian patients, where the enormous authority of the members of the privileged British minority greatly enhanced their powers of hypnosis.

WHAT IS THE MOST REMARKABLE FEAT ACHIEVED WITH HYPNOSIS?

The vast numbers of people afflicted with psychological disturbances as a result of World War II—in particular those involving hysterical deafness or even blindness where no signs of physical damage to the auditory and visual senses had occurred—led to an upsurge of interest in medical hypnosis in an attempt to alleviate these conditions. Some remarkable successes were in fact reported, often through long and careful sessions of hypnotherapy in which the technique of the hypnotist was to lead the mentally disturbed patient back into a slow but steady realization that his afflictions had no physical basis. Many people believe that successes of this kind are among the most remarkable in the history of hypnotherapy. Others choose the celebrated case in which a major improvement was induced in an individual suffering from the rare but unpleasant affliction known as "crocodile skin"—in which the entire surface of the body becomes scaly and reptilian in appearance. Prolonged hypnotherapy alleviated the condition to a large degree, but it was noticeable that the results tended to be confined to the limb or body area which was the subject of suggestion at the time. Skin conditions of a noninfectious kind—eczema, dermatitis—are often aggravated by psychological conditions and, not surprisingly perhaps, frequently respond dramatically to hypnotherapy.

HOW CAN HYPNOSIS REMOVE PAIN?

This is an exceedingly difficult question to answer, for the phenomenon of pain is far harder to define than one might think. High variations in tolerance to pain exist between people, and there is much evidence that hypnosis does not remove the pain itself but leads the individual into a state where he can overcome it, deny it or "live with it." One of the strangest features of hypnotically induced anesthesia is that hypnotized patients being given minor surgery or aided in childbirth will frequently tell the hypnotist that they feel no pain, show no external signs of it, and yet will *afterwards* tell other people that the pain *was* present. It is also significant that in the few cases where patients suffering from so-called intractable pain—as in incurable cancer—have been successfully treated by hypnotherapy as an experiment, the patients will often say that they can still feel the pain but that it does not "bother them." This curious and somewhat contradictory finding could well be the key to understanding the basis of hypnotism, but psychologists and physiologists still find themselves puzzled by it. Recent developments in "painless surgery" through the technique known as acupuncture may be relevant here. So far as one can tell the physiology of acupuncture is more or less nonsense, but nevertheless it seems to work. Though the whole field is controversial, many experts believe that surgery employing acupuncture techniques works only when the patient is absolutely convinced that it *will* work. There are probably close parallels with the early

Animals can appear to be hypnotized. When a cock has its beak placed on a straight line, it can do nothing but follow the line. Humans, contrary to general opinion, cannot be hypnotized against their will, but the causes of hypnotism are not known.

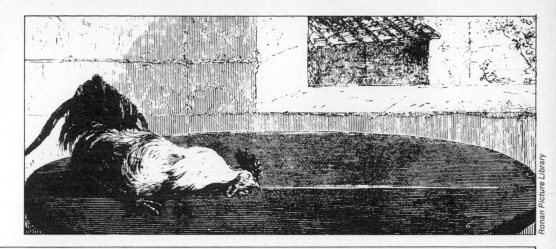

Ronan Picture Library

Mary Evans

surgical experiments using hypnosis performed in British India in the nineteenth century.

CAN YOU HYPNOTIZE YOURSELF?

You can certainly induce peculiar mental states in yourself by meditation, mystical exercises, and by a number of rituals recommended in self-hypnosis manuals. Whether such states are of any significance or of any value to the individual experiencing them is very arguable, but if people enjoy them or believe they benefit from them, then that is probably sufficient justification. Occasionally, by the induction of such states, individuals claim to have been able to break themselves of a bad habit, attain a relaxed state of mind, overcome some personal problem or whatever, and frequently this is referred to as hypnotizing oneself. People who have successfully rid themselves of habits by such means may well be proud of the fact, but in all probability they would have been able to achieve the same result by strength of mind and perseverance. There is however no danger that standing in front of a mirror and making mystical faces will send you to sleep—except perhaps through sheer boredom.

WHAT KIND OF PERSON MAKES A GOOD HYPNOTIST?

There are three main essentials. First, he must believe implicitly in the phenomenon, even if he is not sure what lies behind it. Second, he must have absolute confidence in his ability to hypnotize. This can only be achieved, of course, by experience, and most hypnotists "discover their abilities" by practicing on friends and seeing how easy it is to do. Third, he must learn some of the techniques and skills of inducing hypnosis and the signs or "symptoms" which indicate that his subject is entering into the hypnotic state. It is not necessary for the hypnotist to have brooding, dark eyes or any other kind of physical characteristic—unless these help to inspire the right aura of confidence in his subjects.

WHAT IS POST-HYPNOTIC SUGGESTION?

This involves the implanting of a command or suggestion in the mind of a hypnotized subject, with the requirement that it is executed at some later time when the subject is in a normal waking state. For example,

a person may be told that he will telephone someone at a particular time or, at a less trivial level (as in hypnotically assisted childbirth), that a woman will feel no pain when her child is being delivered. The phenomenon is a curious one but it has no mystical connotations and merely implies that the individual is still in enough of a "state of agreement" with the hypnotist to obey the previously implanted suggestion. He does not go into a "trance" to carry out the command but merely interrupts whatever he is doing in as normal a way as possible.

Associated Press

Boxer Ken Norton prepared for his March, 1973, bout with Muhummad Ali by being hypnotized to "end my overconfidence." It must have worked—he won the fight!

Once again it must be remembered that a person under post-hypnotic influence cannot be induced to do anything which is foreign to his wishes or nature, and there is no evidence that post-hypnotic suggestion can induce any abnormal psychological or physiological feats.

IS THERE SUCH A THING AS AGE REGRESSION UNDER HYPNOSIS?

A skilled hypnotist will induce a suitable subject to describe vivid memories and details of earlier parts of his life, some of which frequently seem to have been forgotten. The difficulties of proving that these are real memories and had really been repressed or forgotten should be obvious, and most psychologists today believe that hypnosis itself cannot drag from the memory any facts that would have been inaccessible to any other deep probing in which hypnosis was not involved. Accounts of people who have recalled their birth through hypnosis are probably nonsense, and those which claim that they have been able to remember "past lives"

are simply unsubstantiated. A particularly good example of the creation of a myth of this kind was the "Bridey Murphy" saga of the 1950s. In this famous case an amateur hypnotist claimed that he had, through age regression, induced a young American woman to recall previous lives, the most detailed of which involved her life as a peasant girl in Ireland in the previous century. Much circumstantial detail, including date and place of birth, various family names, etc., was brought up in the trance, but when the case became world famous, researching journalists were unable to verify any of the details. More skeptical inquirers, however, were able to identify numerous associations in the woman's childhood in America (in this lifetime of course!) which could have given rise to the stories told under hypnosis. All this however just serves as a reminder of the yawning gulf that exists between amateur and scientific investigations of hypnotic phenomena.

CAN HYPNOSIS BE HARMFUL?

Probably not, though it would be difficult to lay down a hard and fast rule. The main dangers of hypnosis may lie in the effect on the relationship between the hypnotist and his subject, and in the effect of hypnosis on the subject's image of himself. In the first case it would be theoretically possible for an unscrupulous hypnotist, by choosing his subjects with care, to make them highly dependent upon him for emotional support. If the hypnotist was being paid for his services, then he would have a financial hold over his subject—but no more of a hold than an unscrupulous psychologist or psychoanalyst could achieve over certain of his own patients. In the second case, an unscrupulous hypnotist could, for one reason or another, decide to amplify the weak points in his subject's personality and character, by consistently drawing attention to them, at the same time playing down the more positive aspects of his personality. In this way the individual might suffer a dramatic loss of confidence in himself and his ability to cope with the problems of life. Occasionally in spectacular court cases, people have been awarded damages because of alleged personality disorders induced by, for example, public demonstrations of hypnosis. These however are probably more a tribute to skillful litigation and the general credulity of juries than to the malevolent powers of hypnosis.

How persistent are you?

Intelligence and other abilities are all fine to have, but one thing that no intelligence test measures, and one quality that makes at least as much difference to our achievements, is persistence. There are many cases on record of men and women who by sheer effort have made themselves successful, in spite of gloomy prophecies by teachers and psychologists.

Eisenhower, for instance, was rated near the bottom of his year at West Point; Winston Churchill was thought to be dull at school. But they did not pay too much attention to other people's estimate of their worth, and went after their own goals with determination.

Aesop's fable of the slow but sure tortoise, eventually winning the race from the fast but overconfident hare, still has its counterpart in modern psychology. Extroverts, in many kinds of tasks, tend to be faster but less accurate than introverts. They also need more involuntary rest pauses as they work, and they tire more quickly when undertaking monotonous tasks.

But this does not mean that extroverts cannot be persistent.

There are two kinds of persistence: the ability to keep on working at something at a particular time, and the ability to keep returning to what you want to accomplish. If you are more extrovert than introvert, you may find it easier to give yourself a break from work when your concentration starts to fail, then return as soon as you feel refreshed. If you are not markedly introvert or extrovert, like most people, experiment with both patterns of effort to find what is best for you.

Persistence In Problem Solving

You have a pretty good idea already of how persistent you are in everyday life. Test out how persistent you can be in solving problems. There is no time limit for working them out, but keep a note of the number of attempts you make and the total time involved.

Problem 1

Using the circles below, place on circle A five coins of different value, with the largest at the bottom, going up in order to the smallest at the top.

(For example, a half dollar, a quarter, a nickel, a penny and a dime.) The problem is to move the stack so that they end up in circle B in the same order as before. The rules are
a. ONLY ONE COIN MAY BE MOVED AT A TIME.
b. COINS MAY BE MOVED ONLY TO ANOTHER CIRCLE.
c. YOU MAY NOT PLACE A LARGER COIN ON TOP OF A SMALLER ONE. (The minimum number of possible moves is 31.)

After Gagne & Smith, 1962.

Problem 2

Solve these three lists of anagrams.

LIST A	LIST B	LIST C
ywons	rtdae	plpae
cansk	reliv	grenoa
gedol	gworn	pgaer
maspt	lrnie	miel
prsto	rbnia	lbbryruee

Problem 3

Make a square from the pieces below. (If you do not want to cut up your page, trace around the shapes and cut them out of stiff paper.)
Now try to make another square from the second set of pieces overleaf.

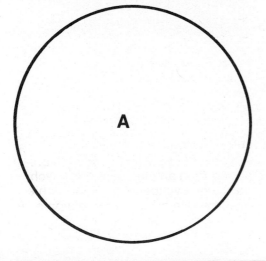
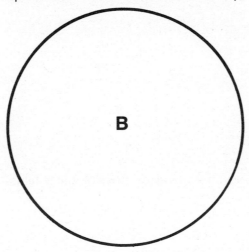
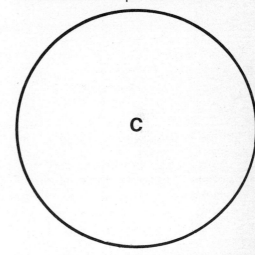

3a

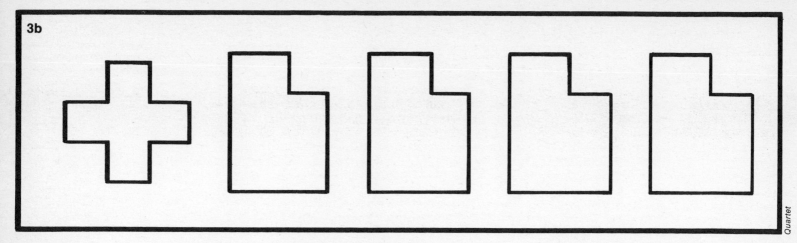

3b

Quartet

Problem 4

Crack the code. What is the message? Clues: Y is the most frequently used letter; A is the next most frequent.
2.12.6 24.26.13 14.26.16.22 18.7 18.21 2.12.6 9.22.26.15.15.2 7.9.2.

Social Persistence

Persistence in solving problems may not be the same as persistence in social settings. The old saying "Faint heart never won fair lady" is sometimes true. One man, neither attractive nor rich, married his beautiful wife after sending her love letters and flowers every day for three years. His gentle persistence worked where more eligible suitors failed. If you want something badly enough, you will try to gain it. Assuming a moderate but not overwhelming motivation, how would you react in the following situations?

1. You want to make a telephone call, but get a busy signal twice in the same hour. Do you
a. forget about it?
b. call once more?
c. contact the operator and check if the line really is busy?
d. call at hourly intervals until you get through?

2. Your girlfriend/boyfriend says she/he is not free on Monday, Tuesday, Wednesday, Thursday or Friday. Do you say
a. I'll call you some other time?
b. Are you trying to tell me something?
c. How about Saturday?
d. When is your next free night?

3. You need to lose weight. Do you
a. think about it, talk about it, but never do anything about it?
b. go on a diet for a few days then relapse?
c. stick to a diet until you are almost the weight you want to be?
d. stick to a diet until you reach your desired weight, and diet again if you move beyond it?

4. You are collecting signatures for a neighborhood petition. Do you
a. collect all the signatures you easily can on one occasion then do no more?
b. try to talk people into signing if they seem doubtful?
c. make more than one trip if people are not home on your first call?
d. keep on until you have asked everyone in your area?

5. You have applied for a new job and have not even been asked to come for an interview. Do you
a. give up hope and hold back from further applications for a year?
b. write that one off but apply for a similar job fairly soon?
c. demand to know why you were not interviewed?
d. apply for several jobs immediately?

Persistence is a quality that needs to be tempered with good sense, of course. To go on with a problem if you are stuck or to keep trying an unfruitful approach is not likely to lead to success. And in a social context, being overly persistent can be objectionable. We have all suffered from others pressing us to drink or eat or give an opinion, when we would prefer to abstain, and being pursued by someone we do not find attractive can be more embarrassing than flattering. Persistence with people should be tactful, and part of the art of influencing people is knowing when to stop!

---

staying power. Or perhaps you were tired at the time of trying the problems?

Social Persistence Scores

1. a.0 b.1 c.2 d.3
2. a.0 b.0 c.2 d.3
3. a.0 b.0 c.2 d.3
4. a.0 b.2 c.2 d.3
5. a.0 b.1 c.3 d.2

Your Persistence Rating

12-15—indicates a high level of persistence.
8-11—fairly high persistence.
4-7—you can be persistent if need be.
0-3—are you persistent enough?

4. You can make it if you really try!

Your Persistence Rating

Give yourself 2 for each problem you worked out until you reached the solution (maximum 8).
Subtract 1 for each time you looked up the answer before working it out.
Subtract 1 for each puzzle partially completed before you gave up.
7-8—good persistence, especially if you did not find all the answers right away.
4-6—reasonably good persistence.
0-3—lacking in persistence in this situation. You probably need to be deeply involved in an activity to show

Problem Solving Answers

1. At some point, you need to have the 4 smaller coins stacked on C in order to move the largest one to B.

2.

LIST A	LIST B	LIST C
snowy	trade	apple
snack	liver	orange
lodge	wrong	grape
stamp	liner	lime
sport	brain	blueberry

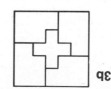 **3a**

 3b

Brian Ward

The Nymphomaniac

Nymphomania may be rare but meet it and you'd better step aside! This female of the species is deadly to the male and will drag anything in pants off to bed to quench her voracious appetite. Addicts must have their fix, so woe betide the man who won't swing on her merry-go-round of sex.

Claudine was a nymphomaniac. Typically, while this caused her little if any concern, her impact upon the circle of friends and acquaintances who were remorselessly exposed to her sexual exhibitionism was of a charmingly explosive nature.

Married to a shipping tycoon, who indulged and adored her, Claudine lacked neither the means nor the opportunities to act the *femme fatale*. Life was a hunt and every man was fair game. This was not to say that the men in her life had to be dragged, scream-ing and protesting, into the desperate sexual abyss which lurked behind her overt attractions; on the other hand it was equally true to say that once they had capitulated to Claudine's vampire greed, her victims tended to discover that she liked to bite off more than they could comfortably deliver. She had a voracious and completely insatiable appetite.

However, that was later. In the early stages of an encounter, for example at one of the frequent parties that her husband liked to throw, she was with-out question the hostess with the mostest. Modesty was not a quality within her repertoire; not surprisingly, if one believes that modesty in a wo-man is an acknowledgement that she *is* a woman and not a man, accepting, to a greater or lesser degree, her non-phallic role.

Claudine, on the contrary, would intrude herself upon a group of men and join in the risqué stories with the best of them. She made no bones about flesh, nor for that matter about the spirit. Alcohol was a fuel for en-

337

joyment, and at the golf club she would stand her own round and drink up glass for glass. She was not, however, coarse or crude. Outgoing, boyishly charming, with her short-cropped hair and enticingly trim figure, she moved about a room with feline grace.

She was a hypermarket of sexual wares, as she half-stalked, half-glided among the guests. No man, other than one totally bereft of sight, could possibly mistake the goods that Claudine offered on her well-stocked shelves. But in order to leave nothing to chance, Claudine employed a number of gift-wrapped tricks to put the issue beyond all doubt. Sometimes she would lift a leg to expose a generous amount of thigh, and proclaim in a loud voice that she had a run in her stocking. At other times she would sit with her hands behind her head to maximize the size of her breasts, in case they might be overlooked, and for good measure—although they already were—would remark about their size.

Man Trap

Predictably this had the desired effect—Claudine not only became the center of attention but also the focus of masculine admiration. She was, to all intents and purposes, as desirable as a siren—and just about as dangerous. For the trap that Claudine laid was to lure every man she could onto her particular brand of emotional rocks.

Her problem, had she been capable of seeing it as such, was that she could show herself, but could not give herself. To her all men were objects, existing for her gratification, from whom she could extract admiration, gifts, wealth and even power, but not, ironically, true sexual satisfaction. Greedily, frantically, she took all she could from sexual relationships, but it was never enough. For while she might experience degrees of physical orgasm—rarely though from vaginal intercourse—the accompanying psychic orgasm eluded her entirely.

The restlessness that drove her from one man to the next was never quelled. Of course she enjoyed her sexual gymnastics; and so, up to a point, did her companions. But when they eventually found, much to their shame and humiliation, that their maleness had apparently failed the test, and that Claudine, with her whims and demands unsatisfied, had been transformed into an Oliver Twist of tyrannical proportions (she always wanted more, please), the relationship,

if one can call it that, foundered on those emotional rocks.

Often there was more to it than injured pride. The vampire showed her teeth. Biting, scratching, there was an element of sadism in Claudine's activities that made going to bed with her an experience to be remembered if not cherished.

However, she saw nothing untoward or even "abnormal" about her behavior. She lived life to the full, and the fact that she was seeking the unattainable in no way diminished the enthusiasm with which she pursued the search. It was her husband who eventually sought treatment, not she, though it was Claudine who brought him to the consulting room, and who was certainly the main cause of his problem. Never a sexually overactive man, it was probably true that one of the reasons he had married her and acquiesced in her infidelities was that he was happy enough not to have his own potency constantly—and rigorously—examined.

But he was, after all, a man. And he did try. Claudine succeeded in reducing him to total impotence. Physically there was nothing wrong with him; he just could not stand up to the sustained sexual hostility and aggression inherent in his wife's nymphomania.

Physically there was nothing wrong with Claudine either. There was no actual "vaginal itch" that had to be satisfied; there was no hormonal imbalance which drove her; there was no medical disorder to account for her behavior. It was, after all, a matter of the mind rather than the heart.

Nymphomania, or Furor Uterinus—madness of the womb—is not, of course, a twentieth century phenomenon. Essentially an hysterical condition, it has manifested itself in a variety of forms throughout the ages. The frenzied dances of the Middle Ages, rituals to ward off evil spirits, the cavortings of the ancient maidens of Greece, and, in this century, the screams of latter-day maidens before the altar of a pop idol are all forms of what we now term nymphomania.

The Male Counterpart—Don Juan

The pseudo hypersexuality of the nymphomaniac is a form of hysteria, and since the time of the ancient Egyptians hysterical symptoms were associated with disorders of the uterus and hysteria was considered a specific disease of women. To this belief men of medicine subscribed for more than 1,500 years, until the seventeenth century when physicians began

to demonstrate hysterical symptoms in male patients. And of course the male counterpart of the nymphomaniac is Don Juan.

While the manifestations may vary from century to century according to beliefs held—for example in the Middle Ages mass hysteria and accusations of witchcraft led to women being prosecuted by the church—the symptoms displayed by the nymphomaniac have remained fairly constant though the same cannot be said of medicine's understanding of the causes.

Bon Appétit

A seventeenth century physician, Philippe Pinel, who made a study of hysteria, had this to say on the subject: "Nymphomania is most frequently caused by lascivious reading, by severe restraint and secluded life, by the habit of masturbation, and extreme sensitivity of the uterus, and a skin eruption upon the genital organs."

Describing the symptoms he writes: "In the beginning the imagination is constantly obsessed by lascivious or obscure matters. The patient is in a state of sadness and restlessness; she becomes taciturn, seeks solitude, loses sleep and appetite, conducts a private battle between sentiments of modesty and the impulse towards frantic desires.

"In the second phase she abandons herself to her voluptuous leanings, she stops fighting them, she forgets all rules of modesty and propriety; her looks and actions are provocative, her gestures indecent; she begins to solicit at the approach of the first man. She makes efforts to throw herself into his arms. She threatens and flares up if the man tries to resist her.

"In the third phase her mental alienation is complete, her obscenity disgusting, her fury blind with only the desire to wound and to revile. She is on fire though with fever, and finally she manifests all the different symptoms of a violently maniacal condition."

In many respects this is a description not too far removed from the behavior of Claudine, though it would, perhaps, be hard to believe that Claudine's condition had much to do with lascivious reading or even a secluded life.

As with any psychic situation—and not until Freud was there any real recognition that the hysterical form of nymphomania was a psychological and not a physical condition—the causes are not so easily determined.

Mary Evans

Kim Sayer

Certainly the high degree of orality in the nymphomaniac is a significant clue. The sucking, biting greediness of the young child, the stage where the mouth plays an all-important part, is a standard phase of its development and one, as emotional development progresses, that will be outgrown.

The Claudines of the world retain, to an unusual extent, this infantile orality. It manifests itself not only in oral sexuality, from which the nym-

phomaniac is more likely to achieve orgasm than by vaginal intercourse, but from her characteristic love of food. Indeed she is liable to find a fine meal infinitely more seductive than sex, and by the same token she enjoys her liquor.

Anality, another stage in the individual's development, is also a component of her personality. The persistence of these infantile traits—they persist, of course, to a degree in all of us—to the virtual exclusion of tenderness and mature affection indicates an emotional immaturity. The boyishness, the fetching babyishness, the consuming hunger for material things, jewelry, wealth, property—these are all characteristic of the nymphomaniac. Add to that the exhibitionism, the constant need for admiration, and one begins to see a woman with many childlike emotions.

Hostess with the Mostest

Perhaps she has not grown up because she never wanted to; because she could not face the ultimate emotional separation from a mother who had given her everything but the final confidence to "go it alone"; perhaps,

Eternally dissatisfied, the true nymphomaniac will exhaust the most athletic of lovers in a seemingly endless quest for the "ultimate" orgasm. The seventeenth century physician Philippe Pinel (left) made some notable early studies on the problem which he claimed was caused by a combination of physical and psychological factors. He, at least, recognized it as an illness, *not* a common case of promiscuity.

on the other hand, her nymphomania stems from the overindulgence of a doting parent. There can be no one formula to explain the origins of her psychic situation, and she would be the last to countenance the psychoanalyst's couch in order to buy her peace of mind.

She is able to live her life according to her lights without experiencing melancholy or depression. There is no depression at the emotional level upon which she operates. There is triumph to be had, there is acclaim and admiration to be gained, but no real horror. Her one fear concerns her physical appearance; she cannot abide the thought of getting fat and prides herself on her lean and hungry looks.

Marriage holds no terrors for her; more often than not she is a good mother, giving her children the emotional security which she herself was perhaps denied. And she can be an alarmingly good hostess, an outgoing companion, an exciting and fascinating woman. Significantly, her ills, in keeping with her psychic situation, tend to be hysterical: aches and pains without physical explanation or medical order and now and again the classic hysterical symptom, Globus Hystericus, a lump in the throat which moves up and down but which has no physical cause.

Dressed to Kill

Of her it can truly be said that she dresses to kill as she stalks her prey, favoring a hectic red and black by night, and during the day short skirts and hunting boots, which is precisely what her ancient Greek forebears wore.

Nevertheless there *is* an important difference between the nymphomaniac of the second half of the twentieth century and her counterparts through the ages. Until quite recently maidens who displayed symptoms described by Pinel were inclined to consider themselves "possessed." The "Cleopatras" of ancient Egypt, flaunting themselves in the brothels of Cairo and Alexandria, retained the conviction that some spirit had taken over their womb. The Greek nymphs had their evil gods to blame; the maidens of medieval Europe were candidates for the exorcists. But what equivalent hysteria of the twentieth century is considered a form of possession? What screaming teenager at a pop concert is overcome by thoughts of the devil? Is there a hypersexual female who would dream, for a moment, that there is a part of her personality which is alien?

Window Dressing

Such unquestioning acceptance of her own behavior makes a "cure"—even if it were desired—as unattainable as the nymphomaniac's very search for complete satisfaction. The possession is total, not perceived as possession at all, with the result that no meaningful communication can be established with any particular part of her personality.

Yvette, the daughter of well-to-do parents, was 17 when her blatantly promiscuous behavior so alarmed and offended them—they were themselves extremely religious and considered they had brought up their daughter to the strict moral ethics of the church

Kobal

—that they took her for psychiatric treatment. Yvette's opening gambit was an attempt to seduce the psychiatrist. She discovered a zip undone and asked for his help. She reclined on his couch in such a manner that only a code of practice delivered him from professional ignominy.

She persisted that she could see nothing shameful, immoral, destructive, aggressive or even unusual about her conduct. She enjoyed herself. For example, the fact that on one occasion

Who are they? How do they act? One amusing answer came from the creators of "Candy," a ravishing young innocent incapable of saying "no." Her excuse: pity for the plight of desperate men! In the film, one of Candy's acolytes (above) bares her heart to the camera. Psychologists have seen certain undertones of nymphomania in the behavior of adolescent girls in the presence of pop idols (right). Their illness is temporary however!

she had chosen to expose herself from her bedroom window to the window cleaner struck her as being one of her finer moments. (The window cleaner may well have shared that view—she was extremely attractive.)

After many fruitless sessions the psychiatrist had to admit defeat. There was no way in which he could make contact on a level other than the one on which Yvette existed. For her part, she became increasingly hostile with each failure to count the psychiatrist among her conquests. Recognizing the danger—at any moment Yvette's vengeance could well take the form of loud accusations that he had attempted to rape her while she lay innocently on his couch—he told her parents there was no point in attempting to continue treatment.

Win or Bust

Yvette was an extreme case. So, too, was Claudine. But there are many like them who find that a permissive society, with its liberal, amoral attitudes, provides a social climate in which—far from being considered children of the devil—they can and do evoke admiration and envy, and in which they can gain the material rewards they consider so essential and prize so highly.

They are to be found wherever exhibitionism needs to be a stock-in-trade, wherever they can flaunt their sexuality, wherever they can elicit the right responses to the somewhat unsubtle signals in their repertoire. Cabaret girls, model girls, airline stewardesses, waitresses, office playgirls, girls in the army, girls in the factory cafeteria . . . no, of course, they are not all nymphomaniacs. But they move in a sphere within which the nymphomaniac can joyfully flourish.

And beneath the outward glamour of some of these occupations, behind the scenes of the top model show or the aircrew's stop-over hotel, the nymphomaniac will, on occasions, reveal something of her true self. She will bitch about the other girls, she will display petty jealousies, she will wail and complain about her food, her surroundings and the arrangements made for her.

Typically, she exists in an emotional world where all is either light or total darkness; and the darkness is most likely to descend if she is unable to achieve her wishes. A failure to make a conquest can, for her, prove literally fatal. That is when the facade crumbles, when she will sometimes stare into that black abyss and attempt to take her own life.

Impotence

Western society sees virility as a major economic asset. It sells automobiles, cigarettes and hang-ups by the dozen. Erection means perfection so the slogan goes. Anything less is unacceptable. Impotence is a dirty word—fail between the sheets and you fail everywhere else too. Yet nearly every man has experienced impotence at some time. Condemn it and we condemn ourselves.

It should have been the perfect ending to a perfect evening. Certainly the setting was all that could be desired—Joanna's Georgetown apartment and the warm afterglow of the concert at the Kennedy Center and the Italian food and wine. For Martin the prize of Joanna was within his grasp.

But it all went bitterly wrong. Something—the excitement, the wine, the sudden aggression on Joanna's part—affected Martin to the point where he found himself physically unable to make love to her. He had become impotent. He reacted by blaming Joanna and the experience not only destroyed a promising romance—it destroyed his self-confidence so completely that he had to seek professional help and treatment.

Happily, however, he recovered quite quickly and the awful experience at the Georgetown apartment left little impression on him. Had he known at the time that practically every adult male at some time in his life goes through precisely the same experience he would have felt better.

Brewer's Droop

But he does deserve some sympathy and understanding. Anyone who has felt the chilling sickness and despair that even a transitory incident can bring will have undergone one of the most distressing of all emotions.

Impotence. The very word arouses soul-shattering images in the mind of the average man. But in the great majority of cases a sexual failure is a "one-time" thing that can be laughed off in a rather shamefaced way. Any football player who has played a hard game and finished his Saturday off by drinking twelve cans of Budweiser will be able to talk about the dreaded "brewer's droop."

She is puzzled and slightly hurt by the idea that he may no longer find her attractive. He is shattered by visions of impotence. The danger is that both will endanger their relationship by reacting coldly.

Anyone worried about a particular business or professional matter, the unsettling situation caused by a merger bid for example, can lose interest in sex entirely for weeks on end, and if he tries to fulfill his marital duties he might well fail.

It is the other cases, the cases where one failure (for whatever reason) leads to another, and another and eventually to a complete inability to "perform" sexually, that are the major concern. For behind each story of prolonged impotence lies personal tragedy and a desolate landscape of broken relationships, broken homes and broken people. It is a prospect so utterly shameful, miserable and desperate that help is often not sought or even considered regardless of its availability.

So what is impotence? And, more important, what can be done to help the sufferers?

An impotent male—and the biological fact of the male's role as the initiator of intercourse effectively rules out the possibility of an impotent female—is one who is physically incapable of achieving successful sexual intercourse with the female (or, indeed, one of his own sex) and therefore incapable of reproducing the species.

About 10 percent of all studied cases of impotence may be termed "organic" and arise from illness or injury. The great bulk of cases, however, stem from psychological factors and may be termed "functional."

A more detailed analysis of the condition appears in Belliveau and Richter's *Understanding Human Sexual Inadequacy*—a layman's guide to Virginia E. Johnson and William H. Masters' major study, *Human Sexual Inadequacy*.

They say: "Anxiety relating to sexual activity and insecurity as a person can be incapacitating enough to overcome completely a man's natural ability to have an erection. Such a man has never been able to have intercourse, either vaginally or rectally, with a female partner or with a male partner."

Masters and Johnson have called this condition "primary impotence."

Problems established by Masters and Johnson as being major causes of "primary impotence" include: the seductive mother—sexual advances by a mother towards her son; religious belief in sex as sin; traumatic initial failure—usually a disastrous encounter, in unsatisfying circumstances, with a prostitute; and, finally, homosexuality.

She's No Lady

Masters and Johnson identified the other main category of impotence as "secondary impotence"—that is, erective failure in at least 25 percent of sexual opportunities. Premature ejaculation, drinking problems, domineering parents, religious restrictions and problems arising from homosexual experiences are enumerated as contributing to this condition.

To illustrate one of these factors—the "traumatic initial experience"—the case of Roger, a 22-year-old insurance clerk working in Buffalo some few years ago, serves admirably.

Roger and two pals decided they would like to see "the lights of New York" and combine this with their other main interest—football. After the game, they went out to "hit" Broadway.

Their progress was the well-trodden path of two or three bars, a Chinese restaurant and, inevitably, a strip club. The "club," as often happens, was a major disappointment and they soon tired of the procession of thin, or blowsy, figures, the bored expressions and the inherent seediness of the setting.

So they adjourned to yet another bar. Inside, after a few more drinks, Roger noticed a smart brunette in a short skirt and black leather jacket staring rather pointedly at him.

She smiled warmly, stood and walked purposefully towards the door. At the door she turned and stared at Roger again. He got the message and followed her out, the derisive hoots of his comrades ringing in his ears.

Marshall Cavendish

"She'll eat you," one shouted. "She'll cost you," said the other.

Roger soon caught on when the girl demanded $30 plus $5 "for the taxi." Arriving at a gaunt, featureless apartment building on the West Side, he began to feel nervous. His head filled with thoughts of "the clap" and other horrors. Inside the apartment his fears began to snowball. The girl looked older, harder. She had stopped smiling and she demanded another $5 "for the use of the room."

Without a further word she whipped up her dress, removed her pants and lay on the bed, staring at the ceiling. "Come on," she said tersely, "hurry."

If Roger had had any desire to possess this girl it now drained away, together with any hope of achieving an erection or indeed having intercourse. He panicked and ran.

Roger's experience would not be likely to have a lasting effect on him, but inside marriage the problem of impotence is often infinitely more distressing. Each partner may feel they are failing the other and both may be too ashamed to seek guidance elsewhere.

A Messy Business

Conversely, what does exist inside a majority of marriages is a fundamental reservoir of love and trust which committed the couple to each other in the first place. This reservoir may often be tapped with the result that impotence can be overcome through mutual understanding and compassion.

From a compendium of different situations, the following scenario serves to indicate the type of problems that married couples may face if the male becomes impotent.

Richard was a young executive in his early thirties, assuredly on the way up. He had been happily married to Kay for four years and they had two young children.

Then Richard suffered a business setback. He had been sent abroad to clinch an important order and had apparently succeeded. The company was delighted and his further advance seemed certain.

Then the troubles started. The order was delayed, the client country's government was overthrown and the future of the company's relationship

Comfort, a declaration of love and confidence in his virility are the ingredients needed by a man who has failed to satisfy his partner. Even when such failures are rare they can still shake a man's ego.

Impotence is undoubtedly one of the problems of age. Male sexual activity reaches its greatest peak during the years of adolescence and steadily declines thereafter as the statistics (right) clearly indicate. Nevertheless, there is plenty of evidence to show that psychological factors are even more important than physiological ones in most cases of impotence. Often it is simply a question of masculine self-confidence. The man who really believes he can make love usually _can_, given the right circumstances.

there put in jeopardy. Richard, seeing how this could affect him, tried to make his position more secure.

He had always been in the habit of having "a drink and a sandwich" with colleagues in the bar nearby. Now, however, as the strain built up, one drink stretched into three. His anxiety to press ahead with other work caused him to be late getting home and when he arrived he was usually a little drunk and very tired.

At first Kay understood, knowing what promotion meant to the family. But the days passed and she realized that Richard had not shown any sexual interest in her for some time. She told him this and his excuse was "tiredness." She did not press the point.

But, inevitably, the moment came when she was "tired" herself—tired of his lack of affection and interest in her. Richard belatedly recognized all this and decided he must make amends. He tried to make love to his wife and found, to his astonishment, that he was unable to achieve an erection. Kay was hurt—but discreet. Two days later the same thing happened. There was a blazing row and the vicious circle was completed. Richard became more and more frightened of his disability—Kay more and more bitter about it.

Female Blackmail

Then a friend advised them to take their problems to their doctor who counseled psychotherapy. The problem was quickly overcome. They were among the lucky ones.

Ian was not so fortunate. He was a victim both of the strictest religious upbringing and of homosexual bullying when in his mid-teens at a boarding school. The evils of the flesh having been preached at him throughout his adolescence, it is easy to imagine the effect that a homosexual assault by a near-psychopathic school acquaintance had on him.

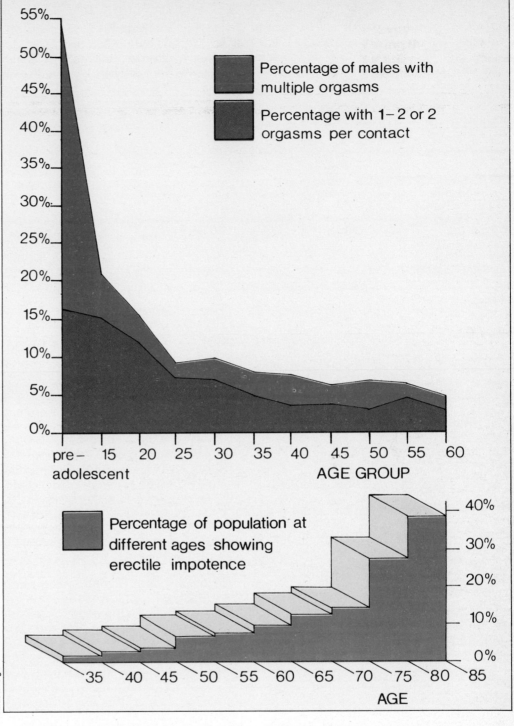

Alias Design

The combination of the two factors destroyed his sexual ability. No doctor was able to convince him that this was a condition which could be treated. He was utterly convinced of the hopelessness of his condition and disappeared into a twilight world of petty crime.

But how do the men who are, or become, impotent—and the wives and girlfriends who suffer as a consequence—view the incapacity?

For the female two main themes tend to prevail: failure by their partner is _their_ fault because, they tell themselves, they are unattractive, too demanding or too uninterested. Or, instead, failure by their partner is

the man's fault, and they deride him.

Both initial responses can be put down to the first shock of the actual physical failure. In the case of loving and understanding wives such feelings may well be replaced by an overriding feeling of compassion and a desire to help their partner to beat his problem.

But there are, alas, numerous instances where the female's bitterness and frustration is of sufficient depth to evoke feelings of malice and spite. She spreads word of his incapacity among friends and even relations with the most hurtful consequences.

And for the male, the trauma of impotence can often affect his whole

Marshall Cavendish

life. If he is not helped and, if necessary, treated, he may never feel himself a "complete" human being. The condition can color his attitude to his job and distort his business judgment; it can affect his whole social behavioral pattern, making him sour and introspective.

The dread of the effect of impotence on his social and business life may be every bit as important as the purely physical aspect of the problem. The thing that must be overcome if the impotent male is to have his sexuality developed or restored is what may be termed the "fear and shame factor." In short, many men in this condition may very well not understand how they came to be impotent and be both ashamed and frightened of seeking help.

A Premium on Potency

In fact a majority of instances of impotence are *not* incurable cases. As we have seen already, most adult males would count themselves extremely fortunate to get through life without experiencing at least one "failure"—probably several.

In the case of married couples what is essential—and, sadly, frequently absent—is a combination of tolerance, courage and love on both sides. Given these advantages, there is a very good chance that the scourge of impotence can be defeated. Mutual love and understanding may well make any medical or psychothera-

Trouble with his job, the high pressures of the business world or financial problems can make a man irritable and moody to the point of destroying all his social pleasures—as well as his sex life.

peutic aid unnecessary. In other cases a doctor may need to be consulted and psychotherapy needed to achieve a similar result.

Belliveau and Richter, discussing the Masters and Johnson therapy techniques, stress the need for educative work that must precede any physical attempt by "primary" or "secondary" cases of impotent males to achieve an erection and proceed to intercourse. "The most important part of this educative process is to convince the male partner that he does not have to do anything to have an erection.

"Erection is a physiological response that happens when effective sexual stimuli are present and when the man is psychologically prepared to respond to them.

"Masters and Johnson's approach is to convince the man that they can and will set conditions right so that he will feel sexual arousal and have an erection," they state.

Out of 32 "primarily" impotent males treated 59.4 percent of cases were successful; of 213 "secondarily" impotent patients 73.8 percent were successfully treated.

Many clinics have reported numer-

ous instances where a man's impotence has been overcome without specific treatment or therapy—merely by his wife's view of the condition being altered through education by the trained staff.

Fundamentally the condition for successful treatment—whether by psychotherapy or not—is desire on the part of the impotent male to overcome the incapacity. This desire must be strong enough to neutralize the understandable fear of seeking help.

For a single man, knowledge of the enjoyment and love being experienced by friends not so incapacitated is a spur, and for a married man the pressures of his partner for a full relationship can act in the same way. But there must be many hundreds of cases where such factors are not sufficiently overwhelming and where, consequently, no help or guidance is sought.

The blatant sexuality inherent in many of today's permissive social attitudes puts, so to speak, a premium on potency. Admitting to anyone, even a doctor, that you are handicapped in such a crucial field can take a lot of heart. Doing so with the conviction that, in any case, nothing can be done to help you is especially difficult.

To overcome impotence or at least to have a reasonable chance of doing so requires physical and mental courage of the highest order. But the rewards stemming from successful treatment scarcely need emphasizing.

Satan at large

Does the Devil exist? For two centuries or so he has been shunted into a siding—an obsolete relic of our superstitious past. Now the occult revival is in full swing, it seems the Devil has ridden out—could it be that all hell has been let loose?

Transworld

Prior to the spring of 1974, the Very Reverend Douglas Bean, former canon of St. Paul's Cathedral, London, and currently vicar of St. Pancras, one of the city's busier central parishes, was skeptical about diabolic possession and the use of exorcism to combat it. Now he is not so sure. His experiences in a London apartment one brittle March morning changed his views on a number of things.

The Reverend Bean is a comparatively young, "progressive" vicar whose hobby is music. During his period at St. Paul's he wrote several modern services for the cathedral, and was instrumental in mounting a controversial performance of *Hair*, featuring the London cast, beneath Sir Christopher Wren's famous dome. He plays guitar and has appeared on British television a number of times, singing his own songs.

Exorcism is a strange business but one which is accepted by the Anglican church as a genuine religious practice provided that it is performed by competent members of the clergy, like the Reverend J. C. Neil-Smith, a noted exorcist.

But he is not the sort of "pop" clergyman who was unduly concerned about the rise of modern witchcraft or the revival of interest in the occult generally; the psychiatrists, he once said, should concern themselves with those fields.

In March, 1974, Mr. Bean's attention was drawn to the plight of a young woman who, though not a churchgoer, lived in his parish. She had been in the care of the psychiatric department of a major London hospital, and experts there were puzzled about her mental condition. She suffered,

apparently, from periods of acute hysteria, during which she claimed to be plagued by several "evil entities." They were, she said, trying to kill her.

After meeting the girl, and after consulting with higher church authorities, Reverend Bean decided to try exorcism. "From the very beginning it was a blood-chilling case," he said. "These 'entities' seemed to be getting at the girl at night, in her apartment, which was part of an old, late-Georgian house in the area. What disturbed me was that when I went into the history of the house I discovered that it had an extremely troubled record. Earlier this century two murders had been committed there, and a suicide had occurred in the girl's living room."

The clergyman went through the unfamiliar ritual of exorcism, increasingly aware of the oppressive atmosphere as he pronounced the sonorous words. The girl screamed, writhed, crashed to the bed, and finally passed out—all phenomena well known to exorcists and psychiatrists alike—and as far as she was concerned, the operation seems to have been successful.

Exorcising the Exorcist

But for the rational, modern-minded vicar the ordeal was just beginning. "The experience shook me rather," he admitted. "Obviously it is a disturbing business for all concerned. But I put it out of my mind and went about my everyday work. That evening I was immersed in other things when I suddenly had a blinding headache, accompanied by a copious nosebleed. I cannot recall ever having suffered from anything like this before. The bleeding and the pain recurred over a period of days, and various pills and medicines appeared to have no effect."

Finally, Douglas Bean felt that there was only one course open to him. He consulted an experienced exorcist, a fellow Anglican clergyman, and his bizarre torments ceased after he himself had been exorcised.

A clear case, many psychiatrists would say, of psychosomatic illness—with symptoms unconsciously induced by the sufferer himself. But what of the girl? She, like Reverend Bean, had known nothing of her apartment's gruesome history until the vicar had investigated the matter: surely the coincidence—both priest and parishioner being "overcome"—was a great one.

This sort of problem, and its solution, has been puzzling and disturbing Roman Catholic and Protestant clergy since the sudden upsurge of the so-called "occult revival" in the late sixties brought black magic, witchcraft, and satanism to the fore once again. The problem of "possession" has also vexed psychologists and psychiatrists, although few will admit to a "supernatural" explanation; their trouble is simply that "hysteria" of the type suffered by Mr. Bean's patient has become increasingly commonplace.

Even before Pope Pius VI made his pronouncements on the existence of Satan and his very real threat in the everyday world following the review of the novel *The Exorcist* in a Roman Catholic periodical, the Church of England, in the person of the Right Reverend Robert Mortimer, bishop of

An age-old remedy for disposing of devils and other representatives of Satan, exorcism has continued to function successfully. One ceremony (below left) took place in Loudun, France, in 1632. The mother superior of the local convent is being cured by the famous "expert" Barré. An Italian priest (right) casts out some modern devils who have possessed a young penitent.

Exeter, had decided to investigate. The bishop convened a special commission to reexamine both the attitude of the modern Anglican church to Satan and the practicability of exorcism as a useful instrument today.

In its report in April, 1972, the commission reported an overwhelmingly "pro-Satan" point of view among its members. The Devil, they said, was still active, and they would welcome diocesan exorcists, appointed by each bishop; they recommended that these exorcists should attend special training centers to be set up in each province, if possible in collaboration with the Roman Catholic church.

Not Playing Ball

Unlike the "liberals" of the Catholic church, the Anglican clergy raised hardly one dissenting voice when the Exeter commission published its report. It seemed that most vicars, even those—or in some cases particularly those—in urban areas, had come across some aspect of the "supernatural" which had baffled local doctors and upset their parishioners. Most of them had been at a loss when faced with such cases, and had either ineptly tackled the problem themselves or, more often, thrown the whole thing in the lap of their particular bishop.

One bishop, the Right Reverend Cyril Easthaugh, of Peterborough, a city near London, had been inundated with "occult" matters and had

Mary Evans

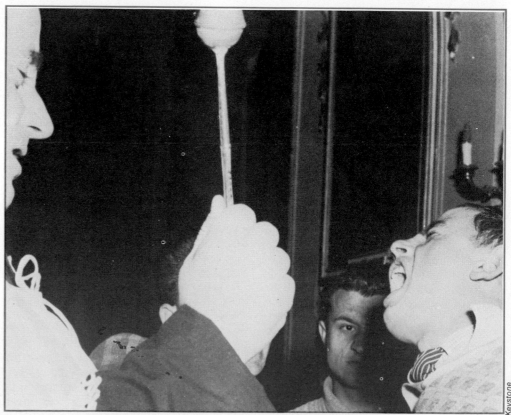

Keystone

anticipated the Exeter findings by appointing his own diocesan exorcist, on the advice of his old friend "black magic" novelist Dennis Wheatley. Wheatley—whose occult books are always prefaced by a solemn warning against dabbling with "dark powers" —was startled to hear that East-haugh's diocese had been the scene of almost every form of "evil manifestation" known. These included thefts and desecrations in churches, young people in abject terror after using ouija boards, satanist groups and witch covens, ghostly happenings, and an outbreak of wild poltergeist activities.

The "ghostly happenings," at least, succumbed to the amateur efforts of the Reverend Jeffrey Bell, vicar of the Ravensthorpe housing project—one of Peterborough's largest. During Lent, 1972, residents—particularly housewives—complained of shapeless apparitions, strange noises in the night, and "icy feelings down their spines," and rather than approach the overworked bishop of Peterborough, Mr. Bell decided to tackle the problem himself. On Palm Sunday he distributed palm crosses to all residents on the housing project, asking that the crosses should be hung on bedroom walls. Then he blessed each house. "The apparitions appeared to cease after that," he said, "but clearly there seems to have been a supernatural being at large on the estate."

Housing projects in general seem to account for a large percentage of Britain's "occult troubles," the pattern being established as far back as the mid-1930s, when a huge and revolutionary block of apartment buildings was built in Leeds, a major industrial city in the northern part of England. As soon as the first residents moved in they began to complain of "ghostly phenomena" and within weeks the project was in a state of panic—or, as psychiatrists might put it—mass hysteria.

But could dark powers dominate anything as mundane as a football stadium? Some people think that they could. The same city of Leeds boasts a football team which sports experts agree is one of the finest to emerge in Britain since the war. Leeds United are, however, dogged by notoriously bad luck in crucial matches, luck which fans claim is "uncanny." The team's manager, Don Revie, finally investigated the history of his club's stadium and found that it had once been a traditional gypsy camping site. The story went that, when the land

was purchased over a hundred years ago for use as a football field, the gypsies laid a curse on it. Mr. Revie sought out a gypsy who tried in vain to lift the curse, and finally the manager was reported to be seeking the services of an exorcist. Meanwhile, the team's ill luck continues to strike.

Perhaps even more mundane than football fields are automobiles, the pride and joy of twentieth century man. But the fact that a ghost may get into the machine is borne out by the experience of young George Becker of Silver End, Essex, in southeast England. Mr. Becker took his girl friend for a spin in his car, a small secondhand model, and the couple parked in a secluded lane on the fringes of Epping Forest, a well-known local beauty spot.

Back Seat Driver

Just as Mr. Becker switched off the ignition, a woman's laugh came from the back seat, and an "icy blast" passed through the car, though the evening was warm and summery. Terrified, Mr. Becker drove home and told the story to his local priest, Father Anthony Mayston, who exorcised the car with holy water and a blessing. Although the ghostly laughter was not heard again, Mr. Becker sold the vehicle shortly afterwards; he still felt uneasy while driving it.

Despite the fact that automobiles, football fields, and modern houses take up a great deal of the exorcist's time, most clergymen agree that these are relatively frivolous subjects compared with people—people in serious trouble. Literally thousands have sought the comfort of exorcism in the past few years, and many have passed through the healing hands of the Reverend J. C. Neil-Smith, vicar of St. Saviour's, in the fashionable London village of Hampstead.

Mr. Neil-Smith performed his first exorcism in the early 1960s and now holds what amounts to a "general license" as exorcist from the bishop of London. By the 1970s, newspapers and television had spread his fame throughout Britain, and the casting out of demons had become a principal part of his priestly duties. In four years he has exorcised more than 2,000 people—around 500 a year— and despite criticism from some quarters about his methods the "customers" still keep knocking on the door of his house. The criticism leveled at Mr. Neil-Smith hits mainly at his "theatrical" style of exorcism.

The "patient" kneels before him on

the marble altar steps of St. Saviour's, while the clergyman prays quietly and recites the service. Then comes a physical struggle, during which Mr. Neil-Smith, his face contorted, sweat running from his brow and his gray hair tousled with effort, grasps the hair of the patient and appears to drag out the offending spirit by the roots. It is a process which leaves both parties drained emotionally, but it seems to be effective.

People come to him from all countries and religions, and he has helped Catholics, Jews, atheists, Buddhists and Hindus—one Hindu became a Christian after exorcism, although Mr. Neil-Smith does not try primarily to win converts. The one common factor in all cases, he says, is that they sincerely believe that some evil power has taken possession of their souls.

Black magic and witchcraft, he claims, account for most of the suffering which he sees. He recounts one moving story of a young woman who had been a "witch priestess" and who wanted to break away from her coven. During exorcism she cursed, screamed and stiffened, then suddenly became calm. Breaking away from him, she ran down the darkened aisle of the church, and threw herself at the feet of a statue of the Virgin Mary, sobbing with relief. Her "possession" never came back.

Devil Hunters

Apart from demonic elements, Mr. Neil-Smith believes that earthbound spirits account for a number of the problems he is faced with. On one occasion, when a nursemaid claimed that she was being sexually molested by a ghost during the night, Mr. Neil-Smith was called to the house and, he claims, "saw" the spirit responsible. It was the shade of a young chamber maid, who had lived in the house during Victorian times. The girl had been a lesbian and, frightened by her "perversion," had killed herself. After exorcism her spirit vanished for good.

Captain Barry Irons, of the British Church Army, is warden of a hostel for boys in Birmingham and has become almost as well-known as Mr. Neil-Smith as a "devil hunter." Like the Hampstead vicar, he believes that the "occult revival" accounts for much of the trouble, and his service includes a rebaptizing of the afflicted person. But—again like Mr. Neil-Smith—Captain Irons always consults with doctors and psychiatrists before taking on a case, and often spends months examining the background to it before taking action. Interestingly enough Captain Irons, like the vicar of St. Pancras, suddenly suffered from high blood pressure and nosebleeds after his first exorcism some years ago.

Many clients of British exorcists are "hippie types" and most leading exorcists agree with psychiatrists that drugs may play a major part in inducing "phantom" takeovers. In the United States, the drug problem is perhaps more acute, and yet the Episcopalian church has been slow to adopt exorcism as a regular feature. One spokesman cagily reported that exorcism lay entirely in the hands of the bishops, and that they rarely authorized more than ten, "perhaps twenty at most," such services a year—a minuscule number considering the population, but such services are increasing.

Manson—a Man Possessed

The ancient ritual does play a major part, however, in the more extreme nonconformist sects which mushroomed in the United States in the early 1970s. The Reverend Dean McAbe, a 32-year-old Vietnam veteran, is pastor and cofounder of the New Church of the Resurrection, specifically established near Fresno, California, in 1967 to "fight the drug and Satan cults."

Dean McAbe sees exorcism as fundamental to his work in achieving the "salvation of young Americans"— a follow-up to baptism where the person being baptized is an adult.

"I have seen many of my contemporaries return from Vietnam with very disturbed minds and I believe that this is in part due to war-weakened souls being taken over by some evil power. I really feel that the Devil is stalking America today, a far greater menace to our country than the Viet Cong ever were."

About a dozen exorcism services a week are carried out by Mr. McAbe, and significantly most of these are for the benefit of ex-soldiers. But California is the center of a new cult movement, where "Jesus freaks" thrive alongside such institutions as the "Church of Satan." Mr. McAbe believes that new-look Christian churches such as his are popular as a direct result of the simmering violence on the West Coast of the United States, which occasionally erupts in the form of tragedies such as the terrible Manson murders. He is convinced that Manson and his followers were possessed by demons, and that if they had been exorcised

Sharon Tate and her friends—ritually and grotesquely murdered—would be alive today.

Oddly enough Mr. McAbe's views are not entirely shared by that prince of evangelists, Billy Graham. Dr. Graham, commenting on the film version of The Exorcist, told a news conference: "I believe in the Devil. Demons can harass people. But I don't think that believers can be possessed by the Devil." There was, he said, a strong psychological element to "possession"—a view taken by most moderate church spokesmen of all persuasions. Sometimes the emotion stirred up in the mind of the sufferer by the very idea of exorcism is enough to trigger the healing process.

Dom Robert Petitpierre, a Benedictine Anglican monk, is another expert on the subject of demonology who does not believe in "possession."

"People are not possessed," he says. "The language for these experiences is mostly fourteenth century and was invented by Dominican monks—nicknamed 'Domine cane' or the 'hounds of God'—who forced the facts to fit their ideas rather than the other way around. The demon tries to dominate the human will, but cannot actually possess it."

Catholic Caution

Most people who come to Dom Petitpierre are persuaded to see a psychiatrist, and even where orthodox medical treatment fails he says, "It does not follow that the trouble is demoniac in origin. This is where the exorcist needs to be trained to carry out preliminary investigations, to 'watch and pray' with the patient."

Despite Pope Paul's 1972 ruling, Roman Catholic priests share Dom Petitpierre's attitude of caution, largely because Catholic canon law is strict on the use of the service. A Catholic monsignor who is a parish priest was quick to point this out. "If a Catholic tells his confessor that he believes himself to be possessed by a demon, the priest examines the person's symptoms very carefully and then, if he feels such a move justified, makes a report to his bishop. The bishop himself may then examine the person possessed and, if he thinks it necessary, appoint an exorcist to conduct the service. The exorcist is always a man of experience in these matters and should be a priest of proven sanctity. Full rituals are performed very rarely, for the Catholic church believes, far more than it did in the past, that most cases of pos-

session are caused by mental illness."

This rather dismissive attitude among "liberal" Catholic clergy is a fairly common one. As another parish priest pointed out, the church does not court publicity on these matters because once a case is reported in the newspapers it is usually followed by a flood of others. "Perhaps some of these may have a basis to them, but most turn out to be publicity seekers."

It's the Cure that Counts

Father Joseph Crehan, a Jesuit who is an acknowledged expert on occult matters, is somewhat uneasy about such light-hearted talk. The younger clergy, he says, are often "unduly skeptical" about exorcism, and points out that even if it is true that, say, 90 percent of disturbed cases spring from mental disorders, this still leaves 10 percent unaccounted for. And the church should accept responsibility for these. As a delegate to a conference on exorcism held in Britain recently, Father Crehan met priests from all over the world; he feels that the Church of England's practical approach to the problem is excellent.

Whatever the truth behind the "medieval" practice, few psychiatrists deny that it can be useful when administered by a sympathetic and understanding clergyman. At best it may well be a positive power for good. Mr. Neil-Smith in particular often has patients referred to him by doctors and psychiatrists, especially where the afflicted person has a religious background.

A practicing London psychiatrist, Jewish by birth but agnostic by inclination, agrees with this viewpoint. "I myself have never sent a patient to an exorcist and I doubt that I ever would," he said frankly. "But I do feel that for certain types of patient the treatment may well be beneficial. I have, in dealing with Catholics or lapsed Catholics with problems stemming from guilt feelings, sometimes suggested that they go to confession, and this course of action has often caused a vast improvement in the patient's general outlook. But I find the idea of a subjective Satan impossible to accept. Unfortunately, there are too many 'Satans' of man's own making."

There is a great deal of drama and tension during an exorcism as the priest grapples with the forces of evil. Roman Catholics may be right in claiming that most cases of possession are caused by mental illness. Still, exorcism works.

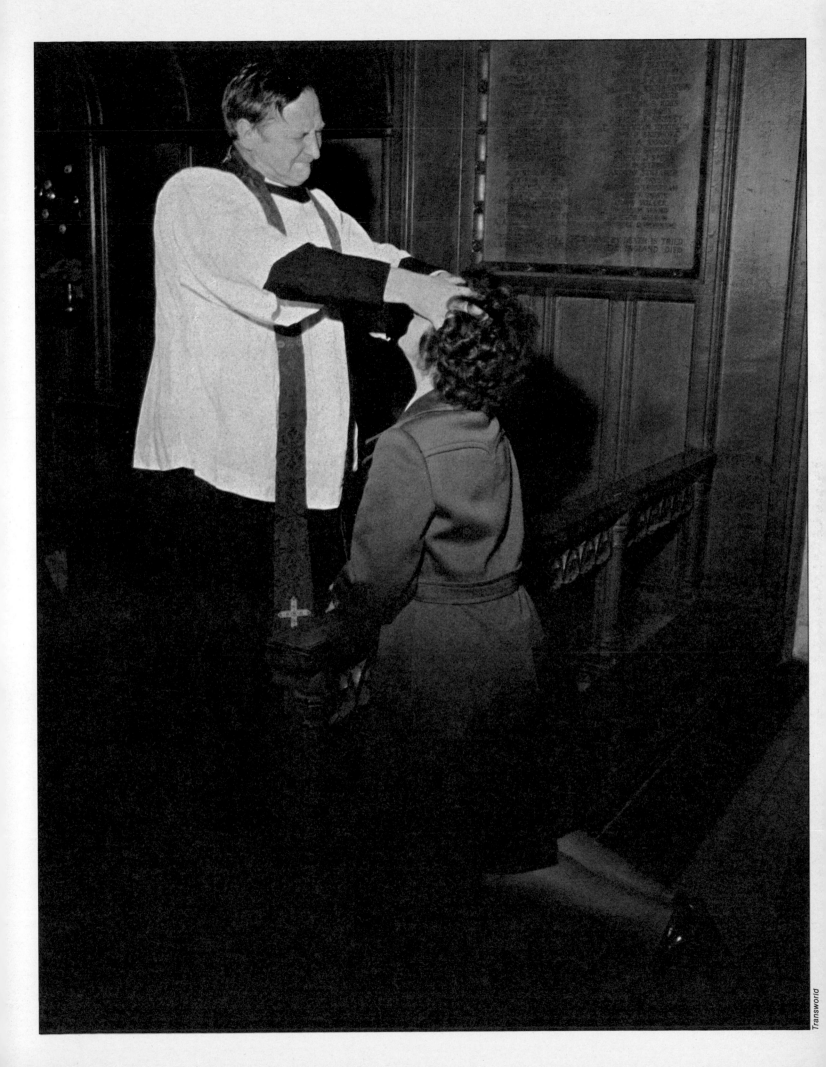

Havelock Ellis: Sex without blinkers

A contemporary of Sigmund Freud, Havelock Ellis saw his mission in life as the demolishing of inhibitions and barriers surrounding the sexual act. Soon, to the horror of all Europe, he calmly and coolly did exactly that in terms which seem as fresh today as when they were first expressed.

Henry Havelock Ellis was unquestionably the greatest sex reformer of his age. He released the nineteenth century from its sexual blinkers and for this we still owe him a great debt.

In his youth sex was barely acknowledged, rarely questioned and never considered a problem. It is largely thanks to him and his lifting of these Victorian taboos that we can discuss sex so freely today and satisfy our seemingly untiring curiosity about its nature.

Born in the days when the art of love was "only known as an improper and immoral subject once written about by Ovid" and when manuals of physiology often made no reference to the sexual organs, he resolved early that his work in life would be the exploration of this subject, "so that it should never be necessary for the youth of succeeding generations to experience the difficulties I had experienced in obtaining enlightenment on a matter so vitally important."

The first volume of his *Studies in the Psychology of Sex* appeared in 1897. After the sixth volume in 1910, Ellis said that he felt like Gibbon completing the *Decline and Fall of the Roman Empire*. "The work that I was born to do is done," he wrote. But he added a seventh volume 18 years later as well as numerous other books, more particularly suited to the layman.

In these books he covered every aspect of sexual activity. He consistently advocated contraception and sterilization; he argued for sexual selection and periods of trial marriage —at the least that both sexes should have the opportunity to assess each other physically before committing themselves to marriage; and he discussed the advisability of divorce.

His researches covered a range of sexual abnormalities (he avoided the word "perversions") from bestiality and necrophilia (or vampirism, the sexual attraction of corpses) to kleptolagnia (sexual excitement obtained from stolen objects) and urolagnia (sexual excitement associated with urinating—a characteristic that Ellis

himself possessed for most of his life, based on a childhood experience).

Frigidity, tumescence or what today we might call foreplay, the menopause, abortion, chastity, masturbation (he named it autoerotism), sexual impulses in childhood, the part played by modesty in sexual excitement, venereal diseases—he had something positive to say on every subject.

But Ellis was not concerned solely with the details of physical manipulation. The other half of the story is the open mind that he brought to his researches, his sincerity of approach and his enormous energy and depth of reading. The psychoanalytic method of Freud, who was born three years earlier than Ellis and died in the same year, sought to explain apparent deviations by working back to their sexual origins. In contrast, Havelock Ellis passionately believed that life embodied all such deviations, and his philosophy embraced them. To him, life and love were together an art with innumerable facets, each of which needed help and understanding. It was central to his teaching that sexual experience was an integral part of everyone's life.

At the time, this concept raised howls of protest from reactionary quarters. Simultaneously, and increasingly as his works spread into translations throughout the world, it brought thousands of letters full of gratitude from men and women confused by their own experiences or frustrated by the repressive attitudes of the time.

To understand this mixed reception it is helpful to remember what these attitudes were. For instance, by the end of the century, neither the public nor the establishment had yet fully recovered from the shock of Darwin's *The Origin of Species*, which had appeared in the same year in which Ellis was born. Then, two years before the publication of the first volume of the *Studies*, which for the first time discussed openly and with sympathy sexual inversion (or homosexuality), Oscar Wilde had been sentenced to imprisonment for homosexual offenses.

Respected physicians still made outlandish statements with regard to the female role in sex—statements which were generally accepted. "The majority of women (happily for society) are not very much troubled with sexual feeling of any kind," wrote one English surgeon. Another stated that only "lascivious women" showed any physical signs of pleasure when in the embrace of their husbands. An Italian added that "woman is naturally and organically frigid."

Remarks such as these may make us laugh because of their absurdity but, even if they are extreme examples, similar attitudes must have caused unimaginable distress and anxiety to countless women.

Havelock Ellis — Sex Spectator

Havelock Ellis dispensed with such nonsense calmly and clearly. The change in attitudes he brought about was deep and long-lasting. By the end of his life he wrote that the "most profound change is that which affects the sexual status of women. They have developed into human beings in general respects on the same level as men, and this has inevitably led to a new attitude towards the former masculinization of all sexual ideas."

He set a new standard of morality, which involved a freedom of sexual expression as much for women as for men. And he concluded, "On the whole it is doubtful whether the total amount of sexual activity has been increased. But it has been placed on a sound foundation and become incomparably more wholesome."

World War I confirmed the collapse of nineteenth century sexual taboos. Within a decade Ellis was complaining that the profusion of sex books on the

Unconsummated romance was just one of the curiosities of Havelock Ellis's life. The pattern began with his first love, Olive Schreiner.

market was only slightly less alarming than the original lack of them.

His own life appears at first a strange paradox after reading his work. He himself would have been the most interesting "case" history of all, had he included himself among those many cases he did quote. "If I had written my own history it would doubtless have been a surprise, to those who could have recognized it, to find how small my experience was and how temperate my estimate of the sexual act. I am regarded as an authority on sex," he wrote in his autobiography, *My Life*, which appeared in 1940, a year after his death, "a fact which has sometimes amused one or two (though not all) of my more intimate women friends. But, after all, it is the spectator who sees most of the game, and it remains true that my experience of sex has been, at all events, ample enough to help me attain a great experience of love."

Although before his marriage he had a passionate and physically close affair, and although he enjoyed affairs outside his marriage, Ellis did not consummate *any* relationship until after his wife's death, when he was already in his sixties.

He was born in Croydon, England, on February 2, 1859. His father was a ship's captain and both his grandfathers had been connected with the sea. He grew up, together with his sisters, chiefly under the care of his mother, Susannah, who, though undemonstrative and evangelically strict, was filled with common sense and kindness.

Throughout his childhood Havelock Ellis experienced virtually no interest in sex. At the age of seven he went on a voyage around the world with his father. But, despite a half-hearted approach by another boy during that voyage, the first experience that touched him was during his schooling years in the suburbs of London.

Passion Potential

An ideal love for his cousin Agnes awoke him to the passionate potential of his own nature. Unhappily for him this was counterbalanced by the beginning of his nocturnal emissions, which, in those days when such occurrences were considered as debilitating and immoral as masturbation, he thought of as a terrible weakness. The emissions continued for the greater part of his life.

His urolagnia, or obsession with urination, also developed from this period of his life. His mother used to urinate on her hands and say that it was good for the skin. He saw her once urinate in public, while out walking at London Zoo. She paused for a moment, he heard the trickle, and when she moved on he saw the small pool that remained behind. "I didn't mean you to see that," she said. But later Ellis inferred that she *had* meant him to see and had herself derived pleasure from his knowledge of her action. It was, he concluded, a form of flirtation. The memory—and the fascination—never left him.

When he was 16 he went on a second voyage with his father and remained in Australia, where he worked as a teacher for four years—though he had never taught before. After holding with varying success a motley variety of teaching posts, he ended up at a remote and lonely outpost called Sparkes Creek, in New South Wales.

It was there that he experienced what he called his "conversion." His sense of depression and isolation lifted and he saw for the first time what he believed and what he wanted. Until that moment Ellis had entertained what appeared to be two contradictory views of the universe. On the one hand was his concept of spiritual love and beauty, which was associated with the religion of his youth; on the other hand was his dedication to scientific values, which seemed to leave no room for either love or beauty.

At Sparkes Creek he began to read the works of the early nineteenth century philosopher and surgeon James Hinton, and from this reading Ellis became satisfied that the conflicting aspects of his life were both part of the same unity. Hinton also believed in free love and, though denying polygamy, preached polyeroticism. But he tied this belief to a moral attitude that affirmed altruism in place of individualism and declared that the moral center of gravity should shift from the self to a regard for others. The influence of Hinton on Ellis's teaching was considerable.

Armed with his new confidence, but deeply conscious of the public attitudes that were partly responsible for his own sexual immaturity, he made a philosophical resolution: "It will be better, I said to myself, to deal with the sex problem first and with the religious problem later." He spent the rest of his life on the sex problem.

Ellis, Freud and Jung

On his return to England in 1881, he took up his studies as a medical student at St. Thomas's, London, and remained there until 1889. He never intended to become a doctor but realized the usefulness of a medical background in his intended field of research.

By that time his first great love affair was over. He had been able to open both his mind and his emotions to the notable author Olive Schreiner, the first woman for whom he had felt any sexual response. Though their relationship was unconsummated—and the sexually experienced Olive perhaps disappointed—Ellis found the deeply involved affair physically and spiritually satisfying. Their correspondence was voluminous and continued for years, though Olive left England in 1889.

Two years later, Ellis married Edith Lees, an apparently tough, intelligent and energetic teacher, with a small amount of independent income, who became a reasonably successful popular playwright and lecturer. Their opinion of marriage agreed. Each required independence within the relationship. After the civil ceremony, both returned to their separate bachelor quarters for the night, though they lived together later.

Not surprisingly, this relationship also remained unconsummated. As a result, Edith's lesbian inclinations developed to the extent that she was able to discover some kind of satis-faction in a number of intense relationships with women, while Ellis in consequence considered himself free to extend his activities to a similar succession of women friends.

On the surface the arrangement seemed neat and amicable; beneath, it was undercut by continual misunderstandings. And yet, though Edith annulled the marriage a few years before her death, she played heavily on her relationship with Ellis during her lecture tours of the United States and once said, "If I lost Havelock, the earth would rock." In turn, Ellis affirmed with absolute sincerity that their love for each other was as complete and perfect as he could have wished for.

In the final twenty years of his life, after Edith's death, Ellis at last found complete sexual and mental compatibility with a French woman, Francoise Lafitte-Cyon, who took the pseudonym Francoise DeLisle (an anagram of Ellis) and remained with him until he died.

By then Ellis was a revered figure. But his *Studies*, the basis of his reputation, had not appeared without a struggle. A court case was brought against the first volume in 1897 and the copies were seized, despite the efforts of Ellis's influential friends. In court, the *Studies* were referred to as "a certain lewd, wicked, bawdy, scandalous and obscene libel." The remaining volumes were published in America.

The themes in this work of "obscene libel" were not altogether new. Some of them originated in Ellis's wide reading of anthropological studies as well as from his admiration of the pioneer work of Hinton. In Germany Krafft-Ebing was analyzing the pathological nature of sexual inversion, while his contemporaries enjoyed greater freedom of expression than their counterparts in England.

One facet of Ellis's work is that much of it is obviously culled from facts and figures quoted in others' books. His was the coordinating and unifying factor that transformed the material, though he also drew on the personal experiences of many of his friends, some of whom, including the influential, were themselves sexual inverts.

In private, long before the *Studies* appeared, sexual attitudes had been slowly changing. By compiling what others were already beginning to feel toward the subject and by adding his own qualities of scientific objectivity and passionate sincerity, Ellis gave voice to the growing dissatisfaction. Discussing the essence of this contribution, he once explained it like this: "My work, I am often told, is cool and serene, entirely reasonable and free from passion, but without that devouring passion of the soul my work would have been nothing."

Far from being nothing, his work extended and grew. Among the best known of those who developed and expanded it were Freud and Jung. Ellis had a certain guarded admiration for Freud, undoubtedly colored by a feeling of pride that he had been one of the first to recommend the importance of Freud's writing.

A Man is his Sex

The modern successors of Havelock Ellis are possibly Kinsey, Wolfenden, even Women's Lib. All owe something to the pioneering work of the grandly bearded, curiously introverted, wise old man who never sought public acclaim.

Many of the attitudes that we take for granted today were first clearly expressed by Havelock Ellis. When he agreed with the person who said, "A man is what his sex is," he might well have added, "A woman is what *her* sex is, also." For it was a fundamental part of his teaching that he emphasized the equal rights of both sexes to enjoyment not only of the orgasm but of the pleasure of sex that went beyond orgasm and to those idiosyncratic tendencies that accompany every physical relationship.

Ellis believed fiercely in a liberated family; in the parallel importance of sexual education and open discussion both between parents and children and between sexual partners and doctors. He held out no hope for any relationship in which there was not this feeling of trust and freedom.

In most aspects we have not advanced far in our sexual attitudes since Ellis died. At times, we have even fallen behind. For instance, Ellis was accustomed to use such words as fellatio and cunnilingus freely and unself-consciously to describe what he considered to be natural and acceptable phenomena.

It is tempting to conclude that most of what we find worthwhile in our present sexual attitudes stems from the teaching of this often misunderstood man, and that many of our difficulties lie in our failure to appreciate that his message was not intended as an incentive to free copulation but as a guide through the sensitive and difficult passage of human relationships towards a natural understanding of the art of love.

All you want to know about...

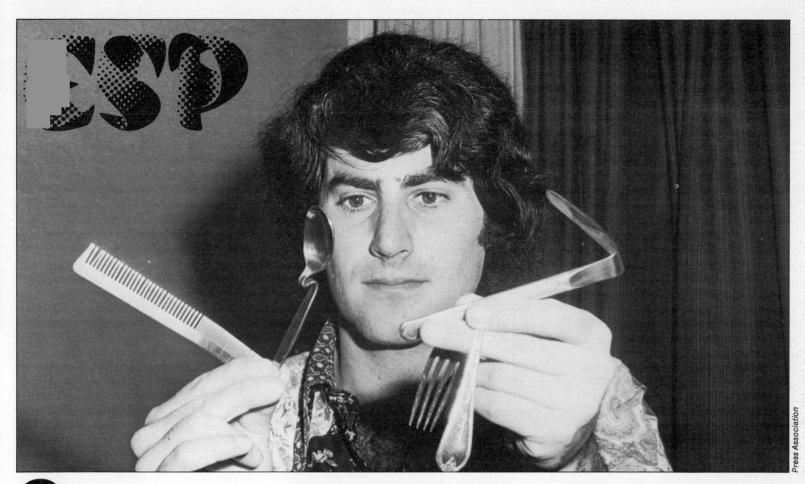

Press Association

Q WHAT EXACTLY IS ESP?

A ESP is the abbreviation used by scientists for "extra-sensory perception," which, as the name implies, relates to any ability to perceive information without the use of the known senses. Human beings and most animals employ five main senses to gather information either close to their bodies or at a great distance from them. The distance receptors—vision, hearing and smell—have evolved over hundreds of millions of years and they are obviously essential to the survival of any creature living in a hostile and dangerous world. The other two senses—taste and touch—are concerned with the detection of stimuli close to the individual. Ever since scientists began to study the nature of these senses and the way in which they work, they have been intrigued at suggestions that human beings and animals occasionally seem to gather information about what is going on in the world in some other way than using the known senses. For example, any animal which apparently correctly detected a dangerous situation—the presence of a predator—which was approaching outside the range of its eyes, ears and sense of smell would by definition be using extrasensory perception. Similarly, a man who suddenly felt an urge to duck and by doing so avoided a tile falling from a roof could be said to have employed extrasensory perception, provided it could be shown that he could not have seen or heard the tile falling, or had any normal information that it was about to fall. These are only two of literally thousands of ways in which ESP might appear. Generally it refers to all situations where information is received by the brain when none of the five "normal" senses are involved.

ARE THERE SEVERAL DIFFERENT KINDS OF ESP?

Scientists who study extrasensory perception believe that it is useful to divide ESP into four distinct categories. These are telepathy, clairvoy-

Uri Geller has recently provided some of the most extraordinary examples of ESP. He appears to have psychokinetic and telepathic powers and seems to have demonstrated them under close scientific observation.

ance, precognition and psychokinesis.
1. *Telepathy*, which means literally "long distance knowledge," refers specifically to communication between one mind or brain and another without the use of the normal senses. For example, if one person looks at a card in a room and another person, a mile or so away, correctly identifies this card, then this is either due to chance, or to the fact that information or a signal of some kind has passed between them. If the experiment is repeated a number of times with the second person continually getting the cards correct so that it becomes almost impossible that it could be due to chance, and if one is absolutely certain that no trickery is involved, then one would more or less have to believe that information has *flowed somehow from one mind to another.*

Information flow of this kind would be called telepathy.

2. *Clairvoyance*, which comes from the French and means roughly "clear sightedness," is quite a different type of ESP and refers to apparently extrasensory knowledge about something in which *only one mind* is involved. For example, if someone was able to specify the order of cards in a pack after shuffling and when no other person knew the order of these cards, then (trickery discounted) you would speak of clairvoyance. This word, incidentally, has acquired a slightly different meaning in connection with spiritualist mediums, who often use it to refer to the ability to "see" the spirits of dead people.

3. *Precognition*, which refers to the apparent ability of some people under some circumstances to "see into the future." Continuing the card guessing example, this could be demonstrated by someone who showed the ability not to guess the card which a person was looking at, but rather the one that he was going to look at! In this category, of course, are all premonitions, hunches about the future which come true, and so on.

4. *Psychokinesis*, the most debatable ESP faculty, literally means "force of the mind." The world refers to the skill claimed by some individuals that enables them to influence an object at a distance without physically touching it, presumably through the power of the will or the mind. In scientific experiments this skill has been studied by testing the ability of people to "will" dice to come up on a certain number more times than would be expected by chance.

WHAT IS THE EVIDENCE FOR ESP?

There are two types of evidence accepted by many scientists for the existence of ESP in one form or another, and these are the anecdotal and the experimental. Many people believe that the anecdotal evidence is the most exciting—it is certainly the most enduring. For thousands of years people have had strange experiences which could be attributed to one of the four classes of ESP. Typically these involve, say, telepathic contact between members of a family during a crisis, strange dreams warning a person of some disaster about to happen, and other inexplicable mental phenomena. Literally thousands of books and millions of words have been written about such experiences. For many people the stories are often com-

pelling enough for them to be counted as true and as denoting that such powers are an integral part of the psychology of man. In fact a recent poll showed that one in four people questioned had had "psychic" or ESP experiences of this kind. But, in the long run, reaction to anecdotal evidence depends upon whether or not you believe in the reliability of the testimony, much of which is impossible to check. It is for this reason that many scientists feel the most important evidence comes, not from these intriguing, exciting and somewhat suspect tales, but from experimental investigation of ESP in which an attempt is made to trap these strange powers in the laboratory. These attempts have been made in research establishments all over the world and tend to be of the card-guessing, dice-willing variety.

WHAT KIND OF SCIENTISTS STUDY ESP?

People who study ESP on a scientific basis are known as parapsychologists. They are drawn from all aspects of academic life and include psychologists, physiologists, engineers, chemists, physicians, mathematicians and philosophers. Many of them have scientific and technical qualifications, but the main bond which unites them is a passionate curiosity about extrasensory phenomena and a belief that comprehending it is essential to the understanding of psychology and human nature.

WHEN DID ESP RESEARCH BEGIN?

ESP research began in the latter half of the nineteenth century when scientists began to realize that the anecdotal evidence suffered from all the weaknesses associated with human personal testimony. The first professional body to be formed was the Society for Psychical Research in Britain, and this was quickly followed by the American Society for Psychical Research, which was modeled on the same lines. Both societies still exist with flourishing memberships and academically oriented research programs. The first laboratory specifically set up to study extrasensory perception, as part of a recognized university, was the world-famous parapsychology laboratory at Duke University in North Carolina. This laboratory, under the directorship of Professor J. B. Rhine, generated thousands of experiments under scientifically controlled conditions and pub-

lished hundreds of papers in learned journals arguing the case for ESP. Despite Rhine's prolific work, however, recognition of parapsychology as a legitimate academic topic has been slow to grow. In the 1950s the State University of Utrecht in Holland formed a small parapsychology laboratory under Professor W. H. C. Tenhaeff. This relatively slow progress, after almost a hundred years of organized research, has been disappointing to parapsychologists and has led to increased skepticism on the part of many critics.

ARE PEOPLE WHO STUDY ESP JUST A LOT OF CRANKS?

Anything but. Every group of people, whether gathered together for a political, economic or scientific purpose, contains a certain percentage of cranks, of course, and parapsychologists probably contain no greater proportion of cranks than any other group. In fact a study of the history of parapsychology reveals that some of the world's greatest scientists and thinkers have taken an active interest in it, and many of them consider that it might well be the most important area of scientific endeavor. Sigmund Freud, for example, once stated that if he could have lived his life over again he would have devoted it to parapsychology—or psychical research as it was then known. Other noted scientists and intellectual figures who devoted some part of their lives to studying it include Sir William Crookes, inventor of the vacuum tube; French physiologist Charles Richet; Alfred Russell Wallace, coauthor with Charles Darwin of the theory of evolution; Sir Arthur Conan Doyle, doctor of medicine and creator of Sherlock Holmes; physicist Sir Oliver Lodge and dozens of other outstanding figures who have made a lasting contribution in the hard and practical world of science. Today the Parapsychological Association is a respected affiliate of the American Association for the Advancement of Science, and other scholarly bodies in most countries of the world, whose sole aim is to collect information and study extrasensory phenomena.

Brilliant minds have devoted a great deal of time and research to the study of ESP. Among them are (clockwise from top left) Sir William Crookes, Sir Oliver Lodge, Alfred Russell Wallace, Sir Arthur Conan Doyle and (center) Charles Richet. Freud was also fascinated.

Psychic News/Mansell Collection/Mary Evans

WHY ARE SCIENTISTS DIVIDED ABOUT ESP?

At the present time the scientific world is split as to whether or not the parapsychologists (those who study ESP on a scientific basis) have achieved definite results or not. Some scientists argue that ESP is *impossible* and therefore feel that all such experiments are a waste of time. This attitude is a bit extreme and corresponds rather to those who think that ESP is so obvious a factor of mental life that it is quite unnecessary to do any further experiments to find out whether it exists or not. The bulk of scientists fortunately take a more balanced view. They can be divided roughly into two groups: those who think ESP has probably been demonstrated, but that more work is required, and those who feel that ESP has probably not been demonstrated, but that more work is worthwhile. The pro-ESP camp tend to point to the fact that research has been going on in parapsychology laboratories for more than fifty years now, and that a large number of scientific papers claiming ESP results have been published. They argue that, while not conclusive, the evidence has been building up slowly but steadily so that it is now more or less irrefutable. The critics on the other hand, while admitting that many scientists believe that they have demonstrated ESP, argue that their results could possibly have been due to some normal means of communication. For example, it is exceedingly difficult totally to rule out cheating, or even deliberate distortion of the ESP results. It is also very difficult to be sure—particularly when the experiments are not conducted in different rooms—that the person guessing has not picked up some information by noting unconscious clues that the experimenter may reveal, such as tenseness at particular moments or significant facial expressions. This kind of argument would be a bit thin if the evidence for ESP was overwhelming, and if subjects in experiments tended to guess very many more cards than would be expected by chance. Unfortunately, "above chance scores" tend to be rather small in most cases, and could just be achieved by carelessness or mild trickery on the part of someone in the experimental situation. These criticisms also might be countered if ESP results could be repeated in any laboratory. But skeptics are quick to point out that the evidence for telepathy, pre-cognition, and so on, tends to come only from the parapsychological laboratories, and that when these experiments are repeated in ordinary psychology and physiology laboratories, no positive results are obtained. Many scientists today are suggesting that a major problem with ESP is that it will not perform to order like other psychological phenomena, and that all laboratory experiments may therefore be doomed to failure. This unfortunately leaves only the evidence of human testimony and personal experience, which psychologists know is exceedingly unreliable.

HOW CAN ESP BE STUDIED IN THE LABORATORY?

By employing the techniques that psychologists use in studying other aspects of the mind and behavior. The principal rule, however, is to make absolutely sure that any phenomena experienced could not have come about by any normal means. For example, in testing telepathy the experimenter and his subject should always be in different rooms, properly soundproofed and with no normal channels of communication open to them. In an attempt to eliminate chance factors, runs of hundreds or even thousands of guesses may be made with specially designed cards using distinctive symbols, such as the circle, square, star, cross and wavy lines—the so-called Zener cards. Packs of Zener cards contain five of each symbol and you could expect therefore to get five right by chance in any run. When lots of runs are used, it is possible to tell by statistical methods whether people are guessing more right than they should by chance. Tests of clairvoyance are performed in the same way by using packs of Zener cards which have been shuffled but whose order not even the experimenter knows—until after the guesses have been made. In precognition experiments, the subject is asked to try to guess one or even two cards ahead of the one that the experimenter is looking at. Unlikely as it may seem, some of the best scientific evidence for ESP has come from such precognition experiments. Finally, laboratory experiments in psychokinesis tend to involve a series of attempts at willing dice to fall in a particular way. Sometimes this involves willing a particular number to come up, sometimes it involves willing the dice, which are automatically ejected down a little chute, to fall into a particular area of a specially marked table. The essence of all these experiments is that ESP phenomena are rather rare and unpredictable when they occur and therefore require numerous experiments before it can be certain that they have been substantiated. There are minor variations on these methods, which were first developed in the 1930s, but on the whole they form the basis of most research in ESP or parapsychological laboratories throughout the world.

IN WHICH COUNTRY DOES THE MOST ESP RESEARCH GO ON?

Quite definitely the United States, where a number of universities and colleges offer courses in parapsychology and encourage research on the part of students and staff. One academic research group in New York have even recently had their parapsychological research funded in part by a grant from the prestigious National Institute of Mental Health. However, despite the growth of interest in the United States, it is a curious fact that the famous parapsychology laboratory at Duke University, which pioneered laboratory studies of ESP, closed down some years ago on the retirement of Professor J. B. Rhine and has not reopened. Britain has some active centers in parapsychology, though none officially part of university academic research. A few universities in Europe—Utrecht and Freiburg notably—have small parapsychology departments. Popular belief that parapsychology is a major topic of scientific interest in the Soviet Union and other Communist countries is based on very little objective evidence. Western parapsychologists who have visited the Soviet Union state that there is not much active research going on and none of this is encouraged by Russian academic authorities. L. Vasiliev, the professor of physiology at the University of Leningrad, did conduct a series of experiments on the relationship between ESP and the hypnotic state, but these studies have not been developed since his death in the mid-1960s. Most Western interest in Soviet research has centered on the alleged powers of a Russian woman to move small physical objects, such as matches, by the power of her mind. Again most Western parapsychologists are hesitant about the objectivity of reports of her abilities, especially in the absence of clear evidence that she can demonstrate them under rigidly controlled conditions.

The art of persuasion

When you want to see one particular movie and your spouse or friend wants to see another, what do you do? Push for your choice, even if it means going separately? Give in, gracefully or otherwise? Or convince him that what you want is what he wants too?

Persuasion is an art that could smooth your life in leisure and working hours. For some kinds of work it is essential: selling of any kind and the more public persuasion of politics, advertising and journalism. Even if you do not plan to make a career of it, you could put into practice the principles of persuasion, as a housewife, a teacher, or in any social situation.

Getting Your Own Way— The Positive Approach

It probably is not good for anyone to get his own way all the time; but some of us seem able to manage it more often than others. Check the questions below, choosing your own most typical response—or the one that comes closest to it.

1. There is one job you hate (at home or at work) and you want to get someone else to do it. Do you

a. pretend to be willing but sick?

b. order someone else to do it?

c. do it yourself, complaining bitterly?

d. bribe someone else to do it?

e. praise the competence of someone else in this field?

2. You want a quiet evening and a lively child does not want to go to bed. Do you

a. promise him candy or money to disappear?

b. put up with his noise until he gets so sleepy that he wants to go to bed?

c. put him firmly to bed and ignore his disappointed yells?

d. get someone else to mind him and go out?

e. read him a story in bed and allow him half an hour to play quietly with an interesting toy?

3. You want to watch a movie or fight on one TV channel, and it conflicts with someone else's favorite program. Do you

a. lead up to your request by being especially considerate beforehand?

b. offer to forgo your favorite program the next evening in exchange?

c. switch on to your program as a matter of course?

d. lose the argument and sulk for the rest of the evening?

e. give in, feeling resentful?

Start With Yourself

Selling products or ideas involves the same basic processes. The first is to make yourself acceptable or credible. Most training programs for salesmen concentrate on building confidence; belief in yourself projects a positive climate for persuasion. Your own personality will determine the style of confidence you show—you do not need to be loud and hearty if you are by nature reserved; quiet confidence can be just as potent.

Some people may not be very adept at persuasion, but everyone is vulnerable to it. Advertising in one form or another has penetrated practically every aspect of our daily life and it is impossible not to be influenced by it in some way.

Many psychological studies show that *who* makes a persuasive communication is just as important as *what* the content of the message is. Over twenty years ago, a classic study by C. I. Hovland and W. Weiss found that people were more convinced by a statement about the practicability of atomic submarines when they were told that it had been made by a well-known physicist than another group who were told that it had appeared in the Russian newspaper *Pravda*.

Being knowledgeable and trustworthy in the eyes of the people you want to persuade is not enough—you also need to be likable. Several investigators have found that messages from an unattractive source have a boomerang effect. No one wants to be identified with the unappealing communicator. Being attractive—presenting a good image—to those you want to persuade can mean very different things with different groups.

In the 1968 presidential campaign, thousands of student campaigners willingly changed their appearance, cut their hair, shaved their beards, wore more conventional dress, to get through to voters they hoped to sway to Senator McCarthy.

Judge Your Audience

Some people seem generally easier to persuade than others; everyone has their more and less approachable moments. You need to gauge both personality and the immediate situation. Pressing someone who is anxious about something else could lead to greater resistance. No one likes to be browbeaten even by a good argument.

Your message has to make people feel *good*. Self-persuasion is highly effective; if you can use the arguments of your audience to lead them towards your point of view, or get them to make statements, or even to complete yours, your task is easier. Let them persuade themselves.

Try agreement on all possible points —"You were so right to say . . ."; show respect for a point of view or wish different from your own. It will make you and your message more acceptable and persuasion, even if it has to take place at a later date, likelier.

Some people find it difficult to change their minds after stating one view; but if they do not feel pressured, a slow change can develop. You may even find them quoting your argument back to you a week later as if they had just thought it up. Saving face is a strong social motive; the good persuader always makes it possible.

Soft Sell or Hard Sell?

To be effective, any message has to be clear and well-organized, but people like to draw their own conclusions. A recent experiment by S. Worchel and J. Brehm showed the dangers of oversell. Two groups of people were asked to read identical statements about the way the government should treat the Communist party. The only difference in the messages was that one contained high-pressure statements like "You have no choice but to believe this" and "You cannot believe otherwise."

The group that was left free to make up their own minds tended to shift their attitudes towards the views in

the message; those with the coercive message tended to move their views in the opposite direction. Similarly, giving only one point of view can be a mistake. Parents naturally want to give their children strong values, but they often push their views and exclude contrary ones. When the children come across conflicting ideas for the first time, their belief is more easily shaken. If you want the results of your persuasion to be long-term, you should include an inoculation of opposing arguments. Give them practice in dealing with opposing views.

Sizing Up the Situation

Persuading those you know well can be both easier and more difficult than persuading strangers. One important factor in dealing with strangers is the amount of physical distance between you. For door to door canvassing, an informal distance of four to five feet seems to be best; any less and you seem to be invading privacy; any more and impact is lost. In a more formal address to a larger group, fifteen feet is found to be a good distance for the speaker to be from his audience.

How Persuasive are You?

Bearing in mind these principles of persuasion, try to work out how you would operate in these situations.
1. How would you persuade a girl of eighteen to stop smoking?
2. Plan an advertising campaign to increase blood donations.
3. Plan the campaign of a congressional candidate.

and creative plans of your own; but here are some suggestions.

1. Research has shown that young people are more worried about their social image than their long-term health prospects. You could boost the attractiveness of nonsmoking (sweet breath, clean-smelling hair, clear eyes, etc.) and the unattractiveness of smoking.

2. The motivational researcher E. Dichter organized such a campaign. He believed that men were unconsciously worried about giving blood as it represented a loss of strength and virility. So he recommended that recruiting should focus on virility, suggesting that each man in the audience had so much that he could easily afford to give some away. He also suggested giving donors a pin

3. You might make use of whatever qualities your candidate has to create a good image. If he has held political offices before, stress his expertise; if he is attractive, it might be advisable for him to avoid controversy and play up personality. How would you angle the campaign to appeal to different sections of the community?

How persuasive are you? Technique is important, of course, but the most vital point of your argument to convince others is that it convinces you yourself!

However fluent the argument, or convincing the speech, if the speaker does not believe what he is saying the insincerity generally comes through.